D1337594

LABOUR'S HIGH NOON

The Government and the Economy 1945–51

edited by
Jim Fyrth

with an introduction by
John Saville

LAWRENCE & WISHART
LONDON

Lawrence & Wishart Limited
144a Old South Lambeth Road
London SW8 1XX

First published 1993

Photoset in Garamond by
Derek Doyle & Associates, Mold, Clwyd.
Printed and bound in Great Britain by
Cambridge University Press.

Contents

CONTENTS

Preface

This collection of essays was conceived as one of two, marking the fiftieth anniversary of Labour's electoral victory of 1945. The second, *Culture and Society in Labour Britain*, is planned for next year.

Contributors to this volume have analysed different aspects of Labour's economic policies, showing their relationship with pre-war Labour Movement discussions, with wartime experience and with Keynesian theory, as well as with colonial and foreign policy. Other writers show the effect of these policies on trade unionists, on women workers, Scotland and immigrants.

Taken as a whole the essays give both an account and a critique of Labour's economic policies. They include a number of topics which other books on the period have either ignored or touched on only lightly. There are, naturally, differences of emphasis between different writers. All to some extent, but some more than others, point to the long-term consequences of what the Labour governments did or did not do. Some topics are treated more critically than others. This is inevitable because, while the post-war Labour governments can be credited with great achievements, they can also be accused of having taken paths which led to the negation of many of the hopes of 1945. The achievements come through clearly in these essays, so do the criticisms.

The quarter of a century following the Labour victory of 1945 was a time both of full employment and, on the whole, economic growth. It can also, with the construction of the Welfare State, be claimed as a time of greater social justice and social stability than the years which preceded or followed it. Looking back from today's bleaker landscape, it is tempting to think of those years as the golden age of social democracy. Yet this would be to forget the discontents of that time and the knowledge that something had gone wrong.

We have also to ask how far the policies of 1945-51 were, in the long run, responsible for the 'stagflation' and the end of full employment in the 1970s, and for the political climate of the 1980s – and the demolition of the post-war achievements which resulted. We have to think, too, whether any conclusions which are useful for the future can be drawn from the history of those years. I hope that this collection of essays will help towards an answer to those questions.

Many people have helped me with suggestions and advice since I first thought of putting this collection together. I would like to thank all of them, and especially the contributors for their help and the tolerance with which they have put up with my editorial demands.

Jim Fyrth, June 1993

Note on the Value of Money

The Central Statistical Office's *Social Trends 23*, 1993 edition, HMSO, Para. 6.9, p86, states; 'by 1991 the 1951 pound was worth just seven pence'. The calculation is based on the Retail Price Index. This would imply that 1951 prices should be multiplied by approximately 14.29 to give 1991 equivalents. There had, by 1951, already been modest inflation during the period of the Labour governments. The Interim Retail Price Index shows a rise from the June 1947 base of 100 to 125 in June 1951 (B.R. Mitchell and H.G. Jones, *Second Abstract of British Historical Statistics*, Cambridge, 1971.)

None of these figures is exact when finding present-day equivalents for sums given in this book. By definition the Retail Price Index does not cover many of the commodities purchased by governments. Nor are the commodities purchased by post-war governments, e.g. for the Health Service or the defence services, the same commodities as are purchased now. Also the Index is itself open to some criticism.

Nevertheless, it would be reasonable, as a rough guide to their present-day equivalents, to multiply by twenty sums spent in the period of the post-war Labour governments.

Notes on Contributors

Ken Alexander is Chancellor of the University of Aberdeen. He taught economics at the Universities of Leeds, Sheffield, Aberdeen and Strathclyde. In the 1960s and 1970s he was a non-executive director in shipbuilding on the Clyde, and from 1977-82 was Executive Chairman of the Highlands and Islands Development Board. He retired as Vice-Chancellor of Stirling University in 1987, and chaired the Standing Commission on the Scottish Economy in 1988-89. He is President of the Scottish National Dictionary Association.

Catherine Blackford lives and works in London, where she is employed as a Research Assistant at the University of East London. She is currently engaged in research for a doctoral thesis on feminism in the 1940s and 1950s.

John Callaghan is Professor of Politics at the University of Wolverhampton. He is author of *The Far Left in British Politics* (Blackwell, 1987), *Socialism in Britain Since 1884* (Blackwell, 1990) and *Rajani Palme Dutt: A Study in British Stalinism* (Lawrence and Wishart, 1993).

Fergus Carr is Principal Lecturer in International Politics in the School of Social and Historical Studies at the University of Portsmouth. Among his research interests are American foreign policy in the Cold War, and post-war British external relations. His publications include work on British foreign policy and European defence issues.

Malcolm Chase teaches history for the Department of Adult Continuing Education at the University of Leeds. He has a particular interest in the history of rural issues and the labour movement, and is author of *The People's Farm: English Rural Agrarianism 1775-1840* (OUP, 1988). He is an active member of the History Workshop movement.

Michael Cunningham is Lecturer in Politics at the University of Wolverhampton. He is author of *British Government Policy in Northern Ireland 1969-89* (Manchester University Press, 1991). His research interests include North Irish politics and political economy.

Roger Fieldhouse is Professor of Adult Education and Director of Continuing Education in the University of Exeter. He was Tutor Organiser for the WEA in North Yorkshire (1964-70) and Lecturer/Senior Lecturer in the Extramural Department of the University of Leeds (1970-86). He has published numerous books on local history and on the history of adult education.

Nina Fishman has taught day-release courses for shop stewards and safety representatives at the University of Westminster, Harrow campus, since 1979. Her book *The British Communist Party and the Trade Unions, 1933-45*, will be published by Scolar Press in 1994.

John Foster is Professor of Applied Social Studies at the University of Paisley, and a member of the editorial board of *Communist Review*. Publications include *Class Struggle and the Industrial Revolution* (1974), *Politics of the UCS Work-in*, (with Charles Woolfson, 1986) and *Track Record: the Caterpillar Occupation* (with Charles Woolfson, 1988).

Jim Fyrth was Senior Staff Tutor in History in the University of London Extra-Mural Department. He now teaches for Birkbeck College, London, Extra-Mural Centre. His most recent books are *The Signal Was Spain: The Aid Spain Movement in Britain 1936-39*,

(Lawrence and Wishart, 1986), and (as editor with Sally Alexander) *Women's Voices from the Spanish Civil War*, (Lawrence and Wishart, 1991). He is a Fellow of the Royal Historical Society.

John Grahl is a Senior Lecturer in Economics at Queen Mary and Westfield College, University of London. A specialist in the economics of the European Community, he has published widely on EC policies. He is joint author, with Paul Teague of the University of Ulster, of *The Big Market* (Lawrence and Wishart, 1990) and *Industrial Relations and European Integration* (Lawrence and Wishart, 1992).

Richard Hyman is Professor of Industrial Relations and Convenor of Graduate Studies, at the Industrial Relations Research Unit, University of Warwick. His writings on labour history include *The Workers' Union* and (with James Hinton) *Trade Unions and Revolution*. Among his other publications are *Industrial Relations: A Marxist Introduction*, *Strikes*, *The Political Economy of Industrial Relations*, and (with Anthony Ferner) *Industrial Relations in the New Europe*.

Kenneth Lunn is Principal Lecturer in the School of Social and Historical Studies, University of Portsmouth. He is editor of *Immigrants and Minorities* and has published extensively on aspects of 'race' and immigration in British history. He is currently writing a history of 'race' and the labour movement.

Jim Mortimer was apprenticed as a ship fitter and later worked as an engineering draughtsman. TUC awards to Ruskin College and the London School of Economics led to work in the TUC Economic Department and membership of the Executive of the Association of Engineering and Shipbuilding Draughtsmen. He was a member of the National Board for Prices and Incomes, and Chairman of the NEDC for Engineering Construction. Later posts were as Board Member of London Transport, Chairman of ACAS and, until his retirement, General Secretary of the Labour Party. He has published nine books on trade unionism and has an Hon.D.Litt from Bradford University.

John Saville is Emeritus Professor of Economic and Social History in the University of Hull, and Editor (with Joyce Bellamy) of the Dictionary of Labour Biography. From 1946–7 he worked in the Chief Scientific Advisor's Division of the Ministry of Works. He has held the positions of Chairman of the Oral History Society, Vice-Chairman and Chairman of the Society for the Study of Labour History, and (1977–9) Chairman of the Economic and Social History Committee of the Social Science Research Council. His publications include *1848: the British State and the Chartist Movement* (1987), *The Labour Movement in Britain: A Commentary* (1988), and *The Politics of Continuity: British Foreign Policy and the Labour Government 1945–46* (1993).

Richard Saville lectures in the Department of Modern History, University of St Andrews, Scotland. He has edited *The Economic Development of Modern Scotland 1950–1980* (1985) and co-edited (with David Crossley) *The Fuller Letters: Guns, Slaves and Finance, 1728-1755* (1991).

Introduction

John Saville

The Labour Party won an overwhelming victory at the general election which followed the end of the Second World War in Europe. The two administrations over which Clement Attlee presided as Prime Minister between late July 1945 and October 1951 are the subject of the essays in this volume. The 1945 electoral result surprised many inside Britain and almost everyone outside. The political and electoral record of the Labour Party in the decades before 1939 had been uninspiring; and the first question to be answered is how did it come about that the dispirited and disunited Party of the summer of 1939 achieved such a commanding position at the end of six years of war, a war that had been conducted under the leadership of Winston Churchill.

During the 1930s, following the debacle of 1931, the Labour Party had been slowly but steadily re-building itself. The 1935 general election, held almost exactly four years after 1931 – years of massive unemployment – showed how far there was still to go. The total number of votes cast for Labour nearly reached the previous peak total of 1929, but the electorate had increased by two and a half million and the turn-out on election day was eight per-cent lower. The main Labour gains in 1935 were in London, Scotland and Yorkshire. The main centres of Labour strength, measured by votes cast, were still the coalfields and selected urban areas. Trade union MPs numbered seventy-nine out of a total of 154, with the miners easily the most important occupational group. Birmingham had twelve constituencies and, as in 1931, had not a single Labour MP returned in the 1935 election.

Labour, throughout the 1930s, failed to win over the very large number of manual workers, skilled and unskilled, who either voted for the Conservatives or the Liberals or who did not vote at all. Even more was this true of their wives and daughters. This failure of the Labour Party to extend its influence within the working class in general provides the major domestic question of the decade. It is a large and complex question. One factor was the quality of the leadership, and here it must be noted that by the time that Clement Attlee became leader of the Parliamentary Labour Party in 1935, the middle-of-the-road politicians had established themselves firmly in control. The central decision-making body became the reconstituted National Council of Labour which had seven seats allocated to the trade unions as against three each for the executive of the Labour Party and the Parliamentary Labour Party; and the block union vote at national conferences withstood effectively any residual opposition. The two leading trade unionists were Walter Citrine, who had accepted a knighthood in 1935, and Ernest Bevin of the Transport Workers. Both belonged to the right wing of the movement.[1]

The Labour leadership derived its political assumptions from the socialist rhetoric which had been added to the labourist ideas of the later 19th century, elaborated most persuasively by the leading Fabians. The practice of the Labour leaders was within the tradition of Fabian constitutionalism and their political attitudes were always, in socialist or labourist terms, cautious. What is so striking in this decade is that the Labour Movement was being offered a series of political platforms from which vigorous campaigns could have been launched. On all the major issues, potential or actual, it was caution which prevailed. There were four national Hunger Marches in this decade: 1930, 1932, 1934 and 1936 and none was given support by either the Labour Party or the Trades Union Congress. In 1930 and 1932 local Labour parties and trades councils were specifically instructed to offer no help. The most extraordinary episode was the denial of help by the National Council of Labour to the Jarrow March of 1936, a denial which illuminated more clearly than any other decisions the narrowness of vision and the prejudiced attitudes of the majority of the political and union leadership. The main reason for the refusal to support the Hunger Marches of the National Unemployed Workers Movement was that its leadership was mainly communist although there was always independent socialist and left

Labour Party support, and this grew rapidly after 1932. The Jarrow March however was organised by Ellen Wilkinson, the sitting MP, and the Town Council, and the Conservative agent for the Division, Councillor Suddick, was among the advance guard of the march.[2]

In the years immediately before the war the two outstanding issues were Spain and the Chamberlain government's policy of appeasement. On Spain the Movement officially supported non-intervention for the first eighteen months of the civil war, the consequence of which was a strengthening of Franco's position, an outcome welcomed by the British Government. The struggle against appeasement led to intense turmoil within the whole Labour Movement, and the attempts to develop a wider national unity against Chamberlain – the story is a complicated one – resulted in the expulsion from the Labour Party first of Stafford Cripps in January 1939 and then of Aneurin Bevan, George Strauss and others who refused to provide the national executive with an unqualified acceptance of the official party line.[3] This was the background to the last annual conference at Whitsuntide before the outbreak of war. By the time it was convened the Spanish Civil War was over and Franco had been recognised by the British Government, Hitler had entered Prague, Italy had invaded Albania, and Chamberlain had given his worthless guarantee to Poland while conducting desultory negotiations with the Soviet Union. The Southport conference was the most listless and the quietest of any during the previous decade. On the basis of by-election results, and other relevant factors, psephologists have always argued that had the war not come and the general election of 1940 been held, the Tories would have won again, for the third time.[4]

The Road to 1945

The years of war radicalised many sections of the British people, a process at times too narrowly analysed. Britain was a deeply conservative society, a generalisation which certainly includes much of the working class, whatever their political affiliation; and the development away from the liberal-labourism of the nineteenth century had been halting and uneven. It was to take two world wars, and the most severe economic crisis capitalism had so far endured, to produce a Labour majority in a country which had still a working-class majority in its population. For the ordinary people of Britain the war was an anti-fascist war, and the entry of the Soviet Union, and above all its central part in the defeat of fascism, were important influences in encouraging changes in popular consciousness. The Beveridge Report, the growing insistence that the poverty and unemployment of the inter-war years must not be allowed to return, the cynicism that was widespread of the 'Homes for Heroes' propaganda in the aftermath of the First World War, all contributed to the metamorphosis in consciousness. The majority of young men, and an increasing number of young women, served in the armed forces, and for many the stupidities of life in the forces – in matters of routine, discipline and organisation – exercised a leavening effect upon minds and hearts. Most of the political writing during the war years, it is necessary to emphasise, came from the Left; the brilliant polemical tracts that Gollancz published – *Guilty Men, The Trial of Mussolini, Your MP, Why Not Trust the Tories* – were only the most coruscating parts of a much broader literature whose general influence was to increase scepticism of the past and to encourage hope for a different future. The impact of the Army Bureau of Current Affairs has probably been exaggerated, although the Cairo Parliament, and its counterparts elsewhere, as well as the political activity that socialists and communists in the Forces engaged in, were certainly not without their influences.[5]

In the long history of the development of an independent Labour Party in Britain, and the slow emergence of a labour-socialist/ socialist consciousness, there has always been a subtle and sophisticated relationship between the unionisation of the work-force and changing political attitudes. In very broad terms, for the half century before 1939 the greater the unionisation of an industry, town or a region, the more likely has been the shift away from the traditional parties to the Labour Party, in voting terms at the least. For the inter-war years the correlation was positive. The problem was the low level of unionisation compared with the years before the General Strike of 1926. After the strike the membership affiliated to the TUC remained under four million from 1927 to 1935; by the end of 1936 the enrolment was about four and a half million but the five million mark was not passed until 1940. The organisation of female workers was much neglected. Out of about five million employed women, only 800,000 were organised, of whom 350,000 were non-manual workers. There was nothing in Britain during these years comparable with the achievements of the CIO in the United States or the French unions in the period of the Popular Front.

The beginnings of the rearmament programme in the later 1930s, and the national mobilisation of resources during the war years, were responsible for the dramatically changed situation within which industrial workers and their unions operated. In the established industries where unionism had already strong traditions there developed a growing strength and confidence as well as new levels of combativeness. Shop steward organisation had already established itself in the aircraft industry before 1939 around the *New Propellor* and the Aircraft Shop Stewards National Council, and these developments expanded rapidly once the organisation of war production got under way. Engineering, in its many different forms, was by far the largest manufacturing industry at the centre of the war effort and the strength of the shop stewards' movement meant that industrial disputes were much more common than has often been recognised. At the end of the war trade union affiliations to the TUC were around seven and a quarter million, and were to increase to over nine million by 1947. Membership was to remain between nine and ten million for the next decade out of a potential union membership of at least twenty million. The unionisation of women remained very limited.[6]

Continuity of Labour Policy

These various changes in social consciousness among the ordinary people of Britain, leading to an acceptance of the need for change – with jobs and wages being for many the central meaning of change – must be set in context with what was happening to the leaders of the

Labour Movement. For them, once they had entered the Coalition government, the experience of wartime administration confirmed their already well-entrenched opinions that the existing structures of government could be used to achieve their own aims and objectives, once a parliamentary majority had been obtained. Most of the Labour leaders who were given office in the Churchill government proved efficient and capable. Familiarity with the Civil Service élites in Whitehall also helped to encourage the belief that wholehearted co-operation would be forthcoming in the event of an electoral victory; and confirmed one of the major assumptions of constitutional practice, that a change of government did not affect the composition of the administrative structures which served successive governments. Thus when Attlee, the new Prime Minister, and Bevin, the new Foreign Secretary, went to Potsdam the day after the election victory in July 1945 in order to resume the Big Three Conference, there was not a single change in the thirty-five member delegation which accompanied them and which had a few days earlier served Churchill and Eden. Attlee had the same Principal Private Secretary as Churchill and even Churchill's valet. Sir Alec Cadogan and all his Foreign Office delegation had remained behind in Potsdam and simply carried on when Bevin arrived.[7]

There is a more general point to be made in this context. Alone among the major powers of Europe in the twentieth century, Britain never experienced either defeat in war and/or a significant upheaval in its administrative organisation and structure; and this was matched by the continuity through war and peace of the members of the upper class élites who occupied the top levels of the Civil Service in Whitehall. The social origins of those recruited had not changed in any significant way throughout the twentieth century and this was especially notable in the key ministries of the Treasury, the Foreign Office and the Home Office. Gladwyn Jebb noted in his memoirs that the Foreign Office was dominated by old Etonians and that this was especially true of the senior officials.[8] Sir Alec Caodgan was the seventh son of the fifth Earl of Cadogan. Like all his brothers he was at Eton, and then went on to Oxford. He became Permanent Under Secretary at the Foreign Office in January 1938, remained in place throughout the war, and was Ernest Bevin's senior official for the first six months. There were large numbers of temporary civil servants in Whitehall from the business world and the academic community, and some reached positions of authority, but they moved out when the war ended and the permanent officials regained full control. It should be added that the top echelons of businessmen continued, as during the war, to provide the many industrial boards, including those of the nationalised industries, with full-time or part-time guidance.[9]

The continuity of people and structures in the post-war period deeply influenced, in conservative ways, the social and political legislation of the Attlee government; but there were important differences between attitudes towards foreign affairs and the social security measures for which the Labour administration is most remembered. In the former, the international policies carried through by Ernest Bevin and his senior officials at the Foreign Office were a continuation of both ideas and policies already in train during the last two years or so of war. French Indo-China is an example, since it was the occasion for the first military intervention in a colonial country by the Labour government. Indo-China, soon to be called Vietnam, was the most important colonial country of the French Empire in 1939. The administration was Vichy-orientated after the fall of France in the summer of 1940, and although the Japanese did not formally occupy the country until the spring of 1945, the collaboration between the French administration and the Japanese was close, and subservient. When the war in the Far East came to an unexpectedly sudden end in the early days of August 1945, the Vietminh – the national liberation movement which had fought the Japanese as well as the French – took control of Hanoi in the north, where they were strongest, and then a few days later of Saigon in the south. There were no French troops in the Far East, and left to themselves the Vietnamese would have remained in control of their own country. The question of what was to follow the Japanese occupation, in Indo-China and elsewhere, had long been discussed in Whitehall and there was full agreement that, as the former colonial power, France was entitled to move back in control once the war was over. South-East Asia Command was under the leadership of Mountbatten, and his formal instructions were to move into the former Japanese occupied territories, repatriate prisoners of war and civilian internees and disarm the Japanese military. British intervention began in the second week of September 1945. The ground troops were mostly Indian and Gurkha, the RAF British. The commander-in-chief, General Gracey, was firmly convinced of the French title to their former colony. Since he was short of combat troops to counter the Vietminh, he began in October to use Japanese infantry in the front line of battle, and the Japanese air force to carry stores, arms and personnel to beleaguered areas. By Christmas 1945 the Vietminh had been effectively contained in Saigon and the southern region, and by now the French had over 30,000 troops under General Leclerc in place, courtesy, mainly, of American ships operating from Europe. The British began to move out in January 1946 – some to reinforce the British-Dutch struggle against the Indonesian nationalists – and Vietnam began to be re-occupied by the French.[10]

Almost no one in the United Kingdom knew these facts about the British intervention and certainly not about the use of Japanese troops at a time, October–November 1945, when British newspapers were full of stories about Japanese atrocities against prisoners of war and the civilians who were interned. The intervention was over within four months, but the fact that the long years of agony for the people of Vietnam might not have taken place without the British action has been almost completely missed by British historians and certainly is not part of the consciousness of the British people. The story has been given here in part because it illustrates the continuity of Bevin's foreign policy with that of his Tory predecessors, in part because it serves to explain the motivation of the new Labour Foreign Secretary. Bevin had no conception of what a Labour, let alone a socialist, foreign policy would involve. He believed fervently in what his leading officials believed in – the Empire and the continuation of Britain as a world power alongside the two other major powers, the USSR and the USA. The further dimension was anti-communism and anti-Sovietism, a central part of British foreign policy since 1917, although it did not attain its all-pervasive significance until the aftermath of World War Two. In the years of the Labour government, foreign policy continued along the lines that had been discussed and debated within the Foreign Office during the closing years of the war, and since Bevin was fervently anti-Soviet in his general approach there were no problems of any fundamental kind to be argued. Thus Bevin, who had publicly supported the Churchill military intervention in Greece in early December 1944, against vigorous opposition from not only large sections of the Labour Movement but many among the general population, continued the same policy as his predecessor. At the other end of the Mediterranean the Foreign Office, before the war ended, had already decided against any kind of intervention to overthrow, or to help overthrow, Franco, and Bevin continued the same policy. Thus we had military intervention in Greece to combat the national liberation front of EAM/ELAS and to restore those who would continue the wholly discredited policies of the exiled Royalists and the old-style politicians, and the second non-intervention with regard to Spain. The first, from 1936, had helped the fascists to victory, the second, after the war against fascism had ended, was a major factor in the continuation of the fascist regime for another thirty years.[11]

Belief in the Great Power thesis was an illusion. Britain's part in the six years war understandably contributed to the general acceptance in public consciousness of the nation's continued role in world affairs, but the reality of the situation was not concealed from those who walked the corridors of Whitehall. Economic stocktaking had provided grim reading in the months before the end of the war in August 1945 although this did not mean that either leading officials or politicians were willing to accept the downgrading of Britain's status in world affairs. Many believed that the serious economic problems would be overcome in the medium to long run, others that an alignment with the United States would provide a successful alliance of American economic strength and British expertise in world diplomacy. What no one appreciated in 1945 was that the economic problems were of a structural kind that could be rectified only by dynamic policies that were never to be implemented, or that the British Empire, understood as the central core of the Great Power thesis, was in process of disintegration before the war itself had ended.

Economic Consequences of Foreign Policy

These are matters discussed in more detail in certain of the chapters which follow. Let it be noted here that in the closing months of the war British exports were around thirty per cent of the 1939 level; that there was now a massive debt, the most important items of which were the sterling balances accumulated in countries such as India, Egypt and elsewhere as a result of large military and other expenditures during the war years. Further it was assumed in the Treasury calculations that there would remain a serious deficit on current account for the first three to five years of peace. All discussion papers assumed a rapid increase in exports and the continuation of wartime restrictions upon imports and consumption in general. With the abrupt cancellation of Lend-Lease by the Americans two days after the formal surrender of the Japanese, the new Labour government was pushed into an application for an American loan. J.M. Keynes led the British delegation to Washington and he went with an optimism concerning the continued 'generosity' of the Americans that was to be speedily deflated. Before the loan agreement was signed in December 1945, there had been much discussion in London concerning the other possibilities that would or might have to be considered if the American loan did not materialise. What emerged as the central problem in a number of specialist assessments, including those by Keynes himself, as the central problem was the high level of overseas military and political expenditures. If these had not existed then it would have been possible to achieve a balance between revenue and expenditure which would not damage the domestic policies to which the Labour government was pledged. Here are Keynes's words on this subject:

> I should be inclined to highlight still more than he [Richard Clarke] that the main reaction of the loss of the American loan must be on our military and political expenditure overseas ...

INTRODUCTION

After quoting the details of expenditure Keynes continued

> Thus, it comes out in the wash that the American loan is primarily required to meet the political and military expenditure overseas. If it were not for that, we could scrape through without excessive interruption of our domestic programme.[12]

Keynes died within two months of writing these words, and there was no one left in Whitehall who commanded the respect he had been accorded. The argument was not therefore heard, and there was no one in Whitehall – of any political weight that is – who could develop and extend the arguments that Keynes expressed in the memorandum quoted above. In the first two years of peace, during which period the basic lines of British foreign policy, above all the anti-Sovietism and the acceptance of American dollars, were clearly laid down and established, there was only one personality among the top élites of the Cabinet, the military and Whitehall, who had serious doubts about some aspects of British foreign policy, and that was the Prime Minister, Clement Attlee. It was Bevin's Middle East policy that Attlee thought wholly misguided, and for two years, until the spring of 1947, he argued the case for a serious revision of priorities. The argument, however, was a private argument which neither the Cabinet nor the Parliamentary Labour Party knew about and which remained undiscussed by historians for some forty years or so. The discussions were carried on through the Private Offices of the Prime Minister and the Foreign Secretary, and in those days Whitehall could keep its secrets. Attlee wanted a much diminished role for Britain in and around the Eastern Mediterranean, not least because of the part that he himself played in the granting of independence to India. The Foreign Office had no effective control over Anglo-Indian negotiations. Bevin would certainly have slowed down the shift of power, but it was not in his political capability, and Attlee in practice became his own Minister for India. The consequences of Indian independence were not at all appreciated by the British Chiefs of Staff or the Foreign Office and their impact upon strategic questions such as the road to India and the greatly diminished importance of the Middle East countries – assuming still the importance of the remaining Empire – was ignored. Attlee lost the argument because Bevin was of such crucial importance to Attlee's own position within the Cabinet; and then, from the summer of 1947, the centre of political debate and discussion moved to Europe and away from the Middle East, at least for the years up to 1950.[13]

Britain, then, continued with a foreign policy which imposed a continuous and heavy burden upon external finances, a burden let it be noted that continued for the next forty years and which is still not properly appreciated. There were several ways in which the military and political requirements overseas could be financed without serious detriment to Labour's domestic plans. The first was to reduce the balance of payments deficit by maintaining wartime controls on consumption and encouraging exports, and this was achieved; the second was to increase the levels of exploitation over colonial countries which had dollar earning assets, such as tin and rubber in Malaya, cocoa in West Africa. The total of sterling balances, representing British debts to mainly colonial countries, actually increased during the Labour governments, and there were physical controls over colonial commerce which also worked in Britain's favour.[14] The third way in which Britain temporarily solved its fundamental economic problems in the immediate years following 1945 was the acceptance of American dollars, first under the loan which Keynes negotiated and then with the implementation of the Marshall Plan. The two countries which received most Marshall Aid were Britain, with about 23 per cent of all dollars made available, and France, with some 20-21 per cent. What is intersting in the British case is that the proportion of foodstuffs financed by Marshall Aid was the largest single category, whereas for France the import of capital goods was much more important. Marshall Aid then was a further component in the general equation which permitted Britain to maintain a high level of military expenditure overseas – although slightly declining to 1950 – at the same time as a very slowly improving standard of living, measured by consumption. What was crucial, of course, for the general support from working people which the Labour government continued to enjoy, was full employment.[15]

Labour's Domestic Policy

There were important differences between the conduct of foreign policy and the implementation of the domestic legislation which had been promised in the 1945 election manifesto. The Labour Party's election manifesto of 1945 was largely drafted by Herbert Morrison. A Campaign Committee had been established in the spring and Morrison launched the new policy programme on 21 April 1945 following with a number of speeches round the country. The policy document was put before the National Conference at Blackpool in late May with Morrison opening the debate in a speech which was enthusiastically received. His central argument was that, 'Permanent social reform and security cannot be built on rotten economic foundations', and that for Labour to provide the extensive social reform to which they would be pledged it was necessary and essential that industry should be socialised. Socialisation meant nationalisation. The proposals in *Let Us Face the Future* were vague on the issues of foreign policy but specific and unconditional in respect both of economic policy and social reform, and it was these latter which the Government put onto the statute book. On social matters the Labour party was reaffirming the main sections of the Beveridge Report on social security and the introduction of a National Health Service. The achievement of the NHS in the summer of 1948 was the outstanding legislative advance of the Attlee years, and it has taken nearly four decades before its basic principles began to be seriously attacked in the Thatcher-Major years. There were weaknesses in the original Act, and the Socialist Medical Association criticised Aneurin Bevan for his failure to introduce a salaried service and a complete end to private medicine. The absence of provision for a comprehensive system of health centres was similarly deplored. Nevertheless it was a major achievement within a very conservative profession. The comprehensive national insurance provision introduced in 1946 by James Griffiths was both progressive and conservative. It was comprehensive in terms of sickness and unemployment and it was added to by the extension of the insurance principle to a large category of industrial injuries previously omitted from the general insurance system. What was noteworthy at the time was the acceptance, as the basis for social insurance, of the contributory principle first introduced in 1911, and at that time severely criticised by a minority of Labour MPs. The contributory principle was regressive in its social impact in that it represented, in considerable measure, a redistribution of income within the working-class population. There were some critics at the committee stage but mostly the policies seemed to be so far reaching when compared with anything that had gone before that critics were silenced without difficulty.[16] We have here a common feature of social reform in Britain throughout the past century and a half. The history of social reform in Britain has rarely been discussed save in terms that are flattering to the sound common sense and political maturity as well as the tolerance of the British people, and reform is assumed to have been a linear process of improved change. British society is not, however, easy to change and the power of vested interests has always been formidable. Reform, in the end, has generally been conceded by the propertied classes in Britain because outright opposition would push the working class towards positions of radical independence. But there are always well-defended structural obstacles to be overcome and change in Britain has always been change by instalments, partly because the barriers to radical measures are always difficult to move, partly because, in the understanding of the politically sophisticated Conservatives, piecemeal change permits the old structures to be maintained more easily in their essentials. As the young Robert Cecil said in the House of Commons in 1861, 'delay is life', and change by bits and pieces can more easily be absorbed into traditional social and political life, and being thus absorbed, its influence in the medium and long term can be correspondingly reduced.

The general election of 1945 produced a political situation unique in the whole of the twentieth century; an overwhelming majority for the party of reform and a willingness for change on the part of large sections of the British people. The party which won this election had promised in its manifesto a far reaching set of provisions for health and social security underpinned by taking into public ownership most public utilities, coal and railways. By 1950 about twenty per cent of the economic structures of Britain had been nationalised, and together with full employment and the newly introduced health and social service provision, the Labour Party claimed the introduction of a new kind of society compared with the unfettered individualism of the decades down to 1939. When however the economic policies of the Attlee government are analysed in detail, it becomes plain that there was never any intention to pursue a radical break with the past. Of the industries which were nationalised, coal and the railways were virtually bankrupt, and any government would have been forced to provide massive financial support for the large scale investment required to achieve some degree of efficiency. Nationalisation was one method out of several, and the way it was carried through in these two industries left unaltered industrial relations, rapidly increased the burden of debt – in the first instance because of much too generous compensation, which provided an increasing rentier income to property-owning individuals and institutions – and offered a cheap service to the private sector of industry and commerce. The same considerations apply to gas and electricity. Radical solutions could and should have been found especially with coal and railways. These are all matters considered in detail in the relevant chapters in this volume. In their dealings with the private sector the Attlee government continued with the type of controls it inherited from the war. For most of the period of the Labour government to 1950 the principal industrial advisor to the Board of Trade was the chairman of the British Rayon Federation. The Capital Issues Committee, set up during the war to approve or deny new issues on the capital market, was taken over by the Labour Government. Its membership was made up of seven bankers, stockbrokers and industrialists, with one representative of the Treasury – no doubt to safeguard the interests of his socialist ministers – who acted as secretary to the Committee but who took no deliberative part in the discussions. The list can be extended throughout the industrial sector; the details can be found in the well-known volume by A.A. Rogow and Peter Shore.[17]

The day-to-day control of the private sector by their own industrial leaders was to be expected by any observer who knew the record of the Labour ministers in the Churchill government, but the absence of any comprehensive analysis of the economic and social processes of nationalisation must be counted disastrous. There were no blueprints for public ownership, and to have to fall back on the example of London Transport was indeed pathetic. Industrial problems, it must be emphasised, were not the concern of economists between the wars at a time when the profession was beginning to grow in numbers and importance. Inevitably, given the existence of large numbers of unemployed during the whole of the inter-war years after 1921, and the aftermath of the world economic crisis which followed the Wall Street crash of 1929, the concentration of economic analysts was with the problem of unused resources. Since the scale of unemployment and unused industrial capacity was so very large it could only be expected that most attention would be given to macro-economic solutions involving interest rates, the stimulation of demand and the role of the State. There were some, like the Robbins-Hayek combination who dominated the London School of Economics in the 1930s, who peddled the free market and the wickedness of wage rate rigidities, but they were to be overwhelmed by Keynes' *General Theory* in 1936. Their voices were not to be heard again in any decisive way until the Thatcher era, and then with the resultant disasters that are afflicting the decade of the 1990s.

A New Society?

The young Labour economists of the 1930s were largely influenced by Keynes and, like their political leaders, were greatly impressed with the experience of wartime controls. What confirmed their general outlook was the continuation of the full employment that war had brought about. The experience of the years which followed the end of World War I was in everyone's mind when the second war came to a close, and the fact that the world economy developed into a period of growth greater than any previous in the twentieth century confirmed the belief that Keynesianism together with physical controls would enable governments to avoid the terrible years of the inter-war period.[18]

The Labour intellectuals, many of them economists who had served in the Coalition administration, were befuddled by the full employment, the growth of industrial production, the expansion of exports, the nationalisation of some industries and most public utilities. They began to believe that the Labour government was actually in process of creating a new kind of society with a range of social services hitherto unknown. Moreover, they believed in a quite uncritical way the arguments coming from the Right, that a very considerable re-distribution of income was taking place. The euphoria found its intellectual statement in the *New Fabian Essays* of 1952. Anthony Crosland in 'The Transition from Capitalism' and John Strachey in 'Tasks and Achievements of British Labour' summed up the prevailing belief that Britain was already moving out of the capitalist phase into something approaching socialism. Crosland was the most persuasive as well as the most far reaching in his claims of what had been achieved. By 1951, he wrote, 'Britain had, in all the essentials, ceased to be a capitalist country'. It was not yet a socialist country but it was certainly one that would not return to the difficulties of the pre-war years. Crosland was to repeat his argument in his well-known book *The Future of Socialism*, first published in 1956, and it was this belief that something of a fundamental change had occurred following the Labour victory of 1945 that provided much of the political and intellectual confusion that has been such a notable feature of British political life in the past forty years. The intellectual bankruptcy of the mainstream Labour intellectuals has never been more strikingly demonstrated.

We must begin with the ideological and political attack that was mounted in a rising crescendo against the Labour government by the Tories inside and outside Westminster. Its successes were especially apparent among the middle classes. In the difficult years after 1945 the components of what constituted a 'good life' for the middle classes were not always immediately obvious. Domestic servants were now increasingly difficult to come by, food and petrol were severely rationed, foreign travel allowances were sharply restricted. But what was especially galling was the argument that the only beneficiaries of Labour's legislative programme were the working classes. It has never been difficult to bring out the anti-trade union prejudices of the British middle classes, because these are built into their traditional ways of thinking, and the continued reiteration by the political Right of the wildest and most absurd stories of the power of 'our new masters' found an easy and vigorous response.[19] At the centre of this propaganda was the widespread conviction that egalitarianism was being pushed forward at the expense of the middle ranks of society. It was a constant theme of the daily and weekly press, and in this important matter no journal was more influential than the *Economist*. After the first two years or so of the Labour government, the *Economist* began its campaign on behalf of the middle classes whom its editorial staff writers clearly believed to be badly bleeding. The debate about income redistribution turned upon the analysis of official statistics, not a subject, it should be noted, that had occupied the attention of economists before 1939. On 3 January 1948 the *Economist* published a major article on income distribution pre- and post-war. Earlier articles, which had emphasised how conjectural any deductions from the official figures must be, were now forgotten, and in this January 1948 article the *Economist* provided the arguments which encouraged and sustained the hysteria that was developing through much of middle-class Britain. The real net income of the average wage earner, wrote the *Economist*, by the end of 1947 was between ten and thirty-five per cent higher than in 1938:

> The total amount paid out in wages in 1946, after the deduction of taxes, was 60 per cent higher than before the war, although there were still hundreds of thousands of men and women in the armed forces. The obverse of this great increase in wage incomes has been a slump in other incomes ... the average salary, in real net purchasing power, has fallen by anything from 20 to 30 per cent, while the real net value of profit incomes has fallen by a quarter; other forms of property incomes (from gilt-edged securities, or from rents, for example), have suffered even more severely.[20]

The literature on this income redistribution became voluminous, among the daily and weekly journalism as well as from academic economists and statisticians, and it went on during the 1950s. Lionel

Robbins, always on the side of the great and the good, wrote in *Lloyds Bank Review* for October 1955, that 'there is nothing particularly neutral in the operation of the present tax structure. Relentlessly year by year it is pushing us towards collectivism and propertyless uniformity'; and Harold Lydall, of the Oxford Institute of Statistics, was still arguing in 1959 that there was a permanent bias in the British economy towards a greater equality of incomes, although he did not expect the trend towards equality to be quite so marked in the future as he thought it had been in the past.[21]

It was all nonsense. The arguments were impressively demolished by Richard Titmuss in his volume *Income Distribution and Social Change* published in 1962. But what matters in the present context is that the mainstream Labour intellectuals and those who provided Labour leaders with their intellectual baggage also believed that income redistribution had gone a very long way. In his abridged and revised version of *The Future of Socialism* published in 1964, Crosland still wrote that 'the distribution of personal income has become significantly more equal; and the change has been almost entirely at the expense of property incomes'. These were words published after the decade of the 1950s which had seen the biggest bonanza for property owners at any time in the twentieth century. After the Tory Party came to power in 1951, and as a result of the post-war growth during the Labour years and the continuation of the world boom, share prices moved sharply upward. As a radically minded City commentator wrote, the average rich man more than doubled his share capital in the thirteen years of Tory rule, 'without having to exercise his brains. If however he had invested his capital shrewdly in equity shares or made use of the professional brains available in the City he would have trebled it.'[22]

A Radical Government?

The long established belief that the Labour government of 1945 was a radical administration stemmed first and foremost from the welfare policies introduced before 1950, with the National Health

Service the most impressive and the most important. With all its deficiencies, the new health service was an important break with the past, in spite of the fact that its political compromises allowed the service to be progressively diminished in its comprehensive coverage in the decades which followed. The additional social welfare legislation, while still within the traditional liberal structures first established in 1911, nevertheless made a deep and long-lasting impression upon public opinion, and confirmed the widespread backing for a general collectivist support of the casualties in modern industrial society. What the mainstream of the Labour Movement has never understood is: firstly, that the property owners in any society will always and continuously fight to retain their privileged position, and secondly, that capitalism as a dynamically evolving system, constantly breeds new types of inequality and new categories of the poor. All state welfare schemes in a capitalist society must regularly be adjusted to take account of economic and social change. If the fundamental structure of society is left untouched, as was the case with the legislative programme of Labour after 1945, then it is only a matter of time before the normal processes of capitalist development erode the benefits and services established in earlier times.

These considerations apply with even more force to the nationalised industries since the legislative approach to public ownership was conceived in such narrow conservative terms. It was the absence of a generous vision of what a different kind of society involves that was so striking in those momentous years after 1945; and nowhere was this more clearly demonstrated than in the area of education. This is the social area above all others where the progressive assumptions of administrators may be tested and analysed. In a modern industrial society education at all levels is a crucial measure of the political intentions and understanding of the administrators and political leaders. After 1945 the educational system accepted by the Coalition government was continued by Labour, and the class structure and class bias which from the early nineteenth century had been such a marked feature of the English educational system was left undisturbed. In the university sector the baneful domination of Oxbridge continued, with the social composition of its student population unchanged. But education was only one, albeit among the more important, of the social structures that remained in place when the Tories came back to office in 1951; and the basic conservatism of British society was never to be challenged.

Britain was never again to be a major world power after the six years of war. The illusion of grandeur remained and nowhere was this illusion more accepted than by Ernest Bevin and his senior officials of the Foreign Office. What they never appreciated – and this was true throughout Whitehall – was that there were structural deficiencies in the British industrial economy which, unless remedied, would ineluctably and inexorably bring Britain down to a second class power, whatever the global situation of world capitalism. Revelations of economic inefficiency across a very wide band of industry were many and damning during the war years, and the evidence of managerial incompetence and technological backwardness accumulated in the files of government departments such as the Board of Trade. By 1945 and in the years which followed there was an increasing volume of published material which closely documented the low levels of productivity compared with other leading industrial economies; and much has been brought together and analysed in Corelli Barnett's massive indictment *The Audit of War*, published in 1986. His political conclusions do not have to be accepted but the evidence he presents is both accurate and quite devastating. Neither the Labour leaders nor the Labour intellectuals understood these matters in spite of the constant encouragement to improve productivity, one of the major themes of the Labour administration. It was the world boom of the third quarter of the century which concealed the inefficiencies of the British economy, at least during the 1950s, and the problems were never seriously understood until analysts began probing into the causes of the British economic decline relative to countries such as Germany, France and Japan. But that was long after Labour left office in 1951, and in succeeding decades Labour politicians remained imprisoned within the political/military relationship with the United States.

The Cold War was a confusing phenomenon, and Stalinism inside Russia made it only too easy to sell the Cold War as a defence of freedom to the British Labour Movement. Peter Weiler's *British Labour and the Cold War* had documented some of the consequences which have been so disastrous, although it remains remarkable how deep-rooted are the myths about 1945 to our day. Throughout the post-war era Britain remained a more or less happy and usually docile satellite of the United States. Viewed from afar and on a world scale, a Labour Government succeeding a Tory administration, whether in 1945 or the 1960s or 1970s was a change from Tweedledum to Tweedledee. There was no change in terms of British influence and policy throughout the world. In a world which has been ravaged by the struggles for colonial liberation and by the fierce nationalisms of the third world, Britain has consistently pursued repressive policies towards the emerging nations. Not, it is accepted, on the scale of American imperialism, but these are matters closely related to economic strength. In Europe Britain underwrote the tensions of the Cold War. The name of Britain, from the end of World War Two, is the name of a country which has steadily fought alongside the old, decaying forces obstructing and where possible strangling progress. The independence of India, it may be granted, was not inevitable, at least at the time it was made; and the Tories, and Ernest Bevin if he had had his way, would have delayed the political process. It was Clement Attlee who recognised the alternative of a massive bloodshed if independence was not granted, bloodshed which would have run wider and deeper than that which actually occurred. For the rest, de-colonisation came because in the end Britain could no longer afford to maintain the forces which would have been required to continue occupation; but before the end was reached life was nearly always bitter and harsh, with many dead and more tortured.

On a world scale and analysed in historical perspective, the social legislation of the Attlee government was long overdue and by comparison with social security policies of the advanced European countries, once the aftermath of war had been overcome, certainly modest. The Attlee administrations engineered a change-over from war to peace with notably little social disturbance; and in the ways that the transition was effected the Labour government disillusioned its own militants, encouraged a far reaching cynicism among the more non-political workers, brought the ideas and ideals of socialism into question and, by the particular ways in which the streamlining of the economy was carried through, provided a spring board for the rich to take off into the profiteers' paradise of the 1950s.

Notes

[1] The history of the Labour Movement in the 1930s will be found in many materials. A selection includes; G.D.H. Cole, *History of the Labour Party from 1914*, Routledge and Kegan Paul, London 1948; C.L. Mowat, *Britain Between the Wars*, Methuen, London 1955; Alan Bullock, *The Life and Times of Ernest Bevin*, Vol 1, Heinemann, London 1960; J.F. Naylor, *Labour's International Policy, The Labour Party in the 1930s*, Weidenfeld & Nicholson, London 1969; J. Saville, 'May Day 1937' in *Essays in Labour History*, A. Briggs and J. Saville (eds), Croom Helm, Beckenham 1977; B. Pimlott, *Hugh Dalton*, Macmillan, London 1985. Among recent biographies are two on Harold Laski; M. Newman, *Harold Laski, a Political Biography*, Macmillan, London 1933; I. Kramnick and Barry Sheerman, *Harold Laski, A Life on the Left*, Hamish Hamilton, London 1993.
[2] Wal Hannington, who led the unemployed workers between the wars, wrote his own lively account, *Unemployed Struggles, 1919-1936*, Gollancz, London 1936, reprinted 1977. See also R. Hayburn, 'The Responses of the Unemployed in the 1930s, with particular reference to South-East Lancashire', PhD. University of Hull, 1970; P. Kingsford, *The Hunger Marches in Britain, 1920-1940*, Lawrence and Wishart, London 1982; R. Croucher, *We Refuse to Starve in Silence*, Lawrence and Wishart, London 1987. Ellen Wilkinson wrote her own account in *The Town That Was Murdered*, Gollancz, London 1939.
[3] M. Foot, *Aneurin Bevan, A Biography, Vol 1. 1987-1945*, MacGibbon and Key, London 1962, pp287ff.
[4] D.E. Butler, *The Electoral System in Britain*, Macmillan, London 1963.
[5] Bill Davidson, 'The Cairo Forces Parliament', *Labour History Review*, Vol 55 No 3, Winter 1990; R. Kisch, *The Days of the Good Soldiers, Communists in the Armed Forces, World War II*, Journeyman, London 1985.
[6] G.D.H. Cole, *Trade Unioins Today*, Allen & Unwin, London 1939; *Trade Unions in British Politics*, B. Pimlott and C. Cook (eds), Longmans, London 1982, esp. Chs. 5 and 6.
[7] K. Harris, *Attlee*, Weidenfeld and Nicholson, London 1982, pp266ff; A. Bullock, *Ernest Bevin, Foreign Secretary, 1945-51*, Heinemann, London, pp25ff.
[8] *The Memoirs of Lord Gladwyn*, Weidenfeld & Nicholson, London, 1972, p106.
[9] A.A. Rogow and P. Shore, *The Labour Government and British Industry 1945-1951*, Blackwell, Oxford 1955, *passim*. See also the chapters in this book by Richard Saville and Nina Fishman.
[10] J. Saville, *The Politics of Continuity, British Foreign Policy and the Labour Government, 1945-6*, Verso, London 1993, Ch. 5.
[11] On Spain there is a brief summary in R. Carr, *Spain, 1808-1975*, 2nd edn., Oxford 1982; and a much more extended treatment in Quasim bin Ahmad, 'The British Government and the Franco Dictatorship, 1945-50', PhD, University of

London, 1987. The literature on Greece is voluminous; H. Richter, *British Intervention in Greece, From Varzika to Civil War, February 1945–August 1946*, London 1986, has a full bibliography.

[12] Sir Richard Clarke (ed. Sir Alec Caincross), *Anglo-American Economic Collaboratiaon in War and Peace*, Oxford University Press, Oxford 1982, p152, entry dated February 22 1946.

[13] The first detailed account of parts of the Attlee heresy were in R. Smith and J. Zametica, 'The Cold Warrior; Clement Attlee reconsidered; 1945-7', *International Affairs*, Vol 61, No 2, Spring 1955, pp237-252.

[14] D.K. Fieldhouse, 'The Labour Governments and Empire-Commonwealth', in R. Ovendale (ed), *The Foreign Policy of the British Labour Governments, 1945-51*, Leicester University Press, Leicester 1984, pp83-120.

[15] The Details of the Marshall Plan allocations are taken from A. Milward, *The Reconstruction of Western Europe, 1945-51*, Methuen, London, 2nd edn. 1987, pp101*ff*.

[16] K. Morgan, *Labour in Power, 1945-51*, OUP, Oxford 1984, Ch 4.

[17] Quoted in Note 9 above.

[18] For an extended discussion of the Labour economists of 1930s, see Elizabeth Durbin, *New Jerusalem, The Labour Party and the Economics of Democratic Socialism*, Routledge and Kegan Paul, London 1985; and see also Morgan, *Labour in Power, op cit*, Ch 1; and Paul Addison, *The Road to 1945, British Politics and the Second World War*, Jonathan Cape, London 1975, esp. Ch 1.

[19] A helpful introduction is *The Age of Austerity*, M. Sissons and P. French (eds), Hodder and Stoughton, London 1961, esp. Chs. 1 and 19.

[20] *Economist*, 3 January 1948.

[21] H.F. Lydall, 'The Long Term Trends in the Size and Distribution of Income', *Journal of the Royal Statistical Society*, vol 122, Part 1, 1959, esp. pp33-5.

[22] N. Davenport, *The Split Society*, Gollancz, London, 1964, p 67.

Part 1 – Economic Policies

'From the Ground Up'?: The Labour Governments and Economic Planning

Michael Cunningham

> Labour will plan from the ground up – giving an appropriate place to constructive enterprise and private endeavour in the national plan, but dealing decisively with those interests which would use high-sounding talk about economic freedom to cloak their determination to put themselves and their wishes above those of the whole nation.
>
> *Let Us Face the Future* – Labour Party Declaration, 1945.

In the decade before the Second World War, the idea of some form of central economic planning was at the heart of the Labour Party's economic strategy. Planning held this pre-eminent position because the two main alternatives to centralised state management were in a relatively weak position in this period. Support for 'bottom up' forms of economic organisation, for example Guild Socialism or the more militant syndicalism, was on the wane, and support within the Labour Party for Keynesian demand management was, as shown below, relatively slow to develop. I shall consider three broad themes relating to Labour government policy from 1945-51: the background to Labour's attempts at post-war planning, the machinery of planning together with the 'Economic Surveys' of this period, and a review of the reasons for the problems associated with a planning strategy.

The Planning Debate

It is not possible here to detail the intra-Party debate on planning in the 1930s; however some broad themes can be highlighted. The justification for planning had at least three different elements for its various proponents within the Labour Movement. Firstly, there was the argument that planning ensured a more efficient use of resources than that which prevailed under a *laissez faire* system. The recession of the 1930s and the distortion of the market by monopolistic trends had dealt a severe blow to the assumptions of classical political economy and made the technocratic case for planning much stronger. Secondly, planning had an explicitly ethical dimension. A diminution, or replacement, of an unfettered market system would promote a sense of common purpose and solidarity within society; competitive individualism would be superseded by shared goals and redistribution based on need, and a conception of social justice would be promoted. Thirdly, for some the ethical dimension, or 'true socialist' planning, was only to be realised under a system of workers' control and industrial democracy. Planning thus had a deeper significance than 'mere' economic efficiency; it involved claims about the nature of power, justice and democracy.[1]

There were, therefore, different theoretical arguments for planning; in practice, of course, many Labour theorists and activists conflated a technocratic and ethical position, and no clear distinction can be made even if the positions are conceptually separable. However, a belief in the efficiency of planning did not resolve the more technical questions and tensions surrounding issues such as the role of the price mechanism within a planned economy and the relationship between Keynesian ideas and planning. If most socialists could agree that planning was both more efficient and more ethical, there was no consensus on the institutional and administrative changes necessary for planning, the question of a pricing policy and the challenge of nascent Keynesianism.

Some of the conflicts over these issues will be outlined here. My purpose is to demonstrate that, despite the upsurge of intellectual

4

activity in the 1930s around issues of what a future socialist government would need to do in the area of practical economic strategy, there was no blueprint which the 1945 government could implement.[2]

The first example is that of the machinery of planning. 'Traditional' socialism, as espoused in Clause 4 of the 1918 Labour Party Constitution, had codified a commitment to nationalisation which was questioned by some of the leading socialist thinkers of the 1930s. For example, Evan Durbin's *The Importance of Planning* (1935) advocated the rationalisation of production units within the same industrial sector and the planning of their investment and output policy by means of a unified authority. To co-ordinate policy nationally, a National Investment Board would be created. The direction of investment by agencies in each sector, agencies which would have a greater knowledge of economic conditions than that available to individual entrepreneurs and managers, was the crux of the machinery of planning for Durbin: for him it was 'the extension of the area of survey and control which is the definitive thing about all forms of planning.'[3]

Although the details of planning outlined by Evan Durbin, Barbara Wootton and Sidney and Beatrice Webb (who advocated the establishment of a parliament to deal with social and economic policy) may have varied, there was a shared conception of Labour representing a national, as opposed to a class, interest, and a related opposition to workers' control or industrial democracy. In *The Importance of Planning* Durbin is explicit in his opposition to workers retaining the surplus made in socialised industries, and of the power of trade unions to influence the size of the workforce. In similar vein, Wootton's concept of a planning commission had elitist implications and no role for workers' control, and was justified by her conception of national rather than class interest.[4] This position was the dominant one, with a minority view represented in the work of G.D.H. Cole, who in *The Principles of Economic Planning* (1935) emphasised the need for democratic control over planners and Treasury officials.

A second issue around which much of the planning debate revolved was that of the role of the price mechanism within a planned economy. Those who argued that prices should not be controlled did so for two principal reasons. The first was on grounds of economic theory; classical theory held that the price mechanism was the way in which the most efficient use of resources was utilised. Consumer preference was indicated by the movement of prices and thus influenced supply and demand. Many advocates of planning argued that this orthodoxy held good under a system of guided investment and larger units of production which would constitute a new planned economy. Supporters of market pricing included Hugh Gaitskell, Douglas Jay and Evan Durbin; the last named argued that, '... there is no formal or logical contradiction between planning and pricing', and he advocated a free market for consumption goods, and marginal cost pricing in nationalised industries.[5]

In addition to the efficiency argument, advocates of market pricing utilised the 'political' argument that the maintenance of consumer choice and freedom was a major feature distinguishing democratic planning from the dictatorial implications of a system of planning by control. This argument was important as a defence against critics who were to equate planning with political unfreedom and the drift to authoritarianism.[6]

G.D.H. Cole, Hugh Dalton and Barbara Wootton were among those who were more sceptical about the retention of the price mechanism. The implication of their position was that the criteria of efficiency utilised under capitalism were not applicable to a planned economy with a large socialised sector. However it was not clear how the deployment of resources would be organised efficiently without them. Indeed, Elizabeth Durbin has described the views of Dalton and Wootton on the price mechanism as vague.[7] Cole, the most 'left wing' of the thinkers discussed here, was the most opposed to the retention of an orthodox pricing mechanism under a planned economy.

A third theoretical question for Labour economists and policy-makers in this period, and perhaps with hindsight the most important, was the relevance of Keynesianism and its relation to socialism and planning. At a 'political' level, there was resistance to Keynesian ideas because they could be, and later were, utilised to

6

reform and stabilise capitalism and thus provide a coherent alternative to socialism. Such suspicion of Keynesianism, and of Keynes himself, who did not share the egalitarian ideals of the Labour Movement, was not restricted to the Left of the Party.

It was only gradually that Keynesian ideas became accepted within the Labour Movement. Evan Durbin had argued that Labour thinking on fiscal and monetary policy remained fairly orthodox until the late 1930s. 'Unorthodox' notions such as budget deficits and fluctuating exchange rates were excluded from the 1937 election programme.[8] Ben Pimlott, in his biography of Dalton, records how Dalton, a key figure in Labour's economic and financial policy formulation in the early 1930s, was resistant to the concept of demand management and emphasised physical planning; this is indicated by the fact that neither *Practical Socialism for Britain* (1935) nor the 1936 edition of *Principles of Public Finance* mentioned Keynes's multiplier principle.[9]

It would be impossible here to chart the impact of Keynesian ideas on leading Labour figures of the 1930s; their effect was uneven, and different individuals would utilise different aspects of the theories. However, two points should be emphasised. Firstly, Keynesian ideas had profound and unsettling implications for proponents of planning; if demand management through fiscal and budgetary policy could stabilise the economy at a high level of employment and stable prices, this cast doubt on the case for physical planning, the associated institutional reform and many Labour figures' conception of socialism. Even as radical a figure as the Marxist John Strachey changed his thinking in the late 1930s partly because of this realisation. Secondly, Keynesianism did gradually permeate Labour thinking. By the end of the 1930s, Labour had adopted expansionist ideas that were, 'at least semi-Keynesian'.[10] Keynesian-inspired ideas about demand management are to be found in James Meade's *Outline of Economic Policy for a Labour Government*, an unpublished paper of 1935, and in Douglas Jay's *The Socialist Case* of 1937. Jay is frequently cited, with Hugh Gaitskell, as one of the more pro-Keynesian thinkers in the party.[11] It has been argued that even Hugh Dalton, often portrayed as unreceptive to Keynesianism in his post-war

Chancellorship, gradually accepted the utility of fiscal policy of a Keynesian type.[12]

In short, the decade of debate over economic policy and planning had provided no clear conception of what the latter would, in practice, entail. Wider theoretical questions, such as whether planning was socialism or a means by which to achieve it, were also unresolved. The rise of Keynesianism had caused further conceptual confusion, as the question of whether it could be used as a supplement to planning, or would ultimately undermine it, had to be addressed. As J. Leruez has argued, in 1945 vagueness and ambiguity surrounded planning after more than a decade of consideration.[13]

The Machinery of Planning 1945–51[14]

The exigencies of total war from 1939–45 had led to the creation of planning machinery which directed virtually all sections of the economy, including manpower, prices, production and investment.[15] The planning sections of the government departments were responsible to two committees. At official level there was a steering committee which comprised the Permanent Secretaries of the main economic departments, and at ministerial level the Lord President's Committee which comprised the Ministers of departments with economic responsibilities. Constitutionally, this was a sub-committee, but in practice it functioned as the supreme planning authority.

Labour's accession to power threw up pertinent questions about the future of planning. These included what was to replace the wartime machinery, which sections of government were to co-ordinate policy, and to what extent planning was compatible with peacetime democratic politics. Although the Labour manifesto of 1945, *Let Us Face the Future*, indicated a commitment to planning, a coherent strategy did not exist, and problems of co-ordination bwtween ministries with economic responsibilities were likely to arise.

The shortcomings of Labour's planning attempts will be reviewed further in the final section, but some preliminary observations may be made about the period 1945–7; that is before reorganisation of the planning machinery. The consensus is that Labour's attempt at planning was flawed, and the following reasons have been cited. Firstly, there was a failure to adapt the wartime planning machinery to peacetime conditions, and a related over-reliance on the continuation of a network of controls. This was probably a result of the lack of clearly defined objectives and the manner in which they could be implemented.[16]

Secondly, criticisms have been made of the role of the Lord President's Committee, and it has been questioned whether Morrison had a clear vision of what planning entailed: his other responsibilities as Lord President, particularly the preparation of Labour's legislative programme, precluded full-time devotion to this issue. Thirdly, and more importantly, there was the necessity of dealing with immediate and externally-promoted economic difficulties beyond the scope of departmental or administrative reform. The most pressing of these resulted from the termination of Lend-Lease in September 1945 and the consequent need to boost export-orientated production to pay for the dollar loan negotiated by Keynes in December of that year. Short-term difficulties might in theory reinforce the need for long-term planning, but tended in practice to reinforce an *ad hoc* approach.

1947 marked the beginning of a period of reorganisation of the machinery of planning, prompted in part by the fuel crisis and the sterling crisis of that year, when short-lived convertibility of sterling resulted in a massive drop in reserves. In March 1947 Attlee announced the setting up of two new bodies to facilitate economic planning. The Central Economic Planning Staff (CEPS) was an inter-departmental agency chaired by the Chief Planning Officer of the Cabinet Office. Its three main functions were to draw up a long-term plan for resource use, to monitor the progress of the economic surveys (see below) and to co-ordinate information provided by departments with economic responsibilities. Although the logic of the CEPS creation appeared to be to centralise economic policy under the Lord President and to improve inter-departmental communication (many of its up to forty members were seconded from other departments), its influence was limited as it had no independent executive power and assumed the status of a 'think tank'. Attlee made it clear that it would not impinge upon existing cabinet and department responsibilities.[17]

The second new agency was the Economic Planning Board (EPB) set up in July. Its membership had a corporate flavour and included representatives of the trade unions and the employers' organisations, Permanent Secretaries of the principal economic departments, members of the CEPS and the Director of the Economic Section of the Cabinet Office.[18] As with the CEPS, the lack of an executive role, and the tradition of departmental autonomy, precluded a significant role for the EPB. Sir Edwin Plowden records that Ministers did not attend meetings and it developed into a talking shop.[19] Keith Middlemas argues that even its corporatist role can be overestimated, if by that is understood a process of bargaining between the government and the peak organisations of capital and labour.[20] Rather, the EPB's role was to keep the representative bodies – the Federation of British Industries (FBI), the British Employers' Confederation (BEC) and the TUC – informed of government plans.

The second period of reorganisation occurred in September 1947 with the creation of the Ministry of Economic Affairs which Stafford Cripps was to head. Under its aegis came the CEPS, the Economic Information Unit of the Treasury and the Economic Section of the Cabinet Office.[21] The Minister co-ordinated two Cabinet committees: the Economic Policy Committee which included the Prime Minister, the Lord President and the Chancellor, and which considered the major issues of internal and external affairs, and the Ministerial Steering Committee, composed of the five production Ministers; Labour, Supply, Works, Board of Trade and Fuel and Power.

It does not appear that such reorganisation marked a serious attempt to improve the machinery of planning and to overcome the fragmentation of the Morrison period. A principal reason for the Ministry's foundation was to assuage the ambition of Cripps, and to provide a way for Attlee to respond to criticisms from within the party of Morrison's shortcomings in the previous two years. The lack of commitment to a powerful, centralised planning ministry is evident; as with the CEPS, the Ministry of Economic Affairs was to be a co-ordinating body and not allowed to impinge upon existing department responsibilities. The Ministry did not survive Cripps's appointment as Chancellor in November 1947 after Dalton's resignation. The CEPS, EPB and the Economic Information Unit became integrated into the Treasury.

There was no significant reorganisation after 1947. The merger of the planning agencies with the Treasury would suggest a *prima facie* remedy to the problem of insufficient co-ordination between the three departments with economic responsibilities in the period 1945–47, the Treasury, the Board of Trade and the Lord President's Council. These departments had responsibility for, or power to influence, one or more important areas; for example, fiscal policy, production, investment, prices and exports. This situation was not helped by personal and inter-departmental tensions.[22] However, the reorganisation of late 1947 contributed to the downgrading of physical planning, since the Treasury's strengthened position militated against the creation of the kind of developmental state which would have been necessary to make planning any more than indicative, or an exercise in vague statements of intent.

The Economic Surveys

To turn briefly to a consideration of the economic plans that the Labour administration formulated: the limited scope of subsequent years' surveys, as they were termed, was prefigured by the unpublished draft *Economic Survey for 1946*. Keith Middlemas argues that most Labour Ministers and officials believed the scope for planning was limited by the need to secure industry's support (which circumscribed the direction of investment), and public tolerance of further controls.[23]

The following year saw the publication of the *Economic Survey* (Cmnd 7046). Compared with subsequent years, it is often seen as the apogee of Labour planning, despite the fact that it was somewhat cautious in approach and unambitious in scope. It indicated the limitations of planning in a democratic society, and the 'essential difference' between this and a totalitarian form. This helps to explain why no direction of labour was contemplated. A second note of caution was the timespan of the survey; long-term (i.e., five year) planning was rejected on the grounds that economic uncertainty rendered this unrealistic.

In essence the 1947 survey drew up balances for manpower and resource distribution and projected the desired distribution between sectors for the coming year. Even this was somewhat tentative; the resources section showed the percentage of distribution of output between sectors of expenditure, but did not indicate the expected increase in output or of the values of expenditure. Four inter-departmental committees at official level were to consider programmes for manpower, materials, balance of payments and capital investment, and a fifth steering committee was to ensure that the claims of the four sectors were kept within the total of available resources. The survey thus acted as an *ad hoc* rationing scheme.[24]

The appendix of the 1948 survey revealed that several of the targets of its predecessor were not met, including coal and steel production, manpower distribution between sectors, and import and export levels. Annual surveys continued until the end of the administration, but increasingly took the form of reviews of the previous year and hopes for the future, often bolstered by exhortation about the need for restrained consumption, to allow goods to be channelled into the export market, and increased production. Caution and conservatism informed the plans as 'targets' became 'estimates', and a contemporary source, albeit an unsympathetic one, described the 1950 survey as a 'humble document, weak almost to the point of being meaningless'.[25]

In addition to the annual surveys, the CEPS and the Economic Section prepared two longer-term economic surveys. The first draft of the 1948-51 survey was circulated among civil servants in May 1947, but much of the detail was rendered out of date by the convertibility crisis and it was never shown to ministers. A second draft document, to cover the period 1948-52, was circulated in the summer of 1948, but it was superseded by the preparation of a document for the Organisation for European Economic Co-operation (OEEC).

This document was prepared under the terms of receipt of Marshall Aid; its main emphasis was on improving the balance of payments via increased production and overseas trade. In general, its predictive qualities proved to be better than the annual surveys, but the question remains: what would have happened without it? The survey did not act as a guide to policy-makers after 1948, and Joan Mitchell's verdict is somewhat qualified – 'its success as a plan, rather than as a forecast, cannot be proved – or disproved'; and Jacques Leruez maintains that the accurate estimates of the plan were largely based on economic policies and mechanisms which preceded it, and thus the plan itself was not the salient factor.[26]

Sir Edwin Plowden argues that the submission of the plan in October 1948 marked the waning of interest in long-term planning and a move towards increased use of demand management. There was a growing belief that important economic indicators (e.g., balance of payments, demand, inflation, employment) could be controlled by fiscal and monetary policy; and the effect of economic shocks, such as the 1949 devaluation, and inflation caused by the Korean War, which made long-term forecasting increasingly arbitrary, also helped to weaken the case for physical planning after 1948.

The Failure of Planning

Commentators on the 1945-51 Labour governments are almost unanimous in their verdict on planning policy; many doubt both the commitment to it and, relatedly, the existence of a clear conception of what it entailed. Adjectives such as 'piecemeal', '*ad hoc*' and 'inadequate' scatter the texts. The politically hostile record the confusion surrounding the term, and the differing concepts held within the Labour Party. Sympathetic commentators, such as Kenneth Morgan, have described the exercise as, 'half-hearted, indirect and in many ways unsuccessful.'[27] Similar verdicts can be found in many texts of the last forty years.[28]

The question which needs to be addressed, then, is not whether planning was successful, but why it was so relatively limited and incoherent. On this question there is less consensus than on the fact of its shortcomings. What must be attempted is a sorting of the myriad of proferred explanations, and a distinguishing of the fundamental factors from the more incidental ones. For analytic purposes, the barriers to more thoroughgoing planning can be divided into political, economic and administrative factors, though this is not to imply that these are practically separable.[29]

The legacy of pre-war confusion over the issue prevented a strategy being adopted between 1945 and 1951 through which important political forces could either be reconciled to, or coerced into adopting, planning. Arguably, if planning were to be more than indicative or exhortatory, involving a statement of aims and an appeal to the altruism or the sense of national interest of employers and trade unions (such as often informed Cripps's speeches), there had to be policies and structures to ensure the fulfilment of investment and manpower policies. The failure to realise these reflects both the Labour leadership's indulgent view of the operation of capital, and the political resistance of capital in Britain to the creation of structures which would more closely integrate state and private investment.[30]

Industrialists were unwilling to entertain the maintenance, or extension, of controls once a period of shortage was over, especially if their former privileged positions as members of production councils were challenged. An example is the hostility shown by industrial interest groups to the government's attempts to establish development councils for each of the main industrial sectors.[31] David Howell argues that the Government's ideology did not fundamentally question the position of capital and that the private sector was treated as a necessary and appropriate partner, and largely on its terms.[32]

The role of labour, or more specifically the Trade Union Movement, as the other part of the corporate equation, has also been cited as a barrier to planning, although this argument is weaker. This view figures prominently in Sam Beer's account of the government's progressive move from manpower planning to accepting the efficacy of Keynesian-influenced national income analysis. A coherent manpower policy, he argues, needed either the direction of labour (unacceptable in a democratic society) or a controlled wages structure. The latter conflicted with the Trade Union Movement's commitment to free collective bargaining which was 'radically incompatible' with the economic planning of the government and largely explains the abandonment of a manpower policy by 1949.[33] However, Beer's thesis can be criticised on three grounds. Firstly, the general thesis is questionable that, even in the immediate post-war years, the power of the Trade Union Movement as a corporate actor was as great as implied, especially when compared with the interests of capital. Secondly, Middlemas has argued that the commitment to planning of both Dalton and Cripps, the first two Chancellors, was weaker than Beer maintains, and that he overestimates the shift in policy away from physical planning towards Keynesian policies in 1947-8. Thirdly, Middlemas contends that the TUC was committed to unprecedented involvement in consultation and planning. 'There is very little substance in the old charge that the unions forced the Labour Government to abandon physical planning in order to safeguard their aggressive wage claims.'[34]

Given the opposition to planning from within industry, Labour's lack of ideological commitment to planning prevented it from formulating a policy which could 'sell' planning to the British people as a positive and innovative way to improve efficiency and social justice. It therefore became an expedient for dealing with post-war shortages which implied removal of controls when these had been remedied; as with the Board of Trade's 'bonfire of controls' in 1948.

These 'political' factors are significant because they help to explain the attraction of alternative economic policies. It was the gradual adoption of demand management which made physical planning largely redundant and precluded the need for thoroughgoing institutional reform, either within the departmental apparatus of government or of the financial and banking sectors. Although there are differences of emphasis, most authors point to the accession of Cripps as Chancellor in 1947 as the period in which Keynesian policies began to establish dominance and the Treasury's primacy was re-established, with the demise of the Ministry of Economic Affairs and the Lord President's Committee as rival economic departments.

It has also been noted that, because full employment was maintained (though more because of the post-war reconstruction fuelled by American expenditure than the result of 'simple' Keynesian expansionism), one of the policies most dear to the Left was effected. This allowed the abandonment of planning with much less opposition from that quarter than might otherwise have been expected.[35]

The third category of explanation for planning's failure may be termed administrative problems. It can be argued that these are of a second order nature; that is, these impediments were not rectified *because* planning was not central to the government's programme rather than their being the cause of its failure. Nevertheless, administrative difficulties did not help the cause of planning. Lack of departmental co-ordination was often exacerbated by personal rivalries between ministers and officials.[36] Rodney Barker has described how many civil service personnel were committed to a *laissez faire* ideology while many of the temporary members who favoured planning had left at the end of the war. The separation of planning and finance resulted in 'muddle and confusion and very often tension' between the Lord President's Office and the Treasury; and the planning machinery stood in an ambiguous position in relation to the traditional civil service organisation and was often by-passed. Barker concludes that the machinery of planning was 'fragmented and lacking in clear channels of advice and decision-making at both official and ministerial levels' and 'was inadequate for carrying out a central plan.'[37] This lack of commitment to planning was also reflected in the relatively small number of trained economists and statisticians in the relevant government departments.[38]

In essence, a lack of ideological commitment to planning and the political difficulties of reconciling important interest groups, especially capital, explain the shortcomings of Labour policy. These were in turn reinforced by the availability of a Keynesian alternative much more congenial to established administrative arrangements.

As Labour's commitment to the key areas of nationalisation, the construction of the Welfare State and full employment were realisable without extensive planning, so the political case for it became progressively weakened over the period 1945-51. This trend was facilitated by external economic shocks and perhaps the very scale of the reconstruction problem which increased scepticism that long-term planning was much more than intelligent guesswork.

Notes

Most of the references below are from secondary sources. For a guide to primary material see, *inter alia*, the references of the relevant sections in: K. Middlemas, *Power, Competition and the State. Volume 1. Britain in search of balance 1940-61*, Macmillan, Basingstoke, 1986; E. Plowden, *An Industrialist in the Treasury*, Andre Deutsch, London, 1989; and A. Rogow and P. Shore, *The Labour Government and British Industry 1945-51*, Basil Blackwell, Oxford, 1955.

[1] B. Pimlott, *Labour and the Left in the 1930s*, Cambridge University Press, Cambridge 1977, pp64-5.

[2] See Elizabeth Durbin, *New Jerusalems: The Labour Party and the Economics of Democratic Socialism*, Routledge and Kegan Paul, London 1985, for a detailed account of this period and the relationship between Keynesian and socialist ideas.

[3] E.F.M. Durbin, 'The Importance of Planning', in *Problems of Economic Planning*, Routledge and Kegan Paul, London 1949, p44. Barbara Wootton's *Plan or No Plan*, 1934, contains similar statist-technocratic implications in advocating a Planning Commission.

[4] G. Foote, *The Labour Party's Political Thought*, Croom Helm, Beckenham 1986 (2nd ed), p180.

[5] E.F.M. Durbin, *op cit*, p48. For Jay's similar views on planning and the pricing mechanism see *The Socialist Case*, Faber and Faber, London 1947 (2nd ed), p128. Foote sums up Jay's position thus: 'Planning was desirable *only* where inequality and insecurity could be diminished without too great a loss of consumer freedom and without the creation of unnecessary state monopolies in industry.' Foote, *op cit*, p202, his emphasis.

[6] The best known advocate of this position is F. Hayek. For a trenchant British critique of planning, see J. Jewkes, *Ordeal by Planning*, Macmillan, London 1948.

[7] See E.F.M. Durbin, *op cit*, pp169-181, for a discussion of the price mechanism.

[8] *Ibid*, p262.

[9] B. Pimlott, *Hugh Dalton*, Jonathan Cape, London 1985, p217.

[10] *Ibid*, p244.

[11] E. Durbin, 'Fabian Socialism and Economic Science, in B. Pimlott (ed), *Fabian Essays in Socialist Thought*, Heinemann, London 1984, p44. James Meade was an academic economist who served in the Economic Section of the War Cabinet from 1940 to 1945 and was director of the Economic Section from 1945 to 1947.

[12] K. Morgan, in *Labour in Power 1945-1951*, Oxford University Press, Oxford 1984, stresses Dalton's wariness of Keynesian ideas. Foote, *op cit*, and Pimlott, in *Hugh Dalton*, record a somewhat more receptive view.

[13] J. Leruez, *Economic Planning and Politics in Britain*, Martin Robertson, London 1975, pp27-30.

[14] For more detailed accounts of planning in this period, see Middlemas, *op cit*, chs. 4 and 5; Leruez, *op cit*, part 1; and J. Mitchell, *Groundwork to Economic Planning*, Martin Secker and Warburg, London 1966, chs. 3 and 4.

[15] For details of the wartime economy, see S. Pollard, *The Development of the British Economy 1914-80*, Edward Arnold, London 1983 (3rd ed), ch. 6. To facilitate wartime planning the Central Economic Information Service within the Cabinet Office had been set up in 1940. It was sub-divided into the Economic Section and the Statistical Section in June 1941.

[16] 'For the most part ... the government was content to rely on using the wartime physical and financial controls to allocate resources on an ad hoc basis rather than according to the requirements of any published plan.' (D. Aldcroft, *The British Economy: volume 1 The Years of Turmoil 1920-1951*, Wheatsheaf, Brighton 1986, p240).

[17] Rogow and Shore, *op cit*, pp19-20. Leruez, *op cit*, argues of the CEPS, 'in essence it was much more concerned with advising on general economic policy than with promoting any particular form of detailed planning' (p49).

[18] For the verdict of its chairman, see E. Plowden, *op cit*, p12.

[19] *Ibid*, p23.

[20] This form of corporate representation was already to be found in the National Production Advisory Council for Industry (NPACI) and the National Joint Advisory Council (NJAC), both of which had been reconstituted after the war.

[21] For details of the Economic Section see the chapter by N. Chester, in G.D.N. Worswick and P.H. Ady (eds), *The British Economy 1945-50*, Oxford University Press, London 1952; and ch. 15 of H. Daalder, *Cabinet Reform in Britain 1914-1963*, Oxford University Press, London 1964.

[22] Cripps and some civil servants were doubtful about Morrison's grasp of economic affairs. See, for example, B. Donoghue and G. Jones, *Herbert Morrison: Portrait of a Politician*, Weidenfeld and Nicolson, London 1973, p354. R.Barker, in 'Civil Service Attitudes and the Economic Planning of the Attlee Government', *Journal of Contemporary History* 21 (3) 1986, pp473-486, records the scepticism of many civil servants about planning.

[23] Middlemas, *op cit*, pp117-18.

[24] Rogow and Shore, *op cit*, p18. See Aldcroft, *op cit*, p241, for an appraisal of the survey.

[25] 'Economist', cited in A. Sked and C. Cook, *Post-War Britain: A Political History*, Penguin, Harmondsworth 1979, p98.

[26] Mitchell, *op cit*, p119; Leruez, *op cit*, p59.

[27] Morgan, *op cit*, p135. For a hostile account, see Jewkes, *op cit*.

[28] A less than comprehensive list includes: R. Eatwell, *The 1945-1951 Labour Governments*, Batsford, London 1979, pp85, 157; H. Pelling, *The Labour Governments 1945-51*, Macmillan, London 1984, p171; M. Ceadal, 'Labour as a Governing Party: Balancing Right and Left', in T. Gourvish and A. O'Day (eds), *Britain Since 1945*, Macmillan, Basingstoke 1991, pp267-68; T. Hutchison, *Economics and Economic Policy in Britain 1946-1966*, George Allen and Unwin, London 1968, p55; Aldcroft, *op cit*, pp204, 238, 248; Rogow & Shore, *op cit*, pp24-5; Pollard, *op cit*, p248 and Plowden, *op cit*, pp48-9.

[29] The problems of post-war planning have, of course, to be set in the context of the economic difficulties of reconstruction; for example, labour shortages, lost productive capacity and the convertibility crisis. These are covered in detail in many of the general histories of the period. Corelli Barnett, in *The Audit of War*,

Macmillan, London 1986, has argued that Labour's pre-occupation with building the 'New Jerusalem' militated against an adequate strategy for industrial regeneration.

[30] These problems were reflected, albeit in different forms, in the failure of the National Plan and the Department of Economic Affairs in the mid 1960s. For the hostility of industry to the Government's plans see L. Johnman, *The Labour Party and industrial policy, 1940-45*, and H. Mercer, 'The Labour governments of 1945-51 and private industry,' in N. Tiratsoo (ed), *The Attlee Years*, Pinter, London 1991.

[31] See Mercer, *op cit*, for an account of the failure of Development Councils.

[32] D. Howell, *British Social Democracy*, St Martin's Press, New York, 1980 (2nd ed), p161. See also Eatwell, *op cit*, p157.

[33] S. Beer, *Modern British Politics*, Faber and Faber, London 1982, pp193-209.

[34] Middlemas, *op cit*, p113.

[35] Ceadel, *op cit*, p268.

[36] See P. Jenkins, 'Bevan's fight with the BMA,' in M. Sissons and P. French (eds), *Age of Austerity*, Penguin, Harmondsworth 1964, p263; and Donoghue and Jones, *op cit*, pp406-10.

[37] Barker, *op cit*, p480.

[38] Rogow & Shore, *op cit*, p46.

Labour, Keynesianism and the Welfare State

John Foster

> It commonly happens that schools of thought and movements in a class society fulfil an objective role which is different from (sometimes contrary to) their subjective design. This, indeed, can be said to be the element of illusion in all ideology in a class society – that the aims its serves are not the aims and ideals with which it beguiles men's minds.
>
> Maurice Dobb, on the politics of Keynesianism in 1950.[1]

There are two quite contrary theses advanced about the Keynesian policies implemented by the Labour government after 1945. One is from the ideological Right, and claims that these Keynesian measures, particularly those associated with welfare and full employment, cost too much and caused Britain's industrial decline. The other is from the Left. This claims that politically, for a Labour government, these measures demanded far too little – in terms of any real transfer of power and resources – and eventually caused the Government's disintegration. Here we will be arguing in favour of this second thesis and against the first. We will begin, however, by examining the quite complex relationship between Keynesian economics and the Labour government.

Keynesianism and Labour Policy

The previous chapter showed how Keynesianism came to the forefront of the Government's presentation of its economic policies only after the acute economic crisis of 1947-1948. It was Sir Stafford

Cripps, as Chancellor of the Exchequer, who first systematically used Keynes's ideas to justify and explain what the Government was doing. Until then Labour had sought to present its policy in terms of socialist planning.

This initial stress was entirely understandable. Labour was elected with a socialist mandate to prevent a return to the 1930s and to overcome the perceived failings of the capitalist system. Its manifesto claimed it would do so by moving the economy sharply in the direction of state ownership and control. Maynard Keynes, on the other hand, was definitely not a socialist. His closest political links were with the Liberal Party, and he had always believed that a regulated capitalism was the best guarantee for the survival of individual liberty and civilised values.

Keynes was no newcomer to the world of policy-making in 1945. From his very first intervention, on the reform of the Indian currency before the First World War, he had been noted for his opposition to the monetarist assumptions which then dominated the British Treasury.[2] At that time most economists argued against government intervention to alleviate troughs in the business cycle. In the 1900s, as in the 1920s, it was claimed that any free-market economy would automatically move towards its optimum equilibrium. By contrast, Keynes sought to stress the real-life structural and psychological factors which could prevent an economy from functioning at full capacity. These included lack of effective demand – which might result from the maldistribution of income domestically, or from imbalances between trading partners internationally – and the associated problem of investor confidence. Keynes's initial proposals focussed on the benefits which might arise from moving away from a rigid gold standard and adopting some form of politically-managed currency by which governments could stimulate economic activity. He urged this for India before the First World War. In 1925 he sharply criticised the terms on which Britain returned to the gold standard.

In the 1920s these proposals were vigorously attacked as short-term and inflationary expedients. Keynes's two major works published in the 1930s, *A Treatise on Money* (1930) and *The General Theory* (1936), sought to answer these charges. Keynes focussed on two central issues. One was business psychology, and the degree to which investors, once convinced that a decline was in progress, would continue to hoard money indefinitely rather than use it productively. The other was on the dynamic effects which would arise from government action to stimulate demand. If the government used credit to provide work and wages for the unemployed, the result, Keynes argued, would be to multiply the impact of the original cash injection throughout the economy and trigger a change in investor confidence. There would be a cumulative demand for goods and as a result the higher output would soak up any increase in money supply. Real growth would suppress inflation.

In the adverse economic circumstances of the 1930s this theoretical package seemed to offer a way of retaining a market-based private enterprise system which could also be democratically managed on socially equitable terms. Support for Keynes's ideas began to extend beyond the Liberal Party to some Conservatives, such as Harold Macmillan, and to some of the younger academic economists in the Labour Party (Douglas Jay, Evan Durbin and Hugh Gaitskell). There were also changes of policy abroad. Australia and Sweden experimented with forms of contracyclical reflation. The New Deal in America also took some of its economic justification from Keynes. Indeed Roosevelt's main foreign policy objective in the 1930s was to achieve an international agreement to establish a managed currency system and thereby create an expansionary framework for world trade.

The British financial establishment remained as suspicious of these American approaches as they were of Keynes's own plans at home. They saw Roosevelt's call for a world monetary system as an attempt by technologically stronger American producers to grab Britain's domestic and colonial markets. They viewed Keynes's economic recovery programme as threatening a return to the wage militancy of the early 1920s and as likely to compromise sterling's standing as a world banking currency.

The key turning point came with the outbreak of war – or, more specifically, the collapse of Chamberlain's efforts to contain and limit the war in May 1940. Once Britain was committed to all-out conflict with Germany two consequences followed. One was full capacity working. The other was reliance on the United States for war materials and finance. Under the terms of the 1942 Mutual Aid Agreement the United States now demanded the elimination of the pound's main pre-war support: the existence of a separate sterling area and the protection this gave to the British trading system.

It was in these radically new circumstances that Keynes re-entered government service in June 1940. It would be quite wrong to imply that Keynes took over the formulation of economic policy. Nonetheless, the most urgent concerns of the Treasury were precisely those which had previously preoccupied Keynes: the financing of a deficit budget within an economy running at full capacity, without incurring serious inflation. By the end of 1940 a number of leading academic Keynesians had entered the Treasury and the Economic Section of the War Cabinet. A close partnership developed between Keynes himself and the Governor of the Bank of England. Keynes's 1940 pamphlet, *How to Pay for the War*, had stressed the need for government control over capital movements and savings to ensure low interest on wartime borrowing. The methods actually adopted were not dissimilar. The 1941 budget explicitly sought to use Keynesian expedients of post-dated tax credits – to be repaid after the war – and food subsidies in order to win the Trade Union Movement to endorse wage restraint.[3]

It was when it came to discussing plans for reconstruction that the arguments started within the wartime Coalition. Churchill was loath to commit the government to any firm proposal that might prove a hostage to fortune in negotiations with the Americans. Others in both the Conservative and Labour Parties were more concerned with issues of wartime morale and providing politically acceptable perspectives to a population that was beginning to move sharply to the left. In March 1941 these generally younger politicians rallied to the proposals of the Keynesian James Meade for continued state intervention to maintain employment. In 1942 they backed the parallel recommendations of the Beveridge Committee on Social Insurance at a time when the Churchill government was withholding support.

Keynes himself spent most of the war negotiating a structure for the post-war monetary system between the Americans and the City of London. It was these negotiations, far more than any fine points of theory, that were to be Keynes's main legacy to the incoming Labour government. The American terms were quite simple: complete free trade in return for underwriting world economic expansion. Faced with these demands, the City of London bankers began to argue for a return to a 1930s type sterling area with economic policies to match. In order to regain their support for an expansionary world currency system, Keynes had to demonstrate that this arrangement was still compatible with London's international banking role, and was in fact the only way of sustaining it. This meant setting very special priorities for domestic economic policy. Internal growth and full employment now started to be presented as inextricably linked to the export drive, the balance of payments and gold and dollar reserves. Economic growth was to be directed almost entirely towards breaking into foreign markets on terms that would ensure British goods were competitive with those of America. Labour costs were critical – and so therefore was some agreement with Labour.

It was in this context that the final wording of the 1944 White Paper on Employment took shape. It contained the famous commitment to government intervention to prevent any recurrence of mass unemployment. But it was also notably cautious. Its definition of full employment was much more conservative than the three per cent unemployment advocated by Hugh Dalton in 1943, and put the threshold for government intervention at around eight per cent. National insurance was to be almost entirely contributory; and it was to be by this method – smoothing wage-earners' consumption through the different stages of the business cycle through national insurance payments – that economic depression was to be avoided – not by increasing government spending. Throughout the document the key concern was the avoidance of inflation. Everything was predicated on this – and the biggest responsibility for avoiding it was placed on the shoulders of the trade union movement.[4]

So when Keith Middlemas states that the White Paper 'stood like a gospel binding whatever party would form the next government', he is not just making the obvious point that it had the support of each of the three parties in the Coalition government.[5] He is also referring to the complex network of assumptions and policy commitments it entailed. The White Paper assumed that post-war Britain would exist within the type of expansionary world currency system agreed at Bretton Woods, and that the consequential link with the dollar would also sustain sterling as a world banking currency. Given the size of Britain's debts, it was clear that the maintenance of sterling in this position would require a drastic increase in exports relative to the pre-war period. Full capacity working would therefore continue into peacetime, and the government would need to maintain wartime controls to channel output towards exports rather than home consumption. Hence full employment would remain – but without any further increase in labour's share of national income.

To this extent Alan Booth is also quite correct when he argues that Keynes's key contribution in 1944–5 was not so much policy innovation as political brokerage. Belief in the theoretical integrity of Keynes's system made it possible for policy-makers to 'negotiate a morass of seemingly inconsistent but irresistable forces'.[6] The City accepted the feasibility of the currency link with the dollar and the necessity of full employment. The trade union movement was won to see full employment and social security provisions as contingent on maintaining wartime levels of wage restraint. The American government saw Keynesian management as guaranteeing a market-based system in the only politically stable non-socialist country remaining in Europe.

In a concluding section we will argue that it was the successive detonation of these contradictions which ultimately destroyed the Labour government. Next, however, we must look at the counter hypothesis: that it was the unique liberality of the post-war settlement, and especially the introduction of the Welfare State, which permanently damaged Britain's economy.

25

The Costs of the Welfare State

In his *Full Employment in a Free Society*, William Beveridge described five giants blocking the road to reconstruction: Want, Disease, Ignorance, Squalor and Idleness. His proposals sought to banish them for ever by massively increasing spending on assistance to the poor, on health, education and housing. These state transfer payments would be used in an actively contra-cyclical way to maintain a high level of employment across the trade cycle.[7] While the policies eventually adopted by the 1945 Labour government were somewhat less far-reaching than those envisaged by Beveridge, Labour could justifiably claim by 1951 that it had laid the foundations of a Welfare State which was already transforming the lives of working people; and it is this achievement that has come under sharp attack during the last decade. The most sustained is made by Correlli Barnett in his *Audit of War*. He argues that the ultimate outcome of the dream of a New Jerusalem was 'a dank reality of a segregated, subliterate, unskilled, unhealthy and institutionalised proletariat hanging on the nipple of state maternalism'.[8]

Barnett is concerned with the reasons for Britain's sharp and continued decline as a leading industrial power since the last war. His starting point is the euphoria of victory which framed the political decision to establish a Welfare State. The basis of this euphoria was, he argues, quite mistaken. Economically, Britain was not a great power. Although the country did apparently achieve high rates of wartime production and mobilisation, it did not do so efficiently and by the merits of its own industry. Britain's war effort was massively dependent on the United States – critically so in high technology areas such as the supply of machine tools and the mass production of electronic equipment. Comparing levels of productivity with those of the German arms industry, Barnett finds output levels per worker up to fifty per cent lower. In these circumstances it was gross political folly to launch into the levels of expenditure demanded by the Welfare State.

Barnett sees the all-party support for the 1944 White Paper as symptomatic of a deeper and more long-standing failure within the British political establishment to understand the requirements of industrial success and survival. The Civil Service, the Established Church and old universities were still dominated by a Victorian ethos of liberal paternalism. It was, says Barnett, this basically Fabian vision which determined the priorities of post-war reconstruction. And the blunder was not simply financial. The 1944 Education Act reproduced a middle class which continued to mimic an upper class disregard for science and technology. The Welfare State itself quickly spawned a culture of mass dependency and spongeing.

Barnett illustrates the economic magnitude of the misjudgement with estimates of expenditure which are generally taken from the planning documents of the wartime years. He cites the costs of the 1944 White Paper proposals for national insurance at £240 million a year and those for the NHS at a further £53 million a year. He compares this with the estimate made by the Treasury in 1943 of a total of £62 million to be spent on new industrial investment once the economy had fully transferred to a peacetime basis in 1948.[9] The proposals for the post-war housing programme come in for particular criticism. Government estimates of 1944 envisaged between three and four million houses over a ten to twelve year period (a figure increased by Labour in its election manifesto to four to five million houses). The cost was estimated to be up to £600 million out of total estimated national savings of £800 million. This left precious little for the redevelopment of the productive infrastructure or for industry.[10] To clinch his argument he quotes a memorandum of January 1945 proposing that £14 million be spent on new buildings for industry and commerce during the first year of peace and notes that already in 1944 significantly more than this, £18.5 million, was being spent on free milk and vitamins for children.[11] He concludes that 'in the long run the welfare state would become, just as Kingsley Wood forewarned, a prior charge on national income of ever more monstrous size, and finally 40% of all public expenditure, uncontrollably guzzling taxes which might have gone into productive investment and spewing them out again indiscriminately to the poor and the prosperous'.[12]

How far, then, is Barnett correct? Can Labour's implementation of the White Paper be held responsible for these dire long-term consequences? Let us consider Barnett's statistics. They are in fact almost all estimates. They may well indicate attitudes of mind in certain government departments during the war. They almost certainly do demonstrate a jockeying for position between them. But they do not tell us what actually happened. When we look at this we find that they have very little bearing on the expenditure policies adopted by the Labour government.

First, housing. By March 1951 the number of public and private sector houses completed since the war had reached only 865,000.[13] This is to be compared with the 500,000 houses destroyed by German bombing and a further 500,000 estimated as rendered unfit for habitation for the same reason. Against this minimal level of housing provision there was very considerable expenditure in the productive sector. Taking 1948, which is the first year for which there are detailed figures, the total cost of all house construction was £337 million as against £501 million on plant and machinery, £249 million on vehicles, ships and aircraft, and £339 million on other new buildings and works. Total capital formation in the private sector was £761 million (with another £180 million by public corporations) as against the net total of all domestic expenditures (or GDP) of £11,751 million.[14]

It is true that transfer payments, including national insurance, health and educational provision did involve a significant increase in expenditure over that in the 1930s. In 1949-50, the total spent on all such payments and social services, including food subsidies, was about £1,800 million (equivalent to a little over 15per cent of GDP). This represented roughly double the expenditure level of 1938. The biggest single new element, £400 million, went to food subsidies, which played an important part in keeping the increase in wages well below the increase in GDP. A further £550 million covered pensions, national assistance, sickness benefits and family allowances – and against this has to be set almost £100 million saved on the 1938 level of unemployment benefit and the £400 million collected in contributions.[15] In fact for these years, thanks to full employments, the contributions to the new national insurance scheme enabled it to run a surplus over all expenditures including pensions, sick benefit, widows' benefit and maternity benefit. The only other items representing an increase on 1938 were education and training (approximately £120 million) and the direct state contribution to health (£180 million). Overall, therefore, the net cost of the Welfare State was quite small – and certainly came to considerably less than the Labour government's military expenditure which at no point between 1945 and 1951 fell below £740 million a year.

Barnett's response would probably be that the figures themselves do not matter, and what was crucial was the effect that this new type of state support network had on social attitudes and economic performance. What evidence is there here? On economic performance we have already noted the relatively high figures of expenditure on industrial investment. According to Sidney Pollard, the figure for net domestic capital formation for the years 1948-1952 was running at 10.6 per cent of net national product (that is GDP minus depreciation). This is to be compared with 7.7 per cent for the period 1934-1938 – and if Germany's post-war investment figure was higher than Britain's, this was largely achieved through a massive influx of US capital.[16] The outcome in terms of growth in GDP was one of the highest this century – with the post-war period seeing export production rising to 50 per cent over the 1938 level by 1950. At this point British manufactured exports comprised 25 per cent of the world total.[17]

On social attitudes, a moment's reflection would also seem to indicate that Barnett's claims are somewhat less than plausible. The virtually complete elimination of unemployment is very difficult to square with the development of a dependent, subliterate and lumpen proletariat. The evidence points in quite the opposite direction. Surveys conducted by Mass Observation during the war indicate that it was the experience of prolonged mass unemployment before the war, especially in the regions specialising in armaments production, that explains the deksilled, demotivated and unproductive workforce in many of Britain's war factories.[18]

If, therefore, the Keynesian Welfare State is to be accused of ultimately having a detrimental effect on the productive economy, it is far more plausible (if not necessarily correct) to argue that it was for quite different reasons: because organised labour became too powerful. This is the claim of Milton Friedman; that Keynesian policies created a cycle of rising expectations which could only be broken by the shock therapy of very high unemployment.[19] From a quite different ideological position, it is also the claim of Claus Offe.[20] He argues that while the introduction of the Keynesian Welfare State did serve to re-legitimise a private enterprise economy in Europe after the last war, its method – the subjection of the market to political control – ultimately generated economically unsustainable demands. This in turn served to de-legitimise the new state system. The consideration of these claims takes us to our final section.

Keynesianism and the Balance of Class Forces

Writing in 1945, G.D.N. Worswick, one of the most influential of the younger Keynesians, assessed the class impact of Keynesian demand management as follows:

> capitalists can tolerate political democracy provided they retain economic power, and this is possible only if the working class is divided. It needs no elaborate theory to see that in a political democracy a *united* working class must achieve all its objectives – including the socialisation of the means of production, which is desirable, both on the grounds of social justice and as a means of accelerating economic progress. If capitalism is to survive the working class must be constantly split, and split again: and unemployment breeds disunity. Not only can the most militant workers be conveniently black-listed and condemned to a life of semi-starvation for themselves and their families, but sectional loyalties triumph over the interests of the working class as a whole.

Worswick continued later in the same article:

> Of fascism as an attitude of mind there is plenty of evidence in Britain even today: but to be effective fascism must become a social force with some mass support, including gangs of men made desperate by prolonged hunger and inactivity. Full

employment will deprive the capitalists in this country of their only hope of recovery from the tremendous blow they suffered on July 26th.[21]

This statement probably represented the strongest and most explicit case for seeing Keynesian economic management as actively creating the conditions for socialist advance. It was a view shared to a greater or lesser extent by the other Left Keynesians, such as Joan Robinson, and also – though perhaps less explicitly – by those younger Labour politicians who had adopted a Keynesian position in the late 1930s.[22] In so far as Keynesianism was to emerge as the dominant ideology of the Labour government after 1945 – displacing the vague corporatism of Herbert Morrison, or Dalton's demand for more directive industrial control – it was at least partly on the basis of such credentials. Conversely, however, to the extent that by 1950-51 the Labour government had lost any real conviction in the political direction of its policies, it must be largely attributable to the deficiencies of this Keynesian perspective. As the programmatic basis for a nominally socialist government, Keynesianism had three key weaknesses. Firstly, it saw economic growth as basically dependent on the subjective motivation of the private investor. Secondly, it gave organised labour only a negative role in this process: as the potential originator of inflation. Thirdly, it provided no way of controlling the quality of investment.

As we have seen, Keynes believed that the essential determinant of economic growth lay in the psychology of the entrepreneur. State stimulation of economic demand was justified only in so far as it created a climate of business confidence which persuaded the owner of capital to invest. The Left Keynesians may have envisaged productive investment by the state as playing an increasingly important role. But whatever their aspirations, this did not happen to anything like the necessary extent.[23] The practice of the Labour government was tightly restricted by the terms of the post-war settlement negotiated by Keynes between 1943 and 1946. The key element of this settlement was the linkage of the pound to the dollar on terms which enabled the City of London to continue its role as a world banker. This arrangement guaranteed an expansionary world monetary system. But the centrality of the banking role for sterling gave the City a dominant position in economic policy formation. The private institutional owners of capital were largely able to set their own terms in relations with the Government. When Dalton tried to force down interest rates in 1945-46, the one element of his policy which had a clear Keynesian pedigree, he was quickly defeated by these same institutions.[24] In the economic crises of 1947 and 1948, each successive outcome moved policy, as Middlemas puts it, towards 'compromises favouring the financial and industrial institutions rather than trade unions and wage earners.'[25] The *Economist* could correctly say, as it did in 1948, that if the government was to apply the principles of Keynes it had to give prime place to the confidence of the investor.[26]

This interlinked with an even more fundamental weakness of Keynesianism as an ideology for Labour. It laid prime responsibility for inflation on wages. Because one of the key ingredients of Keynesianism was a defence of the 'multiplier', that is of the capacity of economic growth to soak up and nullify monetary stimuli, any inflation that did result had to be seen as arising from wage pressure. Indeed, it had been the Left Keynesians, notably Joan Robinson, who had during the war been stressing the dangers of wage-driven inflation and hence the need for a wages and prices policy – no doubt because the political implications demanded the continued presence of organised labour in government post-war.[27]

Yet for a Labour government in power the application of this ideology was particulary disabling. Even though the statistical record shows that wage increases lagged after price increases – and for long periods inflicted sharp cuts in real wages on wage-earners – Labour's newly adopted economic theory involved it in placing responsibility for inflation on wage-earners.[28] The City was increasingly able to insist that if the investor was to be persuaded to expand production, then it was the Labour government's job to deliver an incomes policy. Particularly after the crisis of 1947-8, Cripps had to follow suit. Analysis of the economic propaganda of the Labour government has revealed just how much of its resources were used in 1948 to link the maintenance of full employment to the need to limit wages.[29] As with most propaganda the promoter ended up as its prisoner. The Labour government became locked into a vision of the world, to be fully exploited by the anti-Labour press, in which the active component of growth was the confidence of the private investor and in which organised labour took the villain's part. The impact of this on the Government's relations with the trade union movement and on its own class base are examined in a later chapter. Ideologically, however, for the cohesion of the Labour government, it was all the more damaging because most of its more perceptive members knew that any inflationary pressures coming from *within* the British economy (quite apart from those deriving externally from American rearmament) had nothing to do with wage pressure. They resulted from the weakness of government planning and its failure to stop industry raising prices in what was a relatively monopolised economy. By adopting Keynesian demand management, the Government had surrendered its ability to control and direct investment.

This third weakness of Keynesianism was probably the most fatal for Britain's long-run economic future. Keynesianism provided no mechanism for ensuring that capital was invested in ways that brought continuing increases in productivity rather than short-term increases in production. As with neo-classical economics, the *quality* of investment was left entirely to the market and entrepreneurial psychology. Austin Robinson singles out this failure to direct industry level investment in his retrospective review of the Labour government's economic policy.[30] The same point was also made at the time by Harold Wilson. As President of the Board of Trade in March 1950, he stressed that the key failure on the investment front was the government's inability to influence decision-making in the board room.[31] The City was happy enough to see physical controls used to direct production in exports. It fiercely resisted attempts by the Board of Trade in 1945-6 and after to interfere in the way this production was to be organised. The emphasis remained, as it had over the previous generation, largely on quickly expanding existing systems of production rather than embarking on costly and long-term programmes of innovation. Apart from some isolated areas of the state sector, there was no counterpart to the fundamental restructuring which occurred in

Germany and Japan. The final report of the Anglo-American Council on Productivity made this point in 1952. At a time when the trade union movement itself was co-operating quite strongly in schemes to enhance productivity, there was no corresponding commitment to invest.[32] The precious resources created by post-war economic growth went elsewhere: largely into sustaining the short-run viability of sterling as a banking currency.

Ultimately, therefore, the hopes of Worswick and the other Left Keynesians in 1945 remained unrealised. Full employment did not lead to a consolidation of working-class power or the socialisation of production. When Maurice Dobb spoke in 1950 about the gulf between the subjective intent and objective consequences of Keynesian economics it was largely this failure he had in mind. Writing much earlier, in 1943, Dobb had warned of the dangers of such an outcome. He noted that, after the war:

> it may well be ... that the monopolistic industries, or the larger firms which hope for a monopolistic or semi-monopolistic position, will pursue the policy, not of scrapping the controls, but of adapting these controls to their own purposes ... If this be the case, the post-war issue will not be the simple one of pro- and anti-State controls; but a more complex one, where the dividing lines are more difficult for the politically untrained eye to see: the issue of State controls which simply buttress ... monopoly ... *versus* a policy of State controls aimed *against* monopolistic policies and ... in favour of the maximum planned production for the benefit of the people.[33]

The difficulty with Keynesian economic management was that it did not confront or even properly perceive this problem. While the Left Keynesians talked about working-class power, they did so in an entirely abstract sense. They remained wedded to an ideology that demanded the practical demobilisation of working-class organisation at its most basic level: on wages and conditions. Dobb concluded his 1943 article as follows:

> The central problem is not simply one of devising appropriate economic machinery but, above all, a political problem: a problem of who controls the machinery of State, and for what interests – a problem of power.

34

Notes

[1] M. Dobb, 'Full Employment and Capitalism', *Modern Quarterly*, Vol V, 2, Spring, 1950.

[2] R. Harrod, *Life of J.M. Keynes*, Macmillan, London 1951, pp165-66; Peter Clarke, *The Keynesian Revolution in the Making*, Cambridge University Press, 1988, provides a more balanced and less partisan treatment.

[3] A. Booth, *British Economic Policy, 1931-45: was there a Keynesian revolution?*, Harvester, Brighton 1989.

[4] K. Middlemas, *Power, Competition and the State*, Macmillan, London 1986, (esp. pp76ff); R. Gardner, *Sterling-Dollar Diplomacy*, Oxford 1956; R. Harrod, *op cit*; *Employment Policy, 1944*, Cmd 6527, p30, for the 8 per cent average.

[5] Middlemas, *op cit*, p56.

[6] Booth, *op cit*, p177.

[7] William Beveridge, *Power and Influence*, Hodder and Stoughton, London 1953, pp328-331.

[8] Correlli Barnett, *The Audit of War*, Macmillan, London 1986, p304.

[9] *Ibid*, pp241 and 263.

[10] *Ibid*, p242.

[11] *Ibid*, p263.

[12] *Ibid*, p241.

[13] HMSO, *Housing Return, 31 March 1951*, Cmd 8221; Asa Briggs, 'The Social Services', in G. Worswick and P. Ady, *The British Economy 1945-50*, Oxford 1952, p375.

[14] *Economic Trends*, Annual Supplement 1981, table 48.

[15] HMSO, *Accounts: National Insurance Act, 21 December 1950* and *National Income and Expenditure of UK, 1946-1950*, Cmd 8203.

[16] S. Pollard, *Development of the British Economy 1914-1967*, Longman, London 1969, p375.

[17] A. Cairncross, 'The Post-War Years', in R. Floud (ed), *Economic History of Britain, II*, Cambridge University Press 1981, p389; and A. Cairncross, *Years of Recovery: British Economic Policy 1945-1951*, Methuen, London 1985.

[18] T. Harrisson, *War Factory*, Gollanz, London 1943, esp. pp121-5; and T. Harrison, *Living through the Blitz*, Collins, London 1976, esp. p228.

[19] M. Friedman, *From Galbraith to Economic Freedom*, Institute of Economic Affairs, London 1977.

[20] C. Offe, *Contradictions of the Welfare State*, J. Keane (ed), Hutchinson, London 1984.

[21] G. Worswick, 'Modern Economics', *Modern Quarterly*, Vol 1, 1, 1945, pp25 and 26.

[22] J. Robinson, *The Times* 22 and 23 January 1943, reprinted in *Collected Economic Papers*, I, Blackwell, Oxford 1951, p81.

[23] M. Kalecki, 'The Political Aspects of Full Employment', *Political Quarterly*, 1943.

[24] C. Kennedy, 'Monetary Policy', in Worswick and Ady, *op cit*.

[25] Middlemas, *op cit*, p136.

[26] *Economist*, 10 April 1948.

[27] J. Robinson, *op cit*, and 'Wartime Inflation' in *Collected Economic Papers, I*; for a subsequent discussion, see M. Kalecki, 'Class struggle and Distribution of National

Income', in *Selected Essays on the Dynamics of the Capitalist Economy*, Cambridge University Press 1971.

[28] L. Panitch, in *Social Democracy to Industrial Militancy: The Labour Party, Trade Unions and Incomes Policy 1945-1975*, Cambridge University Press 1976, examined Cripps's use of Keynesian argumentation in dialogue with the TUC in 1948 (pp26-27) – and also documents the 5 per cent fall in real wages between 1946 and 1950 (p26).

[29] S.W. Crofts, 'The Attlee Government's Economic Information Propaganda', *Journal of Contemporary History*, XXI, 1986, pp453-471.

[30] E.A.G. Robinson, 'The Economic Problems of the transition from war to peace', *Cambridge Journal of Economics*, X, 1986, pp165-185.

[31] Cited by J. Tomlinson, 'Labour and the Productivity Problem, 1945-1951', in *Competitiveness and the State*, G. Jones and M. Kirby (eds), Manchester University Press 1991, p53.

[32] A. Carew, 'The Anglo-American Council on Productivity (1948-1952)', *Journal of Contemporary History*, XXVI, 1991, p59.

[33] M. Dobb, 'Industry and Employment after the War', *Labour Monthly*, November 1943, pp346 and 349.

Commanding Heights: the Nationalisation Programme

Richard Saville

> Yesterday Barbara [Castle] quoted from a speech I made some years ago, and she said that I believed the Socialism in the context of modern society meant the conquest of the commanding heights of the economy.
>
> Aneurin Bevan, Labour Party Conference, 1959.

The nationalisation programme after 1945 presented a serious challenge to the private ownership of capital. In the first eighteen months of office Labour passed the Bank of England, Civil Aviation and Cable and Wireless Acts, and nine hundred companies in the coal industry were amalgamated into the National Coal Board. Thereafter, most inland transport – railways, long distance road haulage, inland waterways – (in 1947), electricity (also 1947), gas (1948), and iron and steel (1949) were removed from the private sector, though the highly profitable steel companies were secured only after a bitterly fought campaign which included intervention on behalf of the private sector by the United States government, and vesting day was deferred until after the 1950 election (Table 1). By March 1951 over two million workers were incorporated into new public corporations. They joined 297,000 in the Post Office and 330,000 in government industrial plant and together the public and local authority sectors numbered over four million workers, 18 per cent of the total insured workforce of 22,363,000. By this date around 20 per cent of existing industrial assets were owned by the nationalised sector, and in the 1950s they were responsible for about one-third of the net fixed capital formation of UK industry.

These post-war years marked the pinnacle of 'socialisation'.[1] The Acts were seen by private industry and their trade associations as a political as well as an economic challenge, and the suggestion of further nationalisation of the profitable sectors of sugar, insurance and pharmaceuticals provided the occasion for some of the most intense campaigns in the 1950 and 1951 elections. The programme thus drastically influenced domestic politics, with a legacy felt for the next half-century. At the Parliamentry level the Transport and Coal Acts removed sponsorship from two of the most reactionary groups of Tory MPs, whose commitment to *laisser-faire* and die-hard industrial relations had done much to embitter pre-war politics.[2] While many Tory backbenchers and trade associations remained implacably opposed to government involvement in the economy, above all to further takeovers, the up and coming opposition leaders, including Rab Butler, Harold Macmillan and Anthony Eden, were convinced by electoral defeat that the Tory party had to accept that the war marked a clear divide in British politics. On their return to office all the nationalisations except for steel were accepted as irreversible, even convenient, for reasons which we discuss below.

Arguments for Nationalisation

The case for nationalisation derived from widespread roots in British public life. Firstly, it was a commonplace for town transport, gas, electricity, water, sewage, ports, and waterways to be owned outright by municipalities; in some cities telephones, building contracting and industrial production were undertaken. Previous measures such as the Mersey Docks and Harbour Act of 1857, the institution of the Port of London Authority and the setting up of the Metropolitan Water Board of 1903 enabled economic activity to be dealt with more efficiently than under private, small-scale ownership. This was to be a frequent argument for nationalisation. Those who travelled abroad noticed similar strides in Europe,

Table 1

UK Industrial Nationalisation Statutes, Vesting Day, 1940-1951

		Approx. total employees (1951)
British Overseas Airways Corporation	1 April 1940	16,000
North of Scotland Hydro-electric Board	1 August 1943	8,300
British European Airways Corporation	1 August 1946	7,000
National Coal Board	1 January 1947	730,000
British Transport Commission	1 January 1948	900,000
British Electricity Authority (plus Area Boards)	1 April 1948	170,000
British Gas Council (plus Area Boards)	1 May 1949	140,000
The Iron & Steel Corporation of Great Britain	15 February 1951	235,000

Sources: H.A. Clegg. 'Nationalised Industries', in G. Wadsworth and P. Ady, *The British Economy 1945-1950*, Oxford 1952; Peter Payne, *The Hydro. A Study of the Development of the major hydro-electric schemes undertaken by the North of Scotland Hydro-electric Board*, Aberdeen, 1988; *Labour Research*, 1945-1951.

including Scandinavia, and a growing number of left publications focused attention on diverse public sector schemes across the world. In the British Empire numerous projects of improvement were undertaken by civil servants; in fact by the turn of the century the role of government and municipal schemes was rapidly becoming a part of discussion of economic progress.[3] With so much economic activity conducted through the public sector, pressures were exerted by businesses for reductions of charges for the services they made heavy use of, a matter of concern to many commentators before the Second World War, including the Guild Socialists.[4] A well known example was the British Post Office and Telegraph services; these made substantial profits through the posts (which everyone used) which subsidised the telegraphs (largely a business use) (Table 2). Influence on how local authorities and government ran their commercial activities was seen by the private sector in the UK and Europe as a vital matter.

Table 2

*Statement of the Balances shown in the Postal, Telegraph
and Telephone Income and Expenditure Accounts, 1926–37*

		Surplus or Deficit		
		(After charging Interest on Capital.)		
Year	Postal	Telegraph	Telephone	Total
1926-27	6,853,335	−1,349,112	283,375	5,787,598
1927-28	8,843,786	−1,380,829	107,391	7,570,348
1928-29	9,245,306	−757,237	524,695	9,012,764
1929-30	9,658,770	−800,312	513,214	9,371,672
1930-31	9,849,904	−1,005,669	343,219	9,187,454
1931-32	10,869,520	−809,574	571,848	10,631,794
1932-33	11,484,497	−838,301	409,521	11,055,717
1933-34	11,568,679	−653,591	1,392,929	12,308,017
1934-35	10,910,819	−651,235	1,684,983	11,944,567
1935-36	11,210,238	−797,975	2,126,847	12,539,110
1936-37	11,470,002	−635,603	1,472,370	12,306,769

Source: *Post Office Accounts 1937-38*

Secondly, the case for nationalisation was part of the wider movement for economic and social reform. Ideas on national and regional planning, including town and country planning, on the elimination of social waste and public ownership were beginning to influence more and more people on the centre and left of politics in the 1930s. The reasons can now be seen to be obvious; the large scale unemployment of the depression; the widely held belief that planning in the Soviet Union offered an alternative; the growing criticism of Marshallian economics, and the publication of Keynes's *General Theory* in 1936; the influence of American New Deal policies, though these last were much exaggerated as to their radical nature; all of these and more came together to produce a climate of opinion sympathetic to some degree of state control. A number of senior Labour politicians accepted that the manifold shortcomings of the inter-war years required a broad range of policies which involved government action. They accepted the 1944 White Paper on Employment Policy; the Beveridge Report and the extension of welfare legislation. The approach laid down in the *Royal Commission on the Distribution of the Industrial Population* (the Barlow Commission) and in a succession of wartime reports, organised by Patrick Abercrombie, on the encouragement of smaller industries in a planned context, was to merit a new Ministry of Town and Country Planning.[5] There was thus a widespread commitment to collectivism, though its detailed form remained to be determined.[6]

Thirdly, from their work in the 1930s and their wartime experience, Hugh Dalton, Hugh Gaitskell, Evan Durbin and Douglas Jay, and numerous civil servants, were well aware of how wrong Philip Snowden's budgets during the Labour government of 1929-31 had been, and how misleading orthodox theory was for the maximisation of production. The Board of Trade and every department of war production highlighted major problems of industrial inefficiencies, though the evidence suggested that there was not one type of business problem to which all questions of investment, labour, management and sales could be reduced. The gross inefficiency of the capitalist system required some direction of factors of production with planned output targets. To a world of mass unemployment and gross disparities in basic provision of necessities such as electricity, this seemed reasonable. There were also a number of distinct organisational problems in wartime production where optimum allocation principles guided by marginal costs or market prices were irrelevant; what was important was maximum output. The difficulty was to know when efficiency of factor use and quality of output took precedence over volume, a question raised once it was certain the war would be won. Indeed, such technical comment abounded by 1945 in all industries.

The question of cartels and their unjustified high prices was cited as a case of the inefficiency of capitalist self-regulation; in steel, for example, both D.L. Burn and John Gollan explained how firms, via output restrictions and pricing policy, failed to respond to the supposed advantages of protection.[7] The iron and steel combines were criticised for lack of investment, excessive profits, inattention to modern science and pricing policies that supported the inefficient. It was often suggested that the post-war years might see more of the same, with cartels stifling competition and investment and price policies penalising the efficient. Government was thus urged to intervene, or nationalise, in order to stimulate investment, eliminate inefficiencies in various forms, direct unused factors of production and encourage competition and choice. The contemporary literature underlined the view that nationalisation would tackle these inadequacies, and the new efficiencies would result in lower prices.

The inefficiency of low British productivity loomed large after 1945. The war had provided abundant proof that industry was undercapitalised, often poorly organised and managed, slow at innovation and overstaffed compared with good practice elsewhere. While some of the more recent criticisms have exaggerated these failings, the fact remained that production difficulties dogged the war effort and hindered the proper utilisation of resources.[8] Larger organisations, properly funded and managed were an obvious solution. Great efforts were made by government to tackle these problems; they were part of the remit for the boards of the new public corporations; extensive research was begun, and in 1948 Stafford Cripps founded the Anglo-American Council on Productivity whose reports showed that in virtually every industrial sector most UK firms lagged behind good USA practice and that with wartime capital consumption the gap had grown. In the same year Lionel Rostas published his pioneering work on Anglo-US productivity. The output and employment in thirty-one manufacturing industries in the years 1935-9 indicated a US lead of at least twice the UK level; when allowance was made for the shorter US working week the disparity grew to 2.8 times.[9]

Fourthly, it was generally agreed that the typical unit of production should be much enlarged. The point had been made in a Fabian tract on the Dutch state coal mines. It was emphasised in the Reid report on the English coal industry and similar arguments were accepted for electricity, gas and in the assumed effective size for all public utilities. The benefits of the large scale, which were one of the factors Rostas pointed out as tending to favour higher productivity, would also help to alleviate the shortages of technical skill evident in

42

many small mining companies and elsewhere in British industry.

Last, but not least, let it not be forgotten that at the Labour Party Conference of December 1944 a composite resolution was forced upon the Executive, against its wishes, which insisted upon the transfer to public ownership of the land, large-scale building work, heavy industries, commercial banking as well as the Bank of England and fuel and power. Not all were included in the general election manifesto of the Labour Party in the summer of 1945 and, as we have noticed, the nationalisation programme of the Attlee government omitted many industries included in the 1944 list.

What Kind of Nationalisation?

There were few detailed blueprints for the conduct of nationalised industries. The Fabian Society had extolled some ideas, as had the Labour Research Department, but they were hardly prescribed reading for Ministers, civil servants and businessmen. The *New Statesman and Nation* had much on nationalisation, but little on detail; the efforts of the Post Office union and the Railwaymen to look at the problems of industrial conflict which arose from bureaucratic structures were largely bypassed. James Meade had put forward ideas on pricing in a proposed pamphlet in 1935 for the Fabian Society, but it was not published. The work by Oskar Lange, *On the Economic Theory of Socialism* (1938) was probably the main influential text, but how many civil servants had read it? *Britain without Capitalists*, whose economic sections were penned by Maurice Dobb, was authoritative, but again was not focused in detail on how nationalised industries should be run as businesses.[10] The main left journal which highlighted public corporations after the war was *Labour Research* – influential among some trade unionists, but unfortunately not with Government or the Civil Service.

Where then could Ministers borrow their ideas for nationalised industries? There were some models, of varying usefulness, from the examples of municipal socialism, but the most relevant for Ministers included the London Passenger Transport Board which Herbert

Morrison was responsible for in 1931, and public corporations such as the British Broadcasting Corporation of 1926 and the Forestry Commission of 1919. These were considered, alongside attention to managerial organisation and productivity and the greater efficiency of factors to be achieved under larger scale operations. Morrison, we must note, had argued the case for the LPTB as a public corporation run by business and expert interests. Distance from local authority or government influence was even seen as a virtue. Though the Board was instructed to operate to benefit workers and consumers, both were excluded from any real influence. Morrison had rejected ideas from the Transport and General Workers Union for worker representation and he was opposed to anything but a minimum of information on prices, investment and general operation of the Board. Moreover, he accepted compensation levels above those warranted by the falling revenue and share prices of 1931.

By late 1945 it was decided that a public corporation based on the LPTB model would be too independent. A Post Office structure, with the staff as civil servants and a Minister at its head, went too far in the other direction. Ministers turned to the example of the B.B.C., 'whose freedom in matters of day-to-day administration goes hand in hand with Government control over the policy pursued by the Board, exercised through the terms of its Charter and license, and through its considerable financial dependence on the Government'.[11] These ideas were later refined; Parliament and especially the Select Committees had to be kept at arms length. Thus the Cabinet Committee agreed in January 1949 that, (a) 'Close Parliamentary control was likely to lead to rigid inflexible administration of an undesirable type ... Parliament and the public would judge these industries primarily by the prices which they charged'; (b) there might be commissions of inquiry every 5-10 years on the lines of those which investigated the B.B.C.; (c) recourse would be had to the Production Efficiency Services of the Board of Trade, the Organisation and Methods Division of the Treasury, and the British Institute of Management to encourage modern practice.[12] The administrative format gave the Government and the senior civil servants immense powers. The Minister appointed the Board and fixed the duration of appointments; direction could be given on 'matters affecting the national interest', the lines of reorganisation and development, and significantly on 'advances to the Board to enable them to defray expenditure chargeable to capital account; and the Minister's consent was required for borrowing. When in 1949 it was thought that 'collectively the Boards appeared to take up a more independent attitude', it was considered desirable that this should be checked; the civil servants thought Lord Hyndley at the NCB was in particular need of control.[13]

Ministers were agreed that there would be no major changes in organisation or in the place of the workforce in the new public corporations. Attlee put great stress on worker loyalty in a hierarchy, and the Ministry of Labour launched a number of initiatives, some in association with private managements, to encourage managers to take a more scientific look at human factors in industry. In the coal industry, whose industrial relations record was among the worst in Europe, some innovation in workers control might have been expected. Emanuel Shinwell, the Minister, vetoed such ideas; there was to be nothing more than arbitration in disputes and periodic chats between management and local union leaders.[14] In the case of the hydro-board the management and Scottish Office side-tracked suggestions of worker involvement.[15] Both the National Union of Railwaymen and the Union of Post Office Workers vociferously complained about the absence of worker participation but were rebuffed. The Government thus ignored the experience of over a century of struggle by local authority, post-office and government workers, which showed that public bureaucracies were as capable of provoking strikes and confrontations as capitalists.

Staffing the Boards

Where were appointments to the Boards to come from? Wartime allocation of supplies to industry was controlled by boards comprised of personnel from private companies and their trade associations with a smattering of civil servants and university experts. The myriad industry and trade advisory committees were similarly staffed. The exigencies of transforming an economy from total war to peacetime encouraged the Labour government to adopt the wartime system virtually unchanged. For example, the crucial Capital Issues Committee was made up of seven bankers, stockbrokers and industrialists, with the civil servant there to take the minutes.[16] The principal advisor to the Board of Trade was the chairman of the British Rayon Federation, and the Ministry of Food was overrun with commodity company directors, many on unpaid secondment from industry. Unilever alone had ninety personnel in this Ministry. The Timber Control Board came not, as one might expect, from the Forestry Commission but, apart from some experts, from private firms. Likewise the advisors for non-ferrous metals and steel allocation, chemicals, sulphur and ore imports, leather, cotton, footwear and paper controls came from interested companies. Meat imports were distributed by a board run by the wholesalers, newsprint by the newspaper barons. Over one hundred important controls and boards allocating all the important imports and raw materials were dominated by the private sector. Sir Edwin Plowden, the Chief Planning Officer from 1947 to 1953, came from C. Tennant and Co and, as his memoirs show, was totally committed to private enterprise.[17] The higher reaches of the civil service the controllers and advisors variously reported to, reverted after the war to the narrow Oxbridge dominated cliques who had held sway in the inter-war years.

Appointments to the nationalised boards followed this pattern; even for the National Coal Board (NCB) where a huge body of union and expert knowledge could have been utilised. Shinwell appointed Lord Hyndley, director of the Bank of England from 1931 to 1945, ex-managing director of Powell Duffryn and a director of Guest, Keen and Nettlefold to the chair of the new board. Of the eight chairmen of the new NCB divisions set up in 1946, three were senior military figures, Rear-Admiral N.R.M. Wood (retd.), Major-General Sir N. Holmes and General Sir R. Godwin-Austen, two were knights and one the Earl of Balfour. The eight local boards were flooded with persons associated with the managements of the pre-nationalisation coal industry and many were part of local conservative and old-boy networks. The six members of the Northern Division board in 1948 included a brigadier (also a partner in Feetham and Grievson coal factors), a former director of Londonderry Collieries and the regional labour director of the Ministry of Fuel and Power.

It was a similar tale in other industries. The choice for chairman of the Road Transport Executive was Major-General Russell from army transport; the chair of the Hotels executive was given to the Rt Hon. Lord Inman a former director of Honeywood Hotels; the railways executive chairman was Sir Eustace Missenden, general manager of Southern Railways supported by, amongst others, General Sir William Slim, a close friend of Attlee. The same format was followed for Electricity, Gas, Cable and Wireless, BOAC, BEA, the Steel Board, the Overseas Development Corporation and the British South American Airways Corporation. It may seem extraordinary that so few senior appointees were committed in a fundamental way to the nationalisation programme. There were a few exceptions; the most prominent was Tom Johnstone, the wartime Secretary of State who took over the North of Scotland Hydro-Electric Board in 1946 when Lord Airlie resigned. Where trade unionists were appointed they were always outnumbered by business people. The favouritism shown to the 'right' later rebounded on the Labour government; many of the businesspeople seconded to run the import licence arrangements resigned in the later 1940s amid a welter of recrimination and criticism of Labour, which became especially marked during the campaigns of 1950 and 1951. Even Charles Reid, originally held up as just the sort of expert the NCB needed, resigned from the Board in 1948 and denounced the Government.[18]

There was a fierce struggle over the terms of compensation. Morrison and his department were motivated by the desire to be fair, even generous, to the shareholders and do nothing which might impede investment in the transition to public ownership.[19] There followed a series of extraordinarily generous payments. In this he followed the precedent of the LPTB and the example in 1938 of the nationalisation of the royalties paid for mining coal. These had been one of the last significant feudal remnants; the valuation was 15 years purchase multiplied by the average net annual rent of

£4,430,000 to yield a total payment of £66,450,000. The first compensation by the Attlee Government was to Bank of England stockholders which gave them a yield slightly above the average of the past twenty years' 12 per cent dividend. This involved the distribution of £58,222,000 in 3 per cent stock redeemable at par after twenty years. It traded at a slight premium. As the *Economist* wrote, 'It would take a very nervous heart to register a flutter at what is contained in the Bill. Nothing could be more moderate.' For the coal industry the evidence of serious commentators was that the state of the coal mines was deplorable; the Ministry of Fuel and Power thought at least £200 million would be required to rectify past negligence.[20] As money had been paid out in previous dividends which should have been invested why then pay compensation? Even the Permanent Secretary of the Ministry of Fuel and Power suggested that a payment based on ten pre-war years profits would be too generous, 'unless the Government is to pay something far more than the industry could ever have been worth commercially'.[21] Yet Shinwell, prompted by the Cabinet, was in favour of a 'fairly generous treatment of the owners in this, the first industry to be nationalised'.[22] There was a fierce lobby by the mineowners, which Shinwell largely gave in to, coupled with a complicated process of asset valuation which took only partial account of the requirement to replace much of what was being purchased. This process resulted in £164,660,000 for the 'value' of the mines; another £66 million was paid in cash for existing stocks of stores, railway wagons, and all capital expenditure from 1 August 1945 to 31 December 1946 (the day before vesting day) and other compensation on assets totalled £162 million. Much of this was for plant which had little commercial value and had been kept going by the dedication and ingenuity of the workforce. The Government excelled itself in compensation paid to the railways, the LPTB and inland waterways; the £1,066,800,000 for all assets was based on share prices kept buoyant by Government assurances; even some of the Tory press thought the award generous. The railways were in need of massive funds because of wartime capital consumption on the back of previous inadequate level of investment; again this was largely ignored. The sums granted to electricity, gas and iron and steel were to industries with much out-dated equipment. The total compensation of £2,555,000,000 paid for all nationalised industries was most important for the private sector. Apart from the cash payments, the blue chip tradeable stock could be sold to invest in other outlets. The private owners thus avoided the costs of re-equipment of these industries which would have inevitably reduced their share prices had they remained in private hands and subject to government price controls.

Financial Policy

In 1945 the financial guidelines for nationalised industry and the limits to their business activity were still undecided. Yet how these were arranged would be crucial to their operation and revenues. This was especially the case in regard to the prices they might charge and how finance could be raised for investment. A nationalised business, as any other firm, had to raise the money to invest from revenues, or, if these were insufficient, from borrowing. It was known that the industries required huge investment programmes. Diversification would require new funds. Wage bills were to rise because of shortages of labour. Scientific research had been grossly neglected under private enterprise; the quality of management varied and high salaries had to be paid to improve it.

The central guidelines laid down by the Cabinet and the Lord President's Office after the election sharply limited the flexibility of the new boards. They were first and foremost required to be 'non-profit making' and 'self-supporting', though expected to reduce the prices of their products as a prime object of policy or, when that proved impossible, to limit increases subject to direction from the relevant Minister. Government briefs in June 1946 for the coal industry noted, with regard to coverage of costs, 'this does not mean that the aim is to make large profits either for the State or the Board itself, but, at the same time, it is important that over *a reasonable period* the industry should pay its way and put aside sufficient to renew and repair equipment so as not to constitute a financial drag on the country. Given technical re-organisation there

49

is no reason to suppose that the Board cannot reduce coal prices, maintain or increase wages and cover all its costs.'[23] The Cabinet endorsed the formulation that while the 'socialised industries should not be bound to cover their costs in every single year', there should be a general rule that 'each industry should cover its costs, including the service of capital, over an average of good or bad years, without making an unduly high profit over and above such costs'.[24] In practice this ruled out raising prices to cover both investment and running costs, and therefore forced a recourse to borrowing. It had serious implications for the use of revenues for diversification, one of the key ways in which managers might have sought to reduce dependence on high-cost and unreliable suppliers, or branch out into new products.

The views on prices laid down by Morrison, Shinwell and the Cabinet were enforced by civil service policy committees which dealt with nationalisation in the Lord President's Office and each Ministry. For the process by which policy was made they were easily the most important groups involved; they laid down the restrictions on the new boards and wrote out the clauses for each bill. By the summer of 1946 they developed a growing confidence of their role: (a) that in practice the civil service would be in overall charge of the new public corporations, who would then (b), be stopped from forming a nationalised or 'producer interest' on industrial matters. Thus J.H. Woods of the Board of Trade noted the 'slightly excessive regard for the producer interest on the part of all those who are concerned with planning or running our socialised industries', in contradistinction to the usual civil service view that the private sector buyer came first. The main avenue to control would be through revenues; 'My people here have been arguing with me – and I have a good deal of sympathy with their arguments – that the primary object of a socialised industry must always be to give the consumer as far as possible what he wants at the lowest possible price.'[25] He and his colleagues need not have worried – the reduction of the revenues of public corporations became the main object of the policy process and more important than the need to work out the best business arrangements for the public corporations. There were even echoes of upper-class disdain for the workers; the Under-Secretary in the Lord President's office wrote that 'one gets the impression that the general duty of making coal available "at such prices as may seem best calculated to further the public interest" is apt to be overborne by pressure to provide miners with convalescent homes, pensions schemes and so forth'.[26] What was needed were detailed price and profit orders, 'if they had to sell coal below a maximum price and had to cut their cloth accordingly', such social welfare schemes would not be advanced.

The low price formula was contained in the Coal Mines Act and endorsed in departmental negotiations in subsequent years: (i) that the NCB was to supply coal 'of such qualities and sizes in such quantities and at such prices, as may seem to [the NCB] best calculated to further the public interest'; (ii) to avoid any undue or unreasonable preference or advantage in its price and output policy; (iii) to cover costs over an average of good and bad years. 'In relation to price structure, the most important implication is that the Board must balance its average prices with its average costs' and not use the cost of its marginal production as a guide to price. This meant that huge tonnages of coal, tens of millions of tons, would be produced at a loss, and cross-subsidised by the cheaper production.[27] These were precisely the demands promoted by the Federation of British Industry and the Conservative Opposition within and without Parliament. It was vociferously pointed out by private industry that nationalised companies would be the dominant supplier of transport, energy and steel; it was in the private sector interest to drive prices as low as possible and force the necessary investment programmes on to borrowing. There were thus significant issues of central importance involved in pricing policy.

In the 1940s, energy was a sellers market at the root of which was coal. The two hundred million tons dug in 1950 formed 95 per cent of primary energy usage, either directly or as a feedstock for gas and electricity. International coal prices were above those of the UK; the NCB, the Ministry of Fuel and Power, and the Ridley committee (1952), all estimated that there was a shortfall for inland use of around 30-40 million tons, though much consumption was wasted because of poor energy management by British industry and homes. If prices had risen to cover the costs of the marginal coal output,

Table 3

PRIVATE COMPANIES

CURRENT INCOME AND INCOME AVAILABLE (£MILLION) FOR CAPITAL CONSUMPTION AND NET CAPITAL FORMATION 1948–58

YEAR	1948	1949	1950	1951	1952	1953	1954	1955	1956	1957	1958
Total Income	2374	2360	2860	3181	2767	3010	3419	3784	3955	4108	4016
Less											
Dividend and Interest	−629	−610	−632	−683	−700	−761	−823	−947	−1036	−1113	−1162
Taxes (and remit abroad)	−95	99	106	146	173	144	147	230	238	222	213
UK Taxes on Income	+−626	786	779	746	982	944	856	923	835	925	967
Available income	1024	865	1343	1606	912	1161	1613	1684	1846	1848	1674
Provision for Stock Appreciation	−200	−170	−440	−465	+22	+44	−53	−127	−113	−65	+22
Capital Consumption	−296	−300	−330	−369	−427	−461	−503	−563	−631	−668	−753
A. SURPLUS (+) OR DEFICIT (−)	+528	+395	+573	+772	+507	+744	+1057	+994	+1102	+1115	+943
B. NET DOMESTIC CAPITAL FORMATION											
FIXED	258	290	313	275	220	228	300	419	537	622	606
STOCKS											
Value of physical increase in stocks and work in progress	212	49	−24	426	−62	66	195	353	254	290	−5
FINANCE AVAILABLE (+) or required (−) after providing for invested (A−B)	+58	+56	+284	+71	+343	+450	+562	+222	+311	+203	+342
Capital Transfers (net receipts)	+64	+55	+54	+32	+42	+42	+25	+27	+22	+11	+13
Acquisition of Financial Assets (+) or Borrowing (−)	+122	+111	+338	+103	+375	+492	+587	+249	+333	+214	+355

Source: see Table 4.

Table 4

PUBLIC CORPORATIONS

CURRENT INCOME AND INCOME AVAILABLE (£MILLION) FOR CAPITAL CONSUMPTION AND NET CAPITAL FORMATION 1948–58

YEAR	1948	1949	1950	1951	1952	1953	1954	1955	1956	1957	1958
Total Income	140	179	221	281	305	351	386	359	391	382	405
Less											
Dividend and Interest	−57	−86	−91	−106	−118	−134	−148	−162	−156	−187	−221
Taxes (and remit abroad)	−3	−2	−3	−4	−3	−24	−37	−34	−30	−20	−16
Available income	80	89	127	171	184	193	201	163	205	175	168
Provision for Stock Appreciation	−42	–	−29	−80	+6	+6	−7	−18	−9	−15	+5
Capital Consumption	−141	−176	−191	−228	−271	−288	−287	−306	−333	−357	−379
A. SURPLUS (+) OR DEFICIT (−)	−103	−87	−93	−137	−81	−89	−93	−161	−137	−197	−206
B. NET DOMESTIC CAPITAL FORMATION FIXED STOCKS	39	88	97	129	142	197	245	260	255	295	317
Value of physical increase in stocks and work in progress	−10	33	−15	4	51	−25	−69	22	17	53	40
FINANCE AVAILABLE (+) or required (−) after providing for invested (A−B)	−132	−208	−175	−270	−274	−261	−269	−443	−409	−545	−563
Capital Transfers (net receipts)	+3	+42	+3	+5	+5	+7	+7	+12	+16	+9	+9
Acquisition of Financial Assets (+) or Borrowing (−)	−129	−166	−172	−269	−269	−254	−262	−431	−393	−536	−554

Format follows: John Hughes, *Nationalised Industries in the Mixed Economy*, p9, Fabian Tract, 328 (October, 1960).

then total revenues would have been at least £1 a ton, or £200 million higher. With that price structure, users would have more interest in conservation and the NCB would have had revenues to pay for investment without recourse to borrowing.

In the 1940s a number of civil servants, notably in the Economic Section of the Cabinet Office, did indeed argue for a marginal cost price structure which would indicate costs more precisely than cross-subsidisation. The line of thought of the Section focused on productive efficiency, though they were well aware that 'political, psychological and administrative' circumstances would be critical. General industries which used 'a great deal of capital outlay [were] relatively suitable for centralised control, whether private or public'.[28] They argued that the route to the efficiency of the public corporations in peacetime required a form of incentives and competition, even regional groupings in the major public utilities, rather than central control from London. Their argument on competition followed many commentators in the 1930s who criticised the use made of protectionism by cartels to establish high prices across many industries. These restrictive practices were a target for the Labour government. In this sense, the argument that pooled average costs would not encourage economic efficiency was in line with general anti-cartel thinking. 'The objective is to raise the general efficiency of the socialised industry; and to do this it may be necessary to expand production in the efficient undertakings and contract production in the less efficient.' Each undertaking should account for its own costs. 'In this way state ownership and control may restore to some of the socialised industries the flexibility and progressiveness which they have lost [in the private sector], to some extent as a result of the restrictive practices and protective devices so widely adopted by capitalist industry.'[29]

This meant marginal pricing with differential tariffs. But in 1948 the Civil Service committee responsible for prices confirmed that, 'in general the [NCB] must equate its average costs with average price'. The same year Patrick Jefferies rather sadly summed up the problem of a nationalised industry sector, 'saddled with obsolete price structures', which now gave little incentive to business or the private consumer to minimise the use of their valuable resources.

Unfortunately, these arguments were passed over. The average costs pricing formula, also known as the 'break-even' rule, encouraged waste, reduced the income of public corporations and forced their boards to depend on borrowing for much of their investment. Thus from their origins they were constrained from operating to their own advantage and within a decade were massively indebted for their investment needs. It was a significant victory for the Conservative Party and private business.

What were the results of these pricing policies in the 1950s for the income of nationalised industries? Tables 3, 4 and 5 compare borrowing, capital consumption and profits of the private with the public sector.[30] The figures for net capital formation, for capital consumption and income before provision for depreciation and stock appreciation show that in the years 1950 to 1960 nationalised industries failed to provide for capital consumption, revenue falling over £1390 million short of requirements. Adjusting for inflation, this gap began to grow worse. Nationalised industries had to finance about 41 per cent of their estimated capital consumption, and therefore all of the capital formation as well, by borrowing.

Table 5

Shares of Profits in Net Output of Public and Private Industry, 1950-60 (per cent)

	1950	1955	1960
Nationalised industries	−4.3	−0.4	7.1
Company Sector	23.4	24.9	23.3

Source: Andrew Glyn and Bob Sutcliffe, *British Capitalism, Workers and the Profits Squeeze*, Penguin, 1972, Table 8.1, p164.

The nationalised industries had a large borrowing requirement; by 1958 this reached over £500 million a year. By contrast, the private sector industries generated a surplus, after allowing for depreciation, which allowed them to finance all their net investment. The debt burden on the public corporations mounted fast. Capital liabilities for BTC, NCB, electricity and gas rose from £2.1 billion by 1949 to £5.5 billion in 1959. Interest payments had by then risen to three times those due to the initial compensation. Some of the borrowing in the 1950s could be attributed to the fact that some work was new, like that of the North of Scotland Hydro-Electric Board, in whose case a return could not be expected until the dams were finished and the turbines installed.[31] One could argue that past dereliction was so serious that some corporations would have had a high borrowing requirement anyway. But this does not explain the scale of borrowing nor why the coal industry had to borrow at all. Price policy does. Table 5, from the work of Andrew Glyn and Bob Sutcliffe shows the gross disparity in profits as a proportion of net output between the private and the public sectors; again the cause was the pricing policy laid down by the Cabinet after 1945 and continued by the Conservatives in 1951.

There were many other serious problems for the new public corporations; a few only are mentioned here. Ministers had precious little idea of what breaking even 'one year to another' actually implied for a business. There were problems over 'outgoings properly chargeable to revenue account'; the official position in 1946 was that it meant 'working expenses, depreciation and service of capital', but it was then broadened to include 'sufficient free reserves'. Once the Transport Bill was published, the business users lobbied for either a statutory limit on reserves or amortising, even over ninety years, capital expenditure from borrowing. The Tories opposed any build up of reserves; investment should be financed from loans. Morrison and his Cabinet colleagues failed to appreciate the constraints this would put on a business and the disadvantage they would be under in negotiation for loans and services. Reserves were kept to a minimum. Foreign policy needs obliged the NCB to sell coal under cost to Canada and Denmark; pricing policy forced the Board to import coal from the USA at market prices and then sell it in the UK at the lower NCB prices; from 1947 to 1956 this involved a loss of £30 million. The NCB was saddled with compensation of around £35 million to the steel companies for their coking coal mines. These were in a poor state and needed immediate investment to cope with rising demand. There were serious restrictions on manufacturing. The Coal Act did not ban the NCB from manufacturing, though governments in the 1950s insisted that it did. The huge and successful NCB research programme after nationalisation developed a wide range of mining equipment. Unfortunately the profits from manufacture were made by private companies who sold the equipment back to the Coal Board and launched sales drives abroad. The 1947 Transport Act prohibited the British Transport Commission from a wide range of manufacturing; for example, they were not to build buses, or ships of more than 175 tons. Overall, in the decade 1949-1958 nationalised industries purchased around £12 billion of services and supplies from private industry, with the annual rate at around £1.5 billion by the end of the decade.[32] In fact the exigencies of running these public companies did force managements to build up large and successful workshops. It was often commented on how much more successful they might have been if freed from these constraints.

The take-over of the electricity, gas, and other municipal enterprises greatly weakened the powers and incomes of local authorities across Britain. While some important towns remained Tory or independent after the war, the trend was towards Labour. Here is one cause for the gradual centralisation of British economic and political life in the half century after the war. A nascent regional policy was also weakened as, although there were strong regional boards initially for most industries, the concentration of power in London was most important when investment decisions were affected by government policy. Thus by the middle 1950s the operations of the coal and railways boards began to affect levels of investment in Scotland and the north of England adversely. The lack of democratic controls meant little public, municipal or even parliamentary scrutiny of the activity of corporations; the colossal expenditures on the Magnox and AGR nuclear reactor systems were pushed through with virtually no proper debate and with military considerations in mind. The Left did raise numerous issues of substance, but unfortunately they had little effect compared with the power of the private sector lobbies searching for lower prices and more contracts.

There are, it is clear, quite crucial conclusions to be drawn from this commentary. Firstly, Labour ministers and their intellectual backers from the inter-war years, such as those in the XYZ club, thought that their limited form of nationalisation was really going to solve the problems of coal and railways and the other industries once and for all. Secondly, the basic policy was consumer oriented; in part a response to monopoly and cartel and efficiency problems in the inter-war period, and in part a response to the poor record of industrial relations in the industries concerned. In practice it meant policy was gradually re-focused on the needs of private industry. Thirdly, this focus on low cost and low prices meant that the Cabinet failed to appreciate exactly what the financial consequences for each public corporation would be, in particular as regards the reliance on borrowing and the knock on effect on investment appraisal, particularly in railways and coal. Given the dreadful state of these industries and the scale of reconstruction required, we might have expected a firmer hand on pricing policies. Fourthly, Ministers contained the potential of the public sector by their artificial restrictions on manufacturing. If the nationalised industries had been allowed to diversify they would have been in a better situation to meet the more difficult market situation of the 1960s and thereafter. Fifthly, the scale of the ultimate failure of the Attlee government over nationalisation has had major implications for the Labour Movement and left politics in Britain. Whereas in so many countries the public sector and nationalised companies were seen as essential and progressive parts of the economy, the reverse gradually emerged in Britain. If the Attlee administration had established the public industries on a different basis, then perhaps the notable disillusionment with nationalisation would not have developed as it did, and the economic discussion of the 1980s might have revolved around more, not less, public ownership. The decisions of the 1945 government have thrown long, dark shadows over British politics.

My thanks to the Librarian, Senate House, University of London, for assistance with this work.

Notes

[1] This was the term used by the Cabinet and the Labour Party.

[2] In 1945 the Labour Research Department identified 23 Tory MPs in the coalowners lobby, 19 of whom were directors of mining companies, *Labour Research*, Vol 34, No 7 (July, 1945).

[3] *The International*, (French, German English editions), Dr Rodolphe Borda (ed.), Vol 1, 1907 *et seq*.

[4] John Hughes, *Nationalised Industries in the Mixed Economy*, Fabian Tract, 328, Oct. 1960, Appendix, p40.

[5] The Barlow Commission sat from 1937 and published its final report in January 1940. It had a considerable impact. The work of the Commission and that of Abercrombie was part of a wider reaction to the lack of proper town and country planning in the inter-war years. Abercrombie produced numerous reports, among the best known was his Clyde Valley Regional Plan (1948), his proposals for Coventry and for the greater London area. For a guide to the discussion, see Alison Ravetz, *The Government of Space: Town Planning in Modern Society*, London 1986.

[6] Edwin R.A. Seligman, *Encyclopaedia of the Social Sciences*, New York, 1930-1935, contained several essays on this theme.

[7] John Gollan, *Scottish Prospect: An Economic Administrative and Social Survey*, Glasgow 1948; D.L. Burn, *The Economic History of Steelmaking 1867-1939*, a *study in competition*, CUP, Cambridge, 1940.

[8] Corelli Barnett, *The Audit of War: the illusion and reality of Britain as a great nation*, (Macmillan, London 1986). Several industries met the demands made upon them; these included the chemical and explosive factories, small arms production, and agriculture. The introduction of new fighter aircraft and engines was largely a success story, though the lamentable failure of British industry to manufacture a tank equal to German tanks underlined the backwardness of the vehicle engineering industry.

[9] L. Rostas, *Comparative Productivity in British and American Industry*, CUP, Cambridge 1948, ch.3, p27. The work was co-ordinated by the National Institute for Economic and Social Research and the supervisory committee included Nicholas Kaldor, Joan Robinson, W.B. Reddaway and Richard Stone. Rostas was fully aware of the difficulty of comparison between the two countries.

[10] A Group of Economists, Scientists & Technicians, *Britain Without Capitalists*, A *Study of What Industry in a Soviet Britain could achieve*, Lawrence and Wishart, London 1936; there were many studies on the economics of local authority industry.

[11] PRO, POWE 28/35, clause 3.

[12] Scottish Record Office, SEP 4/24, Cabinet Committee, 'Taking stock'.

[13] Scottish Record Office, SEP 4/24, Cabinet Committee on Socialisation of Industries, 13 January 1949.

[14] A private note from Gaitskell to Morrison, 20 July 1949, may illustrate government ideas:

> My dear Herbert, the proceedings at the Scarborough conference of the TGWU seem to me to provide strong reinforcement of the need which I stressed in my recent paper for the Government to defend the present set-up in the socialised industries. The resolution carried against Deakin to the effect that TU representatives should be placed on the Boards with the right of members to recall such TU representatives as and when considered necessary is a more extreme example of syndicalist tendencies than anything yet put forward. It also – in my view – reveals a hopeless lack of understanding of how any undertaking can be managed and administered ... Even the NUM which has hitherto taken a sensible line is becoming somewhat infected with the same critical and mistaken attitude.

59

PRO, CAB 124/951.

[15] Scottish Record Office, SEP 4/227, Socialisation of Industries, Worker Assistance in Management of Socialised Industries, 6, 8 April 1948.

[16] All examples here are from A.A. Rogow, with the assistance of Peter Shore, *The Labour Government and British Industry 1945-51*, Oxford 1955; *also see, Clive Jenkins, Power at the Top. A critical survey of the Nationalised Industries*, London 1959; Michael Shanks (ed), *Lessons of Public Enterprise: A Fabian Society Study*, London 1963.

[17] Edwin Plowden, *An Industrialist in the Treasury: The Post-War Years*, André Deutsch, London 1989.

[18] R. Saville, 'The Coal Business', *Scottish Economic & Social History*, Volume 8, 1988.

[19] E. Eldon Barry, *Nationalisation in British Politics, The Historical Background*, London 1965, pp164ff; Sir Norman Chester, *The Nationalisation of British Industry, 1945-51*, HMSO, London 1975, ch.3.

[20] The main official criticism of the state of the coalmines was the *Report of the Technical Advisory Committee* (Reid report), Ministry of Fuel and Power, Cmd.6610, 1945; the Left Book Club published Margot Heinemann's, *Britain's Coal, A Study of the Mining Crisis*, London 1944.

[21] PRO, POWE 28/23, Treasury to MFP, 6 October 1945, citing view of Sir D. Fergusson that the number of years purchase 'should certainly not be greater than the 15 years fixed by arbitration for the acquisition of royalties, and may well be substantially less. In our view it should most definitely be less'.

[22] PRO, GEN 98/3, 31 Oct 1945, Memorandum from Shinwell, p3 §9; also in CAB 124/918.

[23] PRO, POWE 28/33, paper for Mr Ausch of the *Vienna Arbeiter Zeitung*, 1 June 1946.

[24] PRO, CAB 124/950, 10 May 1946, official committee report; also the Treasury Economic Section dissenting memoranda on prices.

[25] PRO, CAB 124/950, 8 July 1946, J.H. Woods, Board of Trade to Sir Edward Bridges.

[26] PRO, CAB 124/950, 26 Sept 1947, A. Johnston, Under-Secretary Lord President's office to G.S. Owen, Board of Trade.

[27] PRO, CAB 124/950, 13 October 1948, redraft of *Price Policy of the NCB*.

[28] PRO, CAB 124/915, 'The Socialisation of Industries', note by the Economic Section of the Cabinet Secretariat.

[29] PRO, CAB 124/915, *ibid*.

[30] There are numerous difficulties in doing this and precision will probably always be elusive given the nature of national income accounts. Capital consumption is here defined in the National Income accounts as depreciation of capital assets on a current cost replacement basis, the available funds figure in tables 3 & 4 results after the deduction of capital consumption. These tables follow the format in those in John Hughes, *Nationalised Industries in the Mixed Economy*, Fabian Tract, 328, Oct. 1960. Figures used here are from *National Income and Expenditure 1959–62*, HMSO.

[31] Peter Payne, *The Hydro: A Study of the Development of the Major Hydro-Electric Schemes undertaken by the North of Scotland Hydro-Electric Board*, Aberdeen UP, 1988.

[32] John Hughes, *Nationalised Industries in the Mixed Economy*, Fabian Tract, 328, Oct. 1960, ch. 4, 'Profits for Private Industry'.

Coal: Owned and Managed on Behalf of the People

Nina Fishman

> It is not only our fate that is at stake; our fate as a mining community is wedded to the fate of this country, and if this country fails through lack of coal, then let our power be what we think it is, we shall not remain an oasis in the midst of unemployment and destitution outside the mining industry: we shall be dragged into the whirlpool of depression.
>
> Arthur Horner, General Secretary of the NUM,
> Speech to the union's Annual Conference, June 1947.

It is difficult now to conceive of the unrestrained excitement and euphoria amongst trade unionists and Labour Party members after the Labour victory in July 1945. Moreover, the view that the election result signified a new socialist era for Britain was not confined to Labour Movement activists. I have been mesmerised by descriptions, from men and women working in engineering factories, of their managements' reaction. For a few days, they retreated to their offices, and treated workers with extreme care, in fearful anticipation that the new government would expropriate all private ownership and proclaim the socialisation of all industry.

It was soon evident, however, that Mr Attlee would not use the Emergency Powers Act of 1920 to enact Clause IV of the Labour Party Constitution in its entirety, a manoeuvre which many left-wing ILP and Labour activists had seriously contemplated during the inter-war period. Nevertheless, the conventional wisdom persisted that the electorate had voted in favour of the country embarking on a socialist journey under a Labour government. The great outpouring of collective energy which had enabled Britain to wage the 'People's War' had altered course slightly during the general election campaign and now flowed through into new channels. When Ernest Bevin met the French Foreign Minister in Dunkirk to sign the Treaty of Alliance in March 1947, he addressed the whirring newsreel cameras on behalf of 'the British socialist government' quite unselfconsciously.

Nationalising the Mines

No one doubted that the Government would honour the Labour Party's manifesto commitment to nationalise the coal industry. Attlee appointed Emanuel Shinwell as Minister for Fuel and Power. Shinwell had been Minister of Mines in 1924 and again in 1930-31 in the two minority Labour governments; ironically, he also turned Ramsay Macdonald out of his Durham mining constituency of Seaham in the 1935 general election.[1] In August 1945, Shinwell was seen as the miners' choice for his old cabinet job. He immediately set about mobilisng his department to draft the necessary legislation. As Barry Supple points out, the proposed timetable was so short that the Coal Bill had to be formulated before the Government had finally created the machinery to oversee its general nationalisation programme.[2]

Scholars and commentators have remarked on the evident lack of preparation and forethought given by the Government, and the new Minister in particular, to what was, by almost any reckoning, a daunting prospect. The coal industry had not had a good war. The nation's war factories, the nation's homes, and the nation's electricity industry all depended on coal for energy, heat and light. However, coal production had given cause for concern throughout the period when the total war economy was running at full stretch.

During the war, the coal industry was conspicious for the apparent inability of both management and men to respond to the nation's call for greater effort and more productivity. However, there was no reason to doubt the patriotism and commitment of miners and mine managers compared to their counterparts in engineering. The explanation for the failure of coal stocks to rise lay in a combination of lack of investment in the inter-war period, serious deficiencies in both numbers and physical capabilities of the ageing workforce, difficulties of wartime distribution on the railways, and a history of problematic labour relations.[3]

In the autumn of 1945, sober observers recognised that the many negative factors which had contributed to the industry's poor wartime performance would continue to apply to the new National Coal Board (NCB). For Shinwell, however, sober realism was out of the question. His performances in the House of Commons during the passage of the Coal Industry Nationalisation Bill were marked by an an air of self-confident, almost complacent triumphalism. He had arrived in Parliament as a socialist and also as a representative of working men and women. Their time had now come, and he was loud in proclaiming the bill to be the vindication of his lifetime of socialist conviction.

The *Daily Worker* commented on a meeting between Shinwell and National Union of Mineworkers (NUM) leaders in the summer of 1945 in terms which accurately reflect the mood of the Labour Movement at the time:

> The British people has confidence in the miners. When it voted Labour to the extent that it did in July, it in effect passed a vote of confidence in the miners and of no confidence in the coalowners. It expressed the belief that given the guarantee of good conditions and adequate technical assistance the miners will produce all the coal the country needs. ...
>
> The people are going to ensure that they [the miners] get a square deal. They in turn must reciprocate in producing the coal that the people need.[4]

Before judging Shinwell lacking (something which his Under-Secretary and then successor, Hugh Gaitskell, did not forbear to do at the time),[5] we should examine the grounds for his roseate optimism. The leaders of the National Union of Mineworkers (NUM) certainly shared his view that once the industry was nationalised, miners would work harder and more willingly. They were confident that miners would perform better not only because the coal-owners had been expropriated, but also because they expected the Labour government to grant the miners the fair reward for their labour which the owners had consistently denied. The union had adopted a Miners' Charter embodying these demands, and in discussions with the government, miners' leaders were given assurances by Shinwell that the government shared the Union's commitment to the provisions of the Charter, and expected the National Coal Board to consult the Union in order to bring its objectives to fruition.[6]

The Reid Report, the Coal-owners and the Conservatives

However, it was not only the Union which believed that the industry would have a more successful future under nationalisation. The Reid Committee, whose members were the cream of the industry's professional management, appointed by the wartime Minister for Fuel and Power, had reported in 1944 that sweeping reorganisation and enormous capital investment were essential to secure the industry's future. The Reid Committee Report was as influential in its own sphere as the Beveridge Report was for the Welfare State. During the lively discussion generated by the Report, it became clear that mining engineers, managers and 'progressive' coal-owners who were committed to the survival of the coal industry believed that nationalisation was the only feasible solution. The report put forward such a radically different vision of the industry from its existing status that only the Government had the authority, power and potential financial resources to effect the change.

Indeed, the coal-owners as a whole were not disposed to question the *bona fides* of the Reid Report. Their association put up a token defence of private ownership in the wake of the Report's condemnation of the dilapidation and lack of mechanisation in the industry. Nevertheless, when Shinwell made it clear that the government had no intention of haggling over compensation terms, the coal-owners' will to retain ownership collapsed. The

Association declined to mount any opposition either in the country or Parliament to the nationalisation bill, and instead concentrated on getting the best possible financial deal for its members.[7] The innovative and visionary management and owners took the money, and then switched sides, choosing to finish their careers as employees of the National Coal Board. The Chairman of the National Coal Board itself was Lord Hyndley, who had been managing director of the largest colliery company, Powell Duffryn, since 1931. The Chairman of the Reid Committee, Sir Charles C. Reid, 'an outstanding mining engineer and until 1942 ... manager and a director of the Fife Coal Co., a firm ... which was regarded as a model of efficiency', was appointed to the National Coal Board as member for production, along with T.E.B. Young, another mining engineer/manager from the Derbyshire coalfield.[8]

Though the coal-owners had bottled out, Conservative MPs, including the leftward leaning Harold Macmillan, put up a spirited opposition to the Nationalisation Bill. The Tories' pugnacity on behalf of capitalists who were accepting voluntary euthanasia was fortunate for those on the Labour backbenches who needed to see nationalisation as a victory in the class struggle. The mining MPs spoke from the depths of their hearts and souls about the conditions they had encountered when they first went down the pits aged twelve and thirteen. Justice, or perhaps Nemesis, was finally being meted out to the coal-owners, and it was the lowly pitmen themselves who were doing it. Most mining MPs had strong non-conformist roots, and speaking in the debate must have felt like being present at Judgement Day itself.[9]

The thrust of Conservative opposition was, for the most part, not misplaced. Rather than rebut the principle of public ownership, it pointed instead to the difficulties which the infant nationalised industry would have in living up to the promises being made on its behalf by its Labour supporters. The substance of the conflict was between *utopian* expectations on the Labour side and realistic pragmatism from the Tories, who had the audacity to quote the same passage of Milton twice against Labour's idealism. On the second occasion, Harold Macmillan observed that the National Coal Board, is not nationalisation in the old sense of the word ... This is not Socialism; it is State capitalism. There is not too much participation by the mineworkers in the affairs of the industry; there is far too little. There is not too much syndicalism; there is none at all ...

May not the miner, remembering Keir Hardie, Bob Smillie and Herbert Smith, and all those great figures of the old great days, and contemplating Lord Hyndley, echo Milton's words and say: 'New Presbyter is but Old Priest writ large'.[10]

Vesting Day and Coal Shortage

The Bill received the Royal Assent on 12 July 1946. On Vesting Day, 1 January 1947, about a thousand pits became the property of the NCB and 700,000 miners its employees. It was typical of the austere puritan socialism pervading the Government that no celebrations were organised either by Labour or the National Coal Board to accompany the birth. There were sober, well-attended dawn meetings in South Wales, and large crowds attended meetings at the principal collieries in Durham; in other coalfields, the ceremonies were postponed until the subsequent week-end. Most of the miners who went through the gates that morning were confronted by nothing new except the signs announcing that 'This colliery is now owned and managed by the National Coal Board on behalf of the people.'[11]

At the time, the people of Britain would probably have reacted indignantly to reports in the *Daily Express* and *Telegraph* that miners had taken time off from work to enjoy themselves on this the first shift of their new employment under a socialist government. On 23 January, Britain joined Europe in the grip of the worst winter almost in living memory. Coal shortages were universal, and Britain can be described without exaggeration as experiencing a fuel crisis. The bitterly cold weather and snow continued without a break until mid-March. However, stocks of coal remained precariously low until well into May. Unrealistically, the Government and the nation each expected their new National Coal Board to fulfil the promises made by Labour MPs of increased output and productivity straight away.

In their own phlegmatic, undemonstrative and well-established ways, the miners and the management worked uninterruptedly to meet the enormous demand for coal. As William Ashworth records, it was in part thanks to special efforts by mineworkers that the output of coal in the crisis months of February and March 1947 was more than one million tonnes higher than in the same months of 1946 – those in South Wales volunteered for work on seven Sundays.[12] It was, in fact, the dilapidated railway system, and the Ministry of Fuel and Power's inadequate method for allocating coal supplies, which were largely to blame for the continuing shortages of coal experienced by both industrial and domestic consumers who were not located near to coalfields. The problem of distribution was only addressed competently (and swiftly) after Lord Hyndley had offered the services of the NCB marketing experts to the Ministry.[13]

The immediate management at the pithead and inside the colliery office did not change on Vesting Day; but these men were well aware, and were regularly reminded by local union officials, their superiors at the area and division level, and the press, that they were expected to take a different attitude towards the men underneath them. Moreoever, at the national level, NUM officials not only enjoyed instant and intimate access to members of the Coal Board, they also could count on gaining a hearing from cabinet ministers, and being able to influence their judgement towards the miners.[14] There were, of course, countervailing pressures being exerted on the Board and the Cabinet by the professional management/mining engineer element, notably Sir Charles Carlow Reid. In May 1948, however, it was not the former NUM general secretary, Ebby Edwards, who resigned from the Board in high dudgeon at being consistently ignored and overruled; it was Reid.[15]

The Miners – Conditions and Strikes

During Labour's tenure of office, miners' wages and conditions of work continued to improve. In 1951, they were substantially better than they had been in 1945.[16] There is no evidence, moreover, that the miners of the rank-and-file were dissatisfied with the changes wrought by the advent of the National Coal Board. In 1947, Ferdynand Zweig recorded the mild, but habitual scepticism which the miners whom he interviewed had expressed about the newly nationalised industry.[17] He was impressed by the rich and hermetic culture which he encountered in the Yorkshire coalfield, and reported it with acute sensitivity.[18] Miners went to work and did their stint according to their own and their workmates' lights. They did not feel beholden either to the union or to the new Coal Board. Arthur Horner, General Secretary of the NUM put it pithily: 'There is no power in heaven or hell that can make miners do things against their judgement.'[19]

The Coal Board lifted the wartime embargo on pit-level negotiations about the piece-work rates paid to coalface workers in the second half of 1947; and the number of unofficial disputes in the mining industry dramatically increased. Numerous, small, but militant unofficial pit-level strikes swiftly followed. Much of Zweig's book is an examination of the factors underlying these disputes, with the implicit aim of somehow alleviating them in order to reduce the incidence of industrial conflict.

The Quakers who financed Zweig's researches believed in human perfectibility. Their own charitable efforts at aiding voluntary organisations amongst the 'working classes', and supporting indigenous community organisations, were undertaken with the assumption that it was both possible and desirable to involve everyone in uplifting and improving activity. Zweig and his patrons believed that it was possible for a nationalised industry to exert a beneficent, benign and improving influence on its workforce, and were undertaking their researches in order to further this aim.

The strike of miners at Grimethorpe colliery in South Yorkshire epitomised the apparent ungratefulness of the miners for their greatly improved lot under nationalisation. The strike came to a head at the end of August 1947, the week before the TUC met in Southport. Congress convened in an atmosphere thick with rumours that Ernest Bevin was about to make a bid to unseat Attlee. The well-earned emotional high upon which the Labour Party and the nation had subsisted for two years was dissipated. The reality which emerged when the mists of euphoria had finally dispersed was worrying and grim. The chorus in the Tory press was unanimous that the Grimethorpe strike showed that the working class had deserted the socialist side. They predicted that even greater disaffection and other dire consequences would follow.

The strike was a minor unofficial dispute which meandered on aimlessly for nearly three weeks without anyone outside the pit taking much notice. It attracted attention from neighbouring pits only after the divisional manager, General Mickie Holmes, an ex-champion army boxer, announced that he would summons the strikers for breach of contract unless they returned to work. The threat was particularly ill-chosen,[20] since it had been a method specially favoured by the late and little lamented Doncaster Amalgamated Collieries Ltd., and was always regarded as unwarranted licence and an affront to their native liberties by the miners.

Holmes's intention to prosecute the Grimethorpe strikers precipitated sympathy strikes in nearby pits, which ebbed and flowed without any reason readily apparent to the outside world. There were, however, a number of mitigating circumstances. Glorious summer weather had followed the terrible winter, and its attractions for miners were considerably augmented by a full flat-racing calendar. Most fixtures were being held for only the second time since their wartime suspension. After Mickie Holmes's ultimatum, the next weeks fortuitously (or not) brought race meetings within easy reach at York on 26-29 August, Beverley on 3-4 September, at Manchester on 5-6 September, and the universally popular Doncaster meeting on 10-11 September, culminating on Saturday the 12th with the St. Leger, the oldest and longest classic race in Britain, being that year hotly contested between the Derby winner Pearl Diver and Migoli, with Arbar and the Northern-trained Sayajirao fancied outsiders.[21]

The coalfield's inter-war history was littered with bitter, unofficial strikes in which lodge officials had stood out with their men against the county union leaders in Barnsley. Management routinely waited until the strike had blown itself out, without making any serious attempt to settle. (The vicissitudes of the system for pooling the market for coal under the 1931 Coal Mines Act meant that profitable pits, including most of those in the South Yorkshire field, could not actually sell all the coal which they were capable of producing without incurring a financial penalty.)

In 1947, the mostly mediocre, and even corrupt,[22] union officials in South Yorkshire, and their managerial counterparts, had neither the will nor the facility to move their respective sides out of their entrenched positions towards compromise. However, once the respective national officials on both sides intervened, Arthur Horner for the NUM and Ebby Edwards for the NCB, they quickly and decisively asserted the primacy of the jointly agreed principles and practice of the agreed consultation and conciliation procedures. Negotiations proceeded expeditiously, and a settlement had been effectively concluded by 6 September. But the Doncaster race meeting loomed invitingly ahead in the following week, and the national leaders were powerless against its lure as soon as the Grimethorpe strikers had found a shred of evidence that the prosecutions might proceed, in an unwitting remark made at a meeting by one of the less ept Yorkshire officials.

The conflict involved a third of the South Yorkshire coalfield at its height, by which time there were coal shortages throughout the country – in part because depleted stocks had not been fully replenished from the terrible winter. When the strikers returned to work on 16 September, they resumed producing coal in their normal way. The Grimethorpe men had objected to altering their longstanding working practices under duress, without due account being taken of the web of interconnected mitigating circumstances surrounding their established customs. With the full co-operation of the national union officials, NCB management continued to try to persuade these men to change these 'restrictive practices' in order to increase productivity. In the short run, their combined efforts met with little success.

Memories of the Grimethorpe strike were lodged in the nation's imagination. Conventional wisdom insisted that the strike showed nationalisation would never fulfil the socialists' expectations. The Yorkshire miners had gone on strike for their own narrow ends;

that was human nature, and no Labour government would ever change it. The Labour government recovered its balance in the following year, but their original zeal and crusading enthusiasm for reconstructing a socialist Britain never returned.

Nevertheless, most of the NCB management and NUM activists remained staunchly committed to building the National Coal Board into a more humane, technically proficient and expanding public enterprise dedicated to serving the needs of Britain's industry and people. Divisions emerged and conflicts occurred within each side, and also between the two; mistakes were made by both. However, the joint efforts to achieve better performance and invest in constructive improvements continued. It would be profoundly misplaced for us to dismiss this boldest of Labour experiments in nationalisation merely because it did not live up to the utopian predictions of many supporters.

The NUM and the Coal Board

In 1948, G.D.H. Cole looked forward to the evolution of the NCB from its original Morrisonian model to a more guild socialist institution. Moreover, he defended the Government's decision not to move directly from capitalist ownership to workers' control:

> Why, it will be asked, if the Guild [socialist] solution is best in the long run, will it not do now? The answer is easy. The Guild method implies the existence among all those who work in the industry, from administrators and managers to unskilled workers at the pithead, or at any rate among those of them who have most influence among their fellows, of an attitude of responsible acceptance of the obligation to put the public interest in the first place ... such an attitude cannot in the nature of things come into existence suddenly. Men are creatures of habit; and neither among managers nor among workers can the habits of mind established under capitalism be suddenly transcended as soon as an industry passes from private to public ownership.[23]

The Coal Board did not evolve exactly as Cole had advocated.[24] However, from its inception, both the NCB management and the

NUM leaders conceived a strong commitment to ensure that the union played a stronger, positive and more responsible role in the Coal Board's operations. Successive Conservative governments did not interfere with the NCB management's determination to maintain the Union's new role. The structure of industrial relations built up during the 1950s and 1960s was based on the foundations laid down under Labour. The conventions were unwritten and informal, but dense, mutually accepted, and circumscribed by past custom and practice on both sides. Their operation approximated to the statutory institutional features of 'co-determination' in West Germany.[25]

The other essential pre-condition for these co-operative arrangements continuing was the NUM leadership's commitment to treat the NCB as substantially different from a wholly capitalist employer, even under the Tories. Until the late 1970s, most NUM activists were faithful to this commitment. They continued to honour the co-operative arrangements partly because they perceived that there was a clear difference between the NCB's behaviour and the old coal-owners. But the Union's loyalty to the Labour government's vision of a socialised industry was also remarkably undiminished. NUM leaders wanted to prove that working class miners could contribute to the successful operation of the Coal Board, and moreover that they could ensure that it functioned more effectively than under private capitalism.

One of the strongest influences on the NUM throughout this co-operative period was the Communist Party (CP). The CP never gained large numbers of adherents in British coalfields except Lanarkshire, where its recruits were mainly enthusiastic young Irish and Scots-Irish colliers in full rebellion both against their native Catholicism and, before the war, against the 'almost feudal' Lanarkshire coal-owners. However, from the mid-1930s, a small number of CP mining trade unionists, guided by the example of Arthur Horner in South Wales, began to exercise a disproportionate influence on their county unions and the economic struggle. Far from wielding their power to foment revolt and escalate militancy, they steered the unions towards less conflict and more co-operation with the more progressive coal-owners who were committed to making substantial concessions in return for more orderly industrial relations. By following this lead, CP mining activists gained better wages and conditions for miners, and also led successful assaults on the 'non-political' unions which had been a running sore since 1926.

Horner's outstanding intellectual abilities and charismatic leadership ensured his election as the first General Secretary of the NUM in 1946. He threw himself heart and soul into achieving the socialist goals implicit in the National Coal Board. When Arthur Deakin, Vincent Tewson and Herbert Morrison declared open season on Communist trade unionists, Horner and other CP colleagues declined to enter into open conflict with Labour political leaders despite continued provocation. The most capable Labour men inside the NUM leadership, notably Sammy Watson and Jim Bowman, refrained from attacking Horner and other Communists unnecessarily.

Horner was accused of exceeding his Executive's instructions when fraternal delegate to the 1948 Congress of French Communist led unions; but labour and Communist NUM leaders backed away from all-out confrontation. Horner remained a very active General Secretary. For both groups, the underlying motivation for refusing to enter into political conflict was union loyalism. The deep commitment to placing the union first had marked the CP's approach to the economic struggle since the early 1930s. CP activists espoused rank-and-file militancy, but when the economic struggle forced them to choose between the two ideological imperatives, Communist mining trade unionists were firmly guided by Horner, Abe Moffat from Scotland, and Harry Pollitt and Johnnie Campbell at the Communist Party centre, towards union loyalism.[26] It is not surprising that capable Labour activists realised that it was not only possible but also essential to work with their CP colleagues. Though they remained a small numerical minority, Communists continued to play an important part in NUM activity at every level.

It would be incredible, nevertheless, if the profound political polarisation and rigid geographical division affecting the whole of Europe had failed to have some impact inside the union. There has been insufficient research of this aspect of the NUM during this period, but at first sight, it appears that one of the most serious results was the cessation of lively political discussion and debate inside union institutions. Another negative effect was the failure of Communists in the NUM to articulate and draw the political logic from the support which they continued to give to the NCB.

Party mining activists were *de facto* evolutionary socialists in their behaviour towards the National Coal Board. When challenged by disgruntled rank-and-file members or Trotskyists, they usually equivocated or even flatly denied that they were treating this nationalised industry any differently than private capitalist enterprise. Eventually, this schizophrenic conduct sapped their ability to think constructively about the way forward for the union and the industry. The union suffered, because Communists had previously made the most powerful intellectual contributions towards the NUM's strategy towards the Coal Board.

After the Labour Government

If the Labour government had continued on into the 1950s, the NCB would no doubt have conducted its business differently, and the NUM might have played an even larger part in its dispositions. However, though successive Conservative governments altered and re-defined the NCB's remit to include the positive duty to take making a profit seriously, they left the Board's commitment to provide a public service intact, despite contradiction between the two goals. We have just observed that the Tories allowed industrial relations to continue upon the lines clearly drawn by the 1945 Labour government.

If the demand for coal had continued to expand, the NCB, the NUM, and the hundreds of thousands of miners and their families would have faced a very different situation. Experts were still confidently predicting coal shortages into the early 1960s, and the NCB had accordingly proceeded with plans for ambitious capital projects to make British collieries and British miners more productive. Many of these new investments were made, but they came on stream when the market for coal was contracting precipitately. The NCB responded with a far-reaching programme of pit closures, with which the NUM co-operated – ensuring favourable terms for redundancy and relocation. However, in an industry whose long-term future was increasingly uncertain, it became increasingly difficult for the NUM to play the positive co-operative role envisioned by its leaders in 1945.

The utopian socialist expectation that the rank-and-file miners' attitude towards their work would be transformed under nationalisation, held in varying degrees by Communist and Labour politicians and union activists, was not fulfilled. The division which Zweig had observed in 1947 continued between the majority of miners, who were not 'believers', and the union leaders who had felt both socialist faith and a call to lead their workmates. Many union leaders had initially tried to move their men to see the socialist light which they felt would be brighter now that they worked for a nationalised industry. With time, they learned not to ask their men to make many sacrifices for their industry and their country, and accordingly the 'rank-and-file' did not disappoint them.

Notes

[1] With the boundary changes enacted in 1948, most of the Seaham constituency was included in the new seat of Easington, which Shinwell moved over to represent in 1950.

[2] Barry Supple, *The History of the British Coal Industry*, Vol. 4, 1913-1946, The Political Economy of Decline, Clarendon Press, Oxford 1987, p632.

[3] For the coal industry and the war, see Supple (1987), Chapters 11 and 12. The official history of coalmining in the war is W.H.B. Court, *Coal*, HMSO 1951.

[4] *Daily Worker*, 20.8.1945.

[5] P.M. Williams, *Hugh Gaitskell: A Political Biography*, Jonathan Cape, London 1979, p135.

[6] R. Page Arnot, *The Miners One Union One Industry*, A History of the National Union of Mineworkers 1939-46, Allen and Unwin, London 1979, pp125-7. The Charter also contained a commitment to expand and modernise the coalmining industry, and implicit acceptance of the need to close some pits, whilst opening other new more productive collieries.

[7] Supple, *op cit*, p633. For the Reid Committee and the public response see pp615-624; for the coalowners' reaction, see pp621-627.

[8] William Ashworth, *The History of the British Coal Industry*, Vol. 5, 1946-1982, The Nationalized Industry, Clarendon, Oxford 1986, pp122-3. Both Hyndley and Reid had held important positions in the Ministry of Fuel and Power during the Second World War. Hyndley had also worked with the government in administering the coal industry in the 1914-18 war, and been commercial adviser to the Mines Department from 1918-38.

[9] For the debate see Arnot, *op cit*, pp130-147. There were about 35 Labour MPs

sponsored by the NUM. Arnot points out that over a third of them were in the Government, and that five of them were in the Cabinet (p120).

[10] *Ibid*, pp158-9. Peter Thorneycroft was the other Tory MP who had quoted the same passage earlier in the debate (p139).

[11] Supple, *op cit*, p696. He notes. 'The pithead ceremonies, where they did take place, were universally accompanied by serious appeals for application and productivity, co-operation, forgiveness and dedication.'

[12] Ashworth, *op cit*, p133.

[13] *Ibid*, pp130-7. He points out that the civil servants in the Ministry of Fuel and Power had warned Shinwell of the serious shortcomings of their system of allocating coal supplies, inherited from the war. '[They] thought that it was only with luck and ingenuity that a crisis had been avoided in the winter of 1945-6' (p134). Shinwell had not responded, and had reassured the government and stated in parliament in the summer of 1946 that there would be no coal shortages.

[14] See, for example, Ashworth's description of the negotiations between the NCB and the NUM on the five-day week agreement and its subsequent alterations, pp147-50.

[15] For Reid's resignation, see Ashworth, *op cit*, pp184-6. Ebby Edwards had specific responsibility on the Coal Board for labour relations. A second Board member had responsibility for manpower and welfare. Lord Citrine, former general secretary of the Trades Union Congress (TUC) held the post for a short time, and then left in May 1947 to become Chairman of the British Electricity Authority. He was succeeded by Sir Joseph Hallsworth, another former trade union official. The practice of appointing trade union leaders to the Board continued under Conservative governments. For example, James Bowman, vice-president of the NUM in 1945, became deputy chairman of the NCB in 1955 and chairman from 1956-61.

[16] Ashworth, *op cit*, pp223-4. See also L.J. Hardy, *Wages Policy in the British Coalmining Industry: a study of national wage bargaining*, Cambridge University Press, Cambridge 1981, p172.

[17] F. Zweig, *Men in the Pits*, Left Book Club, Victor Gollancz, London 1948, Chapters XXXI-XXXIII, pp152-65. Zweig noted that his inquiry, *Men in the Pits*, had been prepared at the suggestion and on behalf of the Industrial and Social Order Council of the Society of Friends, and was 'really a continuation of the Inquiry 'Labour, Life and Poverty', prepared for Seebohm Rowntree's Trust (p1).

[18] Chapter III is entitled 'Strong Habits'. Zweig begins it: 'I had never realised, until I came into contact with miners, how strong can be the force of habits and how great is their functional value. One can say without exaggeration that the miners are simply addicted to habits' (p8).

[19] *Daily Worker*, 2.8.1947, quoting Horner's speech at the TUC on the 'coal crisis', which had been precipitated by the escalation of the Grimethorpe strike.

[20] Arthur Horner, *Incorrigible Rebel*, Macgibbon & Kee, 1960, pp196-7. Holmes acted on his own initiative without first consulting the National Coal Board's legal department (Ashworth, *op cit*, fn.1, p186).

[21] The first wave of sympathy strikes began on 27 August, when the Ebor, one of the biggest handicap races of the flat season, was run at York. The number of pits on strike continued to rise during the final two days of the York race meeting.

[22] Gaitskell gloomily recorded a conversation with General Holmes. Joseph Hall, President of the Yorkshire area of the NUM, had asked Holmes how much he was going to pay, and boasted about having £45,000 in the bank. Holmes had told Hall that he could not behave like Doncaster Amalgamated Collieries (*The Dairy of Hugh Gaitskell, 1945-1956*, edited by Philip M. Williams, Cape, London 1983,

p84). There are short descriptions of the Grimethorpe strike in Ashworth, *op cit*, pp167-8, and B.J. McCormick, *Industrial Relations in the Coal Industry*, Macmillan, London 1979, pp180-1.

[23] G.D.H. Cole, 'The National Coal Board, Its Tasks, Its Organisation, and Its Prospects', Research Series No. 129, Fabian Publications, London, September 1948, p10.

[24] Ashworth's official history of the NCB provides a valuable overview. But for reasons of time and space, the author refrained from any detailed examination of how the Board functioned away from the centre. We do not yet possess an adequate picture of the NCB's twelve large divisions, of the areas administered by each division, nor of the daily rhythms of working life – relations between miners and lodge officials, miners and management, and lodge officials and management at the furthest periphery of the Board, its many hundreds of pits.

[25] Co-determination is the conventional English translation of the German *mitbestimmung*, which describes the system promoted by the British Labour government in the Ruhr pits and steel mills.

[26] See Nina Fishman, 'The British Communist Party and the Trade Unions, 1933-45, the dilemmas of revolutionary pragmatism', PhD, University of London, 1991, chapters seven and eight. See also Alan Campbell, 'Communism in the Scottish Coalfields, 1920–36: a comparative analysis of implementation and rejection', in *Tijdschrift voor Sociale Geschiedenis*, 18e jaargang, nummer 2/3 July 1992. Horner justified his opting for union loyalism in *Incorrigible Rebel*, *op.cit*, pp184-90.

'Nothing Less Than a Revolution'?: Labour's Agricultural Policy

Malcolm Chase

> In the policy which this Government has introduced for the land I see something broad in its conception, solid in its foundations, an edifice which I believe will still be there in its main outlines long after time has gathered up those who built it. No other country in the world can boast anything like it.
>
> Laurence Easterbrook, *News Chronicle*, 8 July 1948.

Towards the end of 1949 there was published a four volume collection, *Progressive Farming: the Maintenance of High Production*. By January 1951 it had been reprinted three times. Its title encapsulated the almost-universal contemporary view that progress in agriculture meant higher production. It contained, 'the best technical advice on the practical application of the latest results of scientific and technical research', and was intended to complement the recent establishment of the National Agricultural Advisory Service.[1] The work was prefaced by Tom Williams, Minister of Agriculture and Fisheries, and accompanied by a foreword from the President of the National Farmers' Union (NFU) – symbolic of the partnership that had been forged between the post-war Government and the farmers. Assured markets and guaranteed prices, annually negotiated with agricultural capitalists through the NFU, had been combined with security of tenure for those farmers who did not own their land. However much nationalisation was the principle of Labour policy for other primary industries, agriculture was the polar opposite – with the salient exception of research and development, from the financing of which the industry was relieved.

Consolidating Wartime Practice

In agriculture, as in so much else, the post-war Labour governments set an enduring agenda. Yet it was not quite 'nothing less than a revolution in British agriculture', as Labour was wont to claim.[2] It consolidated the practice of the wartime Coalition government, which had in turn benefitted from the incorporation of a previously narrow and defensive NFU into the administration of agricultural policy during the 1930s, notably through Labour's 1931 Marketing Act and the subsequent efforts of Walter Elliott, Conservative Minister of Agriculture 1932-6. By the early 1950s broadcaster and writer farmers tended to see the agricultural measures of the 1945 government as part of a seamless garment. This was true whether they supported them as did the farming editor of *The Field*, or deplored them as did A.G. Street.[3] Subsequent commentators have tended to the same view. In the words of a *Financial Times* correspondent, a Wiltshire farmer:

> Governments since the war have all been faithful to the principles of the Agriculture Act of 1947. Although the Act has had its critics – none more inexorable than the classical economists – successive Ministers of Agriculture, all of them in the Cabinet, have never questioned its philosophy, which basically is the philosophy of one of their predecessors, Walter Elliott. He saw, as they have seen, that quite a high price should be paid by the State to underwrite domestic food production in the unsettled conditions of a hungry world. The only dispute has been over the size of the premium, in fluctuating economic conditions.[4]

That underestimates, though, the enormity of the task confronting the Labour government in 1945. Britain's most precarious moment, as far as feeding its citizens was concerned, came not during the war but in 1946-7. This was affirmed, in the most dramatic manner, by the decision to ration bread in 1946, a policy from which the Churchill coalition had shrunk and which was effectively without precedent (it had last been rationed in 1802).[5] The war-torn British economy was sustained principally by massive dollar loans. And the balance of payments deficit meant that economic energies had to be divided between domestic reconstruction and earning much-needed foreign currency. World agriculture, except in North America, had been acutely disrupted by the War. However, given the economic crisis, importation of high-priced foodstuffs purchased in the dollar market was not a feasible option. This was the background against which Labour's agricultural policy was drawn up. The overall objective was to minimise British dependence upon imported foodstuffs, drive out inefficient farming practices, and feed the nation at a time of general European austerity.

In the event, although Britain remained on rationing until 1953 (bread was released in 1948), the policy achieved rather more than just overcoming austerity. The spirit of the 1947 Act, if not its detailed prescriptions, underlay farming and food policy until the United Kingdom entered the European Community.[6] The longer term influence of this policy, however, was ambiguous. The only unequivocal beneficiary was the farmer – not the government, consumer, landworker nor, one might add, the environment.

Managing Agricultural Capitalism

Although a great deal was owed to wartime precedent, the 1945 Government's agriculture policy represented a departure for farming in peacetime, and arguably a departure too for Labour Party policy. In retrospect, the acceptance by Labour of an agricultural policy of private enterprise, sponsored rather than directed by the State through assured markets and guaranteed prices, was a decisive point in the redefinition of Party ideology. The acceptance may even, in retrospect, be seen as conceding that Labour's task in government was to manage the capitalist economy rather than engineer its transformation into a socialist one.

The declared objective of the 1947 Act was a comprehensive plan for a 'stable and efficient agricultural industry'. 'Guaranteed prices and assured markets', the first part of the Act, provided for an annual review of fat stock, milk, eggs, grain, potatoes and sugar beet – some 75 per cent of agricultural output in all. However prices of the remaining quarter of farm output were also closely affected: for example, the prices of dairy cows indirectly determined milk prices, fat cattle those of store cattle, and eggs those of chickens. The review was to be conducted each February by the Ministry of Agriculture and Fisheries (MAF), in consultation with representatives 'of producers in the agricultural industry'. The exclusion of farm-workers and consumer organisations from this process was controversial. The NFU was effectively enshrined as a quasi-autonomous instrument of government, and this gave rise to suspicions that the farmers were being 'feather bedded' (a famous remark by Labour's junior Food Minister in 1950, for which he was forced to resign).

Part Two of the Act set out, in necessarily general terms, rules for good husbandry. Farmers judged to be failing these rules could be placed under 'supervision', and directed how and what to farm. Failure to comply could result in compulsory dispossession, be the land freehold or tenancy. This, on the face of it most draconian, measure was inherited from Coalition policy, and it was politically and socially very emotive. In 1940 a recalcitrant Hampshire farmer had been shot dead by police whilst resisting dispossession, one reason why the new Act incorporated a right of appeal to a Tribunal. However, in practice there were few post-war dispossessions (157 in the years 1948-51).

Part Three of the Act concerned the relations between landlord and tenant. It significantly increased security of tenure, and the extent of compensation from the landlord for improvements carried out by a tenant farmer on quitting his farm. Although it had to some extent been anticipated by the 1923 Agricultural Holdings Act, this section has had enduring and far-reaching effects on rural life. By contrast Part Four has not, being devoted to measures to encourage smallholdings – a favourite radical shibboleth – but only through the medium of enabling legislation which placed the onus for action on local authorities.

81

Administrative procedures through which the Act was to be implemented were set out in the fifth and final part: an Agricultural Land Tribunal to deal with dispossession appeals; an Agricultural Land Commission to manage farms vested in the Ministry; and an Agricultural Executive Committee for each county. The latter were to promote agricultural development and efficiency, and had extensive responsibilities (including supervisions and dispossessions) delegated to them by the Ministry. They replaced similar wartime committees, which had been very largely responsible for the local direction of farming's war effort. Here at least a concession was made to the claims of agricultural workers, two representatives of whom sat (with two landowners and three farmers) on each committee. Although these Committees survived until 1971, their teeth were drawn after 1957 when a Conservative government repealed Part Two of the 1947 Act.

Complementing the 1947 Act were other measures, which can be more briefly dealt with. A central feature of wartime agricultural policy had been a 'plough-up policy', transfering grassland to arable. Labour further encouraged this process in its earliest agricultural measure, a 1946 Act paying a subsidy to farmers of £2 per acre ploughed of grassland that had been down to grass for three years or longer. In the same year a Hill Farming Act encouraged the preservation of upland agriculture with livestock headage payments not available to lowland farmers. As Howard Newby points out, this measure was a unique example of agricultural policy actually taking account of the *social* impact of farming changes.[7] Also in 1946 the National Agricultural Advisory Service was set up, with a staff of eighteen hundred, 350 district offices, fourteen experimental farms, and a brief to advise farmers in the application of the latest technology. Finally, in 1948 the government gripped the nettle of closely-guarded professional independence to increase the supply of veterinary surgeons.

Agricultural workers' wages were dealt with by another Act of 1947, which created a wages board for the industry to determine a national minimum wage: this was a progressive measure in that it replaced the previous peacetime policy of regulation via county committees. Its shortcomings were firstly a failure to establish a wages structure for the industry, leaving recognition of skill to precarious individual negotiation, and thus exacerbating the decline and demoralisation of the farm workforce. Secondly, although the labourer's incremental gains under the Act were significant (from eighty shillings to ninety shillings a week in 1947, and to ninety-four shillings in 1949) they failed to achieve anything like parity with industrial wages. Even at a peak in 1949 they equalled only some 75 per cent of average industrial wages. The disparity is revealing. The Labour Party (like the farmers) pointed to the achievement of wage parity with road-menders and railway labourers, and failed to recognise the growing skills-base of a workforce which was at the heart of a second agricultural revolution.

The Party's lines of communications with farm labourers and the National Union of Agricultural Workers were less than satisfactory. It neglected the emotive issue of tied cottages. It misconceived the nature of farm work and the pace with which it was changing; and it divided its attention between the NUAW and the Transport and General Workers, which latter represented only a minority in the industry, a role it had acquired in absorbing the Workers' Union in 1929, along with the energetic George Dallas who had organised its agricultural section.[8] Dallas's retirement from Labour's National Executive Committee (NEC) in 1944 robbed the farm workforce of its voice inside the citadel of the Party. Although the NUAW had increased its membership massively during the war, and increased its sponsorship of Labour MPs to seven (from none in 1935), this hardly made it a powerbroker inside the Party. Its leadership was not respected, either within the Labour hierarchy or by Williams personally. Partly out of dismay at the Party's lack of interest in rural affairs in the inter-war period, the NUAW's president Edwin Gooch had become estranged from Labour. Alfred Dann, its secretary from 1945, was held in little more than contempt by Williams, as his correspondence with Morgan Phillips reveals: 'the usual characteristic Dann letter … entirely wrong' … 'One would imagine from Mr Dann's letter that little had been done for the workers and everything for the farmers which, of course, is just moonshine.'[9]

One detects a degree of sensitivity in Williams's last remark. 'Tom, the farmer's chum' (as he admitted being called by some inside the Party)[10] arguably had much to be sensitive about in this respect, but the NUAW's own policies tended to the same ends. A disastrous strike in 1923, disaffection with Labour during the inter-war years, and the problems of organising a dispersed and often deferential workforce – these factors had reinforced Gooch's instinct to seek 'common cause with the NFU on agricultural policy matters'.[11] Insofar as Labour seriously considered the interests of the farmworkers, the NUAW's concentration on pay and conditions (in preference to restructuring the industry) reinforced the Party's own conclusion: to wit that the farmers were the only channel through whom an effective agricultural policy could be delivered. To the logic and consequences of that conclusion we now turn.

Agriculture had had a 'good' war. The industry had been called upon to make massive, rapid increases in output and reduce Britain's dependency upon imported foodstuffs: gross output for 1941-2 exceeded by two-thirds that for 1938-9. The industry submitted to the closest regulation by the War Agricultural Executive Committees ('War Ags') for each county – on a field by field basis – and there was a massive transfer of acreage and resources from livestock to arable cultivation. In return landowners' revenue from rent, farmers' incomes and labourers' wages all rose. This was achieved with minimal impact on the consumer, since much of the cost was met by the government. The policy had to address the extraordinary circumstances of war, and marked the strongest contrast possible to the peacetime pattern of prodigious imports and 'dog and stick' (low efficiency and mainly livestock) farming. Yet both the essential features and much detail had been framed as early as 1936 by Baldwin's National Government. Total war necessitated extensive state interference in farming, and unprecedented measures to coerce and encourage increased output; yet at the same time a certain sensitivity towards those required to achieve that output was required. Technology, marketing, distribution and the landscape itself were transformed, but the essential infrastructure of agricultural capitalism remained unchanged. This was Labour's inheritance in 1945.[12]

'The Farmers' Friend'

Tom Williams, the new Minister of Agriculture, had been closely involved as a junior minister in the direction of wartime farming. It was a subaltern role, however: his principal reponsibilities were to chair the Dig for Victory Campaign, the Domestic Poultry Keepers' Council and the Young Farmers' Club Advisory Committee. After the general election, Viscount Addison's name, as much as Williams's, was the one canvassed as the new minister. As a minister in both Lloyd George governments, and as Minister of Agriculture in the second Labour government, Addison had considerably greater experience: but this also made him an obvious choice for Leader of the House of Lords, and this he duly became. Williams, a bluff but personable Yorkshireman, went to Agriculture.

It was not an imaginative appointment, and having made it, Attlee was not rewarded by imagination. Williams was a conscientious minister, with a good eye for detail; but he tended to rest on the laurels of his Coalition record, with whose policy regarding agriculture he was very largely content. The immediate needs of the post-war period differed little from the War, only 'the submarine menace had given place to the dollar shortage'.[13] Consolidation of the Coalition inheritance was a sensible short-term policy and Williams – who knew the thickets of emergency directives intimately, and had relished his new-found popularity with farmers – was an obvious person to direct it. He had lost touch, though, with the perspectives of farm-workers and consumers alike. His autobiography, with a title (*Digging for Britain*) consciously evoking his Coalition service, is revealing as much for its silences as for the information it contains. Williams had more to say about horse-racing ('a special bond' with his fellow Coalition junior agriculture minister, the Duke of Norfolk) than he did about farm-workers. As a cabinet minister he was swept along in a mood of convivial association with the NFU. The *Dictionary of Labour Biography*, with appropriate piety, records that when he departed from office in 1951, 'a hundred of his permanent officials in his Ministry inscribed an album to "Dear Tom".' Williams, for his part, remembered only 'a small dinner party at Claridges ... organised by the Duke of Norfolk'.[14]

There is little evidence, however, that the Government's policy was other than to consolidate and refine the achievements of wartime agriculture: if Williams had any aspiration to effect a more thorough-going restructuring he kept them to himself. In one sense both are surprising. He had been Parliamentary Private Secretary to the Minister of Agriculture in the first Labour government, and had taken a close interest in the Party's rural policies during the inter-war years. As author of the rural volume in the 'Labour Shows the Way' series edited by Attlee, Williams had produced one of the fullest statements of the Party's agricultural policy: 'There can be no moral title to private ownership of land'; furthermore, private landownership as a system was no longer adequate to service the capital investment needs of modern farming. 'In a word, the first essential step to a complete rehabilitation of agriculture is the transfer of the land to the State'.[15] 'As soon as administratively possible', all agricultural land would pass into national ownership, with compensation based on the values calculated for Schedule A Income Tax purposes. A National Agricultural Commission would then manage the land through a network of county committees (not an anticipation of developments under Baldwin's National Government but rather an echo of the Great War). There was nothing maverick about Williams's enthusiasm for land nationalisation, which had good claim to be considered the earliest and most enduring political objective of British Radicalism and Socialism. Other Party publications on the subject at this time were equally uncompromising.[16] The approach of land nationalisation seemed almost inevitable in the 1930s. Not only were there loud calls in its favour from the Liberals, long committed to policies of extensive land reform, but even (with qualifications) from certain Conservative and Unionist quarters.[17] There was also extensive interest in nationalisation from the non-politically engaged.[18]

Land Nationalisation Rejected

Some sections of the Party, however, were prepared to reassess the historical commitment to nationalise the land. As early as 1923, a sub-committee of the NEC had suggested that policies grafted on to the agricultural tenancy system were to be preferred to outright nationalisation. Though Addison felt it was a benchmark in the evolution of Labour policy, this idea was rebuffed.[19] However, unease about the electoral appeal of land nationalisation prompted the Parliamentary Labour Party to take more interest in the issue than did the movement as a whole. Early in 1939 there was a heated debate when a group set up by the PLP to advance proposals for the taxation of land values, as a substitute for nationalisation, were met head on by the NEC Policy Sub-Committee.[20] Opinion within the Fabian Society was similarly divided.[21]

It was thus becoming respectable to argue that land nationalisation was not in the best interests of the Party. A combination of electoral calculation and Labour's relatively slender interest in rural issues (to which should perhaps be added the NUAW's equivocal view of nationalisation during most of the inter-war years) led to a situation in which both pro- and anti-nationalisers could draw comfort from Party policy. *For Socialism and Peace*, the programme adopted at the 1934 Conference, stressed 'only a unified ownership of the land can provide a satisfactory basis' for Labour's proposed reforms. However, it drew back from a complete policy of nationalisation (promising instead 'a General Enabling Act, giving the state power to acquire any land, rural or urban, at any time'). Yet it confirmed that the nationalisation of agricultural land would be accorded priority. Hence Attlee could claim that, 'The Labour Party stands for national ownership of the land', whilst presiding over a Party sections of which were increasingly ambiguous about the feasibility and appeal of land nationalisation at the ballot box.[22]

By 1945 therefore, the Labour Party was attuned to compromise on the land issue. Official policy statements were habitually hedged with 'as soon as administratively possible', whilst an influential section within in the Party were prepared to abandon land nationalisation altogether. In terms of electoral *real politik* this is comprehensible. Only in the light of the long history of agrarian reform within British Radicalism does it surprise – hence maybe the care with which the 1945 manifesto spelt out that nationalisation remained a long-term policy objective.[23] Why was land nationalisation unobtainable in 1945? The sheer scale of the undertaking has to be appreciated. It would have required a feat of legislative architecture which would have dwarfed the Government's health or mining measures. There were only 1900 mines: there were at least 260,000 farmers.[24] Labour faced a dilemma of how to govern the countryside, and of how to deliver its policies for feeding the nation. It was tied by habit and deeply practical considerations to the 'War Ags' model. It was likely that any attempt to nationalise the land would be greeted by wholesale resignations from the County Committees, leaving MAF and the government without the means to apply policy at ground level.

One might note too the significant expansion of land ownership since the Great War. As a political objective, land nationalisation had emerged in the era of the great estate, as a thrust at the economic, social and political power of the aristocracy. Aristocratic landholding, however, whilst still considerable was in obvious decline, as the Party recognised when it spoke of the 'lost leadership' of the traditional landowners. The government's agricultural policy was in effect a compact with agricultural capitalists: it could ill afford to alienate any of them, and a significant section were now owner occupiers.[25] It was not just the wrath of owner occupier agriculturalists that Labour would have had to confront. A deep-rooted pastoralism suffused English popular culture. It had been particularly apparent in wartime, and the farming lobby had not been slow to cultivate the nation's sense of indebtedness. Proposals to nationalise the land, however secure the tenure for active agriculturalists, would have run into the sands of a public opinion hostile to large scale disruption of rural life, and also imbued with the sentiments that the catchphrase 'an Englishman's home is his castle' sums up.

A more tangible consideration was the need for careful management of the House of Lords. The Government's legislative programme made huge demands on parliamentary time, and the capacity of the Lords for obstruction and delay could not be underestimated. Any substantial agriculture bill was going to exercise the upper house a great deal: no other issue would have been more likely to awaken the enmity of the Lords, or encourage backwoods peers to take a sudden and critical interest in all apsects of Labour's programme, than land nationalisation.

Finally, consideration had to be given to the financial cost of nationalisation. Labour's policy was that all landowners would be compensated with 'Land Bonds' of equivalent value to the property nationalised. Not only would such a system have been costly to administer (in comparison, for example, to the procedures for recompensing the far smaller number of mine-owners and railway shareholders), but the interest payments on such bonds would have been problematic. Meeting them from the income from nationalised land would have placed pressure on rents, which would have been highly unpopular with farmers and also incompatible with a cheap food policy. To attempt to supplement them from other exchequer revenues would have undermined the financial basis of other urgent government projects. It was both financially and politically expedient, then, for the Labour Party to forget its commitment to land nationalisation in 1945.

Much of the reasoning that informed Labour's decision not to pursue land nationalisation when in government also shaped other aspects of the agriculture policy, which could in essence be described as a refinement of the *status quo*. Subsequently there was obvious political capital to be made from claiming that the 1947 Act *was* a revolution in British agriculture, and in the new electoral climate Labour was not slow in doing so. The sheer scale of the 1945 victory seemed to redefine the electoral landscape, and 'a widespread belief in the 1950's and 1960's that the farmers' vote was important was apparently confirmed by the existence of several rural marginal seats within the reach of Labour and not fixed upon the Tories'.[26] The supposed strategic significance of the farmers' vote, however, arguably served only to restrain Labour in the formulation of its rural policies. This was a cause of heated criticism – from the NUAW, from some inside the Party, the Co-operative movement, and more widely. For example the *Daily Mirror*, by the end of 1947, was vocal in demanding the resignations of the Ministers of both Food and Agriculture.[27]

Restructuring Farm Practices

It would be a mistake, however, to dismiss Labour's policy as one that protected agriculture and threw the cost of doing so on the consumer. The burden of state support for agriculture was met from progressively structured taxation rather than directly by the consumer. In this way the Government squared the circle, keeping faith with the popular, and increasingly consumer-driven electorate, whilst paying to farmers the premiums that were necessary to ensure an adequate supply of foodstuffs in a time of acute shortage. The term 'premium' is rather simplistic, and the complexities of government finance to the industry need to be analysed. The annual price review (which took place in February) set price levels for the year ahead, guaranteeing a market for commodities scheduled under the Act. The guarantee could take the form of acreage or tonnage subsidy, but the Act also provided for limits to be placed on production – either by restricting acreage subsidies or by rationing seed. The annual review thus constituted the first tier of a policy to restructure farm practices.

The second tier was provided through improvement grants. One of these, for ploughing-up grassland of three or more years' standing has already been mentioned. Others included extensive subsidising of lime and artificial fertilisers, of field drainage to help render heavy clay soils suitable for arable, and of other major capital improvements (buildings, machinery, etc). Security of tenure was intended to encourage the tenant farmer to undertake such improvements. The National Agricultural Advisory Service assisted the process of restructuring, and in working with the County Agricultural Committees was directly able to influence the application of coercive measures on recalcitrant farmers. Inefficient dog-and-stick livestock farming was to be replaced by high-productivity arable and mixed agriculture.

Feeding the Nation

The post-war years were ones of austerity, but not starvation: Labour's policy achieved its primary objective of feeding the nation. The efficiency with which it did so, however, was and is open to question. Classical economists held that the only test of good husbandry was a free market: a sitting tenant might be a good farmer, but another potential tenant even better: freedom of the landlord to maximise rent tested this, controlled rents and security of tenure prevented it. 'The Agriculture Act ... has preserved as farmers the maximum number of duds in living memory'. Whereas war-time had generated in the community a willingness to concede the need for punitive measures, in peacetime sentiment and neighbourliness made the County Committees reluctant to punish inefficiency. 'Post-war legislation has meant freedom for any tenant but the most blatantly incompetent to retain his occupancy'.[28] Whilst the doctrinal purity of the free market was incompatible with both Labour's ideology and the nation's need for a guaranteed food supply at a time when parts of Europe were on the verge of starvation, the 1947 Act certainly starved aspiring farmers of opportunity, and made a nonsense of the popular notion of 'a ladder for the farmworker'. Its provision for smallholdings was scant compensation. A related issue was that rather than acting as an effective incentive to the less-efficient cultivator, the guaranteed price mechanism worked primarily in favour of larger and already-progressive farmers, that is those 'whose farm structure [was] sufficiently flexible to take advantage of changes in relative profit margins'.[29]

A second problem was the relationship which emerged between the NFU, the Advisory Service, MAF and its minister. The 1947 Act was in effect formulated round the tacit assumption that farmers could hold the government to ransom, because the gift of adequate foodstocks was alone theirs to make. The combination of a highly professional and single-minded NFU and a weak Minster susceptible to flattery meant that at annual reviews the producers' claims tended to prevail. It should be said that Thomas Dugdale,

Williams's Conservative successor, was barely different. So integrated into the structure of government policy did the NFU become that it actually opposed the repeal of the coercive second part of the Act by the more robust Heathcote Amory in 1957. In 1948 a Fabian pamphlet rather pointedly resurrected a criticism, levelled at MAF as early as 1942, that its staff were 'demoralised by long subservience to the N.F.U.'.[30]

Labour's Legacy

Perhaps the 1947 Act's greatest legacy was to translate policies designed to overcome wartime and the immediate post-war austerity into a lasting peacetime prescription. 'The 1947 Agriculture Act acquired a monumental significance, not so much for what it contained as for what it represented as the token of a government promise to look after agriculture'.[31] The wider policy of which the 1947 Act was part appeared more questionable once the crisis years of 1946-7 were negotiated. By 1949 government subsidies to agriculture exceeded £400 million a year, resources which might indirectly have generated more food had they been devoted instead to export-generating industries.

Post-war governments of both parties have defended interventionist agricultural policy with particular reference to the high productivity achieved by farmers. Labour's policy, however, was a formative stage in the evolution of a post-war myopia where agricultural science and economics were concerned. Underlying it was an uncritical acceptance that science and technology offered a readily accessible and uncomplicated pathway to economic efficiency. Among Labour's earliest measures was the establishment of the National Agricultural Advisory Service and its associated network of experimental farms. Technical proficiency, however, is not necessarily economic efficiency. Not only was the growth of farming's prodigious outputs per acre and per man-hour not matched by growth per unit of capital investment, they were probably not matched by growth per unit of energy either – certainly not if allowance is made for the longer-term costs of the environmental damage inflicted by many modern farming methods.[32] By relieving the industry of all responsibility for the support of research and development, and by cocooning it within a blithe equation of technical proficiency and macro-economic efficiency, the agricultural policy of the post-war Labour governments can be seen as having had an enduring, detrimental effect on the landscape and environment.

Earlier this essay noted Tom Williams's 'special bond' with the Duke of Norfolk, and suggested that this – and his Coalition service generally – compromised him as a Labour politician. However, it has also been argued that Labour had no option but to surrender its historic commitment to land nationalisation and with it the comprehensive restructuring of the industry that might have facilitated. Even the strongest and most adroit Minister of Agriculture could not, in 1947, have envisaged all the wider consequences of post-war farm policy as set out above. So convinced have governments of every political persuasion been of the need to maximise growth, that it might also be considered unfair to single out Labour in 1945-51 for criticism on the basis of the environmental impact of its policies.[33] A more independent Minister, however, especially if operating within a Government and Party more closely attuned to a wider range of opinion on agricultural affairs, might have made a distinction between the emergency legislation necessary to maximise output in the post-war economic crisis, and a longer-term corporate policy for food and farming.

I am grateful to Jack Brocklebank and Joan Maynard for their help and interest in the research on which this article is based. I remain responsible for the opinions expressed. Special thanks are due to Shirley Chase.

Notes

[1] J.A. Hanley (ed), *Progressive Farming: the Maintenance of High Production*, Caxton, London 1949, quotation from vol. 1, pxiv.

[2] Clement Attlee, preface to Tom Williams, *Digging for Britain*, Hutchinson, London 1965, p8.

[3] Ralph Whitlock, *The Land First*, Museum Press, London 1954; A.G. Street, *Feather Bedding*, Faber, London 1954; see also Anthony Hurd, *A Farmer in Whitehall: Britain's Farming Revolution, 1939-1950, and Future Prospects*, Country Life, London 1951, esp. pp90 and 103.

[4] Tristram Beresford, *We Plough the Fields and Scatter: Agriculture in Britain Today*, Penguin, Harmondsworth 1975, p16; see also Howard Newby, *Country Life: a Social History of Rural England*, Weidenfeld, London 1987, pp184-6.

[5] R.J. Hammond, *Food: Studies in Administration and Control (History of the Second World War, U.K. Civil Series)*, HMSO, London 1962, pp703-718.

[6] For analysis of the 1947 Act within the context of long-term policy developments see: Peter Self and Herbert J. Storing, *The State and the Farmer*, Allen & Unwin, London 1962; J.K. Bowers, 'British Agricultural Policy since the Second World War', *Agricultural History Review*, 33, 1985, pp66-76; B.A. Holderness, *British Agriculture since 1945*, Manchester University Press 1985, pp12-41; B. Burkitt and Mark Baimbridge, 'The Performance of British Agriculture and the Impact of the Common Agricultural Policy: an historical review', *Rural History*, vol. 1, no. 2, October 1990, pp265-280.

[7] Newby, *Country Life, op cit*, p191.

[8] For details of Dallas's career see J. Bellamy and J. Saville (eds), *Dictionary of Labour Biography*, vol. 4, Macmillan, London 1974.

[9] National Museum of Labour History, Manchester, Labour Party Archives, General Secretary's Papers, GS/Ag/44 (22 March 1949); GS/Ag/74 (27 March 1950).

[10] Williams, *Digging for Britain, op cit*, p189.

[11] Howard Newby, *The Deferential Workers: a Study of Farmworkers in East Anglia*, Allen Lane, London 1977, p236.

[12] K.A.H. Murray, *Agriculture (History of the Second World War, U.K. Civil Series)*, HMSO, London 1955; Jonathan Brown, *Agriculture in England: A Survey of Farming, 1870-1947*, Manchester University Press, 1987, pp125-146.

[13] Hanley (ed.) *Progressive Farming, op cit*, vol. 4, p202.

[14] *Dictionary of Labour Biography, op cit*, vol. 2, 1974, p407; Williams, *Digging for Britain, op cit*, p180.

[15] Tom Williams, *Labour's Way to Use the Land*, The Labour Party, London 1935, p89.

[16] Christopher Addison, *Labour's Policy for the Countryside*, Labour Party, London 1937, pp8-9, and *A Policy for British Agriculture*, Gollancz, London 1939, pp91-105; *The Labour Party and the Countryside: A Statement of Policy with regard to Agriculture and Rural Life*, Labour Party, London 1924, pp2-3; *A Labour Policy on Agriculture*, Trades Union Congress and Labour Party, London 1926, pp5-8; *Labour and the Land*, Labour Party, London 1935, p7; *Our Land: the Future of Britain's Agriculture*, Labour Party, London 1943, pp4-5; see also Hurd *A Farmer in Whitehall, op cit*, pp14-5.

[17] e.g. Viscount Astor and B. Seebohm Rowntree, *British Agriculture: the Principles of Future Policy*, Penguin, Harmondsworth 1939, pp247-50; F.N. Blundell, *A New Policy for Agriculture* [with a foreword by Neville Chamberlain], Allan, London 1931, pp83-4.

[18] e.g. Frances Donaldson, *Four Years Harvest*, Faber, London 1945, pp113-15; John Drummond, *Charter for the Soil*, Faber, London 1944, pp192-5; Arthur Smith, *Agriculture's Challenge to the Nation*, Heinemann, London 1942, pp192-5; A.D. Hall, *Reconstruction and the Land: an Approach to Farming in the National*

Interest, Macmillan, London 1942, pp171-213; C.S. Orwin, *Speed the Plough*, Penguin, Harmondsworth 1942, pp79-124.

[19] Christopher Addison, *How the Labour Party has Saved Agriculture: the Story of Six Great Years*, Labour Party, London 1951, p5.

[20] Labour Party Archives, NEC Policy Sub-Committee, Minutes, 21 February 1939.

[21] John Parker, *Labour Marches On*, Penguin, Harmondsworth 1947, p67; F.W. Bateson, *Towards a Socialist Agriculture: Studies by a Group of Fabians*, Gollancz, London 1946, pp168-186.

[22] *For Socialism and Peace*, Labour Party, London 1934, pp20-1; Clement Attlee, *The Labour Party in Perspective*, Gollancz, London 1937, p181.

[23] *Let Us Face the Future*, Labour Party, London 1945, p9.

[24] Holderness, *British Agriculture, op cit*, p123. The number of agricultural holdings was even greater, at around 400,000.

[25] Malcolm Chase, 'This is no Claptrap, this is our Heritage', in C. Shaw and M. Chase (eds), *The Imagined Past: History and Nostalgia*, Manchester University Press 1989, pp134-5; Williams, *Labour's Way to Use the Land, op cit*, pp5-7.

[26] Holderness, *British Agriculture, op cit*, pp12-13.

[27] Williams, *Digging for Britain, op cit*, p169.

[28] Street, *Feather Bedding op cit*, p191; Anne Martin, *Economics and Agriculture*, Routledge and Kegan Paul, London 1958, p147.

[29] E. Whetham and J.I. Currie, *A Record of Agricultural Policy, 1939-1958*, University of Cambridge School of Agriculture, 1958, p11.

[30] F.W. Bateson, *The Challenge of 1950: Socialism and Farming*, Fabian Society, London, 1948, p23.

[31] Holderness, *British Agriculture, op cit*, p12.

[32] See Bowers, 'British Agricultural Policy since the Second World War', *op cit*, pp74-6.

[33] It should however be pointed out that there was already by this time an extensive literature on the environmental effects of modern agriculture. Williams himself was aware of some of it, see *Labour's Way to Use the Land*, p58 where he quotes Viscount Lymington, perhaps the leading authority on soil erosion at this time. On Lymington and early ecologism see Chase, 'This is No Claptrap', *op cit*.

Education and Training for the Workforce

Roger Fieldhouse

> To-day there is a palpable need for fully-trained citizens, and we have the opportunity to train them. The need is implicit in the responsibilities of a democratic society. The opportunity is provided by the greater leisure of a scientific age. There is here a vital challenge to our educational system. For the training and preparation appropriate to the times must and can extend far beyond the statutory school-leaving age.
>
> Ministry of Education, Pamphlet No 9, 1947, *Further Education*.

Until the 1860s Britain's position as industrial world leader was largely unchallenged, and little attention was paid to scientific and technical education, in spite of Lyon Playfair's appeal, during the Great Exhibition of 1851, for an Industrial University. In 1887 T.H. Huxley and others launched the campaign which became the National Association for the Promotion of Technical Education, which led to the 1889 Technical Instruction Act and the technical education committees established under the auspices of the new county councils. But in spite of these and the foundation of the Polytechnic Colleges, the number of scientists and technicians trained in Britain in the first quarter of the twentieth century in no way came up to that of Germany and the USA, its main economic rivals.

The Second World War left British industry with an immense need for new industrial equipment and skilled workers to overcome the immediate shortages of production. For the more long-term future, the rapid development of new science-based technologies and the emphasis put on science in wartime indicated that future economic success would depend upon research and development in the field of industrial technology. And for this there must be a greatly increased number of technologists and scientists, as well as managers and leaders of a technological society. There were scientists pointing this way to the future, such as Ritchie Calder who urged in 1943 that Britain should become a 'kind of research laboratory'.[1]

Both the Special Committee on Higher Technological Education under Lord Eustace Percy (1944-45), and the Committee appointed in 1945 to investigate scientific manpower needs under Sir Alan Barlow, Second Secretary at the Treasury, found that serious shortcomings in the training of technologists and scientists were undermining the effectiveness of British industry.[2]

How far did the post-war Labour government respond to this advice? Was there a vision or plan for the long-term educational needs of a more technological society? Despite some indication of concern, of which the establishment of the Barlow Committee was the most conspicuous, the new Government did not show a real commitment to the improvement of technical education and training. When a Ministerial group concerned with central government planning and economic development was establishing priorities in 1946 in the face of worsening economic conditions, education was not included. Nor was any educational development included in the initial list of priorities, although educational building work was added later.[3]

Within the field of education, there is no doubt that implementing the 1944 Education Act was the Government's priority, and within that policy, top priority was given to raising the school leaving age by 1 April 1947.[4] The only reference to education in the King's speech after the 1945 general election was to raising the school leaving age.[5]

Secondary Education

The 1944 Act provided for a tripartite system of secondary education – secondary modern, technical and grammar schools. The emphasis was very much on extending the opportunities of the elitist system to more working-class children rather than destroying its elitism. Both Ellen Wilkinson, Minister of Education 1945-47, who had fought her own way up through the system from elementary school to university, and George Tomlinson who succeeded her as Minister in 1947, and who was determined that the grammar school education he had missed should be available to deserving children of the next generation, put great store by the grammar schools.[6]

The second leg of the tripartite system, the secondary modern schools, was much the biggest and took the bulk of the pupils, although its real status was something less than the 'different but equal' position envisaged by the 1944 Act. The third, technical, leg hardly existed at all. Very few technical schools were created. This was partly because technical education did not enjoy as high a priority as other forms of education in the Ministry of Education. Before and during the war the technical education ('T') branch had been very much the Cinderella. There was little traditional awareness of, or sympathy for, the needs of industry. It was assumed that much of the necessary technical education after the war would take place in part-time further education classes.[7]

Further Education

The 1944 Act made the local education authorities legally responsible for securing the provision of 'adequate facilities' for full-time and part-time education for persons over compulsory school age. As a consequence, further education expanded rapidly after the war. In the decade between 1947 and 1956 the total number of further education students (full-time and part-time) increased from 1,595,000 to two-and-a-quarter million. This represented an 80 per cent increase in student hours during those ten years.[8] It has been claimed that this expansion was achieved with few resources for new building and in the 'absence of any form of major regional or national planning'.[9] However, the Ministry did produce a comprehensive national plan for further education and required LEAs to formulate local plans or schemes.

The circular instructing the LEAs on how to draw up their further education schemes was issued in March 1947, after a six month delay and three revisions which attempted to take account of the acute shortage of available capital for new buildings without strangling the plans at birth. It required the LEAs to submit their schemes within a year.[10] The circular was accompanied by 'an official publication designed to survey the whole field of further education as an entity'. This was the Ministry's pamphlet on *Further Education* with the FE Branch adopted as its 'bible'.[11] While the LEAs's schemes did produce something of a 'patchwork-quilt' of local or regional FE plans,[12] the two hundred page 'bible' must be regarded as a reasonably comprehensive and coherent national plan or blueprint.

According to this blueprint, there was to be a college of further education (which might have originated as a technical, commercial or art college, an institute of adult education, or a village or county college) in every centre of population. They were to 'serve as power houses ... (and) provide the framework of further education as a whole'. Within this framework a pattern of smaller centres would be fitted: 'community centres, youth clubs, village halls and the like'.[13] Different patterns of organisation were laid down in detail for large urban areas, smaller towns and scattered rural communities.[14] It was felt that 'the replacement of a great deal of evening class work by part-time study during the day (was) long overdue, especially for young people'. Hence the central role conceived for the FE colleges and their satellites. 'Preparation for work' was their primary purpose: 'to produce both skills and social leadership'.[15] The great majority of vocational students were expected to receive their training in local colleges, but plans were laid for more specialised and higher-level regional and national colleges[16] (see the section on higher technical education below). The LEAs were also encouraged to make discretionary scholarship and maintenance grants available for full-time further education students.[17] Between 1946-47 and 1955-56 the number of such awards increased from 6000 to nearly 17,000 per annum.[18]

Of all aspects of the blueprint for a re-vitalised vocational further education system, the most innovative, positive and far reaching was the proposal for compulsory part-time education up to the age of eighteen for all who had left school, to be provided in new county colleges, as recommended by the 1943 White Paper on Educational Reconstruction. The 1944 Act made provision for such part-time education, and in 1945 the Ministry published a pamphet entitled *Youth's Opportunity* to help local authorities prepare their plans for county colleges. Ellen Wilkinson was very firmly committed to this section of the Act. She argued that 'for a very large number of children, County Colleges might be a more creative part of their education than continued education at school'.[19]

However, shortage of funds for capital expenditure, and a growing belief that improvements in primary and secondary schools should take precedence, held back the plans for county colleges. Gradually, voluntary day release came to be favoured over the county college scheme, until it was quietly abandoned in 1950.[20] It is true that the development of voluntary part-time education and training for young employees between 1945-51 did lead to a very considerable expansion. In 1939 some 42,000 young employees were released during working hours: by 1951 the number had risen to over 250,000. But a large part of this expansion was accounted for by the introduction of apprenticeship schemes. In these, and indeed in other voluntary schemes, there was not necessarily the breadth of general education that had been envisaged in the county colleges. Moreoever, the voluntary system was only catering for about one in eight of the fifteen to seventeen age group.[21] The failure to implement the section of the 1944 Act relating to county colleges must be regarded as 'one of the most disappointing features in the post-war development of further education'.[22] Although there were many practical difficulties, the failure was really a consequence of the absence of the kind of determination to succeed which Ellen Wilkinson showed when pushing through the raising of the school leaving age to fifteen in 1947.

Higher Technical Education

In 1944 the Special Committee under the chairmanship of Lord Eustace Percy was set up to recommend how best to organise higher technical education and the respective contributions to be made by the universities and technical colleges. By the time its Report was published in the autumn of 1945, the Labour government was in power. The Report recommended that industry should look to the universities for the training of scientists, but that there should be a strictly limited number of higher technical colleges which would promote technical courses of a standard comparable to universities, including postgraduate courses. It also recommended that there should be a few national schools of technology to meet the needs of small but highly specialied industries; that full-time sandwich courses of degree level should be established; that a national council of technology be set up to advise the Minister and the University Grants Committee (UGC), and a number of regional councils should co-ordinate technology studies on a regional basis; and that all technology students should receive some management training.[23]

In accordance with the Percy Report, the Government established a National Advisory Council on Education for Industry and Commerce in 1947 and ten regional advisory councils in England and Wales in 1948. Their function was to advise the Ministry of Education and to assist the development of technical education in technical colleges, and co-ordinate this with the universities.[24]

The Government was cautious about the creation of university-level technical colleges. Hugh Dalton, the Chancellor of the Exchequer, was probably expressing a majority Government view when he informed the Deputy Chairman of the Parliamentary Scientific Committee in January 1947 that it would be wrong to upgrade certain technical colleges into universities for fear that technology would be neglected for academic work, with a consequent loss of skilled workers for industry (what is now called 'mission drift').[25] The Ministry of Education was likewise opposed to the technical colleges producing science graduates – their function was to produce technologists. It marshalled the same 'different but equal' argument that was used to justify technical secondary schools vis-a-vis grammar schools. 'There should be no difference in status between technologists trained in a technical college and the holders of a University degree in technology'.[26] But there was a world of difference in practice! Eustace Percy felt that the Government had failed to implement this, the main recommendation of his Report, to supplement the university higher education system by the creation of a select body of self governing higher education technical colleges.[27] In 1951 the Labour government postponed the establishment of a new technical university on the grounds of cost.[28]

In April 1946 the Minister did accept the Percy recommendation that a number of national schools specialising in particular branches of technology should be set up, but recommended that they should be developed in existing colleges by the appropriate industries, which were expected to give general support. Three months later the regulations were amended to allow the Ministry to pay 100 per cent of the costs. Within a short time, six specialist national technical colleges and the Royal College of Art were set up under this scheme.[29]

Policies for agricultural education formulated during the war were later implemented by the Labour government. These entrusted higher agricultural education to certain universities and agricultural colleges, and more practical training to farm institutes run by LEAs.[30]

The further education and training grants which the Ministry encouraged the LEAs to make available to full-time further education students also assisted students taking higher level courses at the technical colleges. These grants particularly helped ex-servicemen and women not accepted for university to undertake degree and diploma courses, including external London University degrees, at the technical colleges.[31]

Altogether, the Labour government made little real advance in technical education. Some of the administrative recommendations of the Percy Report were quickly implemented, but the development of advanced technology courses progressed very slowly. Although the number of part-time students increased very considerably, these were mainly on relatively low-level further education vocational courses. The number of full-time students on advanced courses increased scarcely at all. The Government had in fact adopted the more conservative philosophy of the Percy Report, maintaining the traditional pattern of part-time technical education, thus condemning it to inferior status, rather than opt for a genuinely equal-status technological higher education.[32] This was partly due to financial constraints. The Ministry of Education's Annual Report for 1949 stated that the lack of suitable accommodation had prevented any real progress in technical education.[33] And on 28 June 1951 George Tomlinson, the Minister of Education, in reply to a parliamentary question, revealed that the reduction of the national investment programme necessitated a delay in any increase in the provision of technical education.[34] But an equally valid reason for the Government's unimpressive record in developing higher technical education was probably a widespread inherent belief in the superiority of a traditional education with the humanities and pure science at its pinnacle. Higher technical education, beyond the part-time vocational further education, was still not invited to the ball.

Higher Education

The 1944 Act contained little that directly affected the universities, but indirectly it was a very considerable reforming influence on higher education, through its promise to increase the potential number of university applicants by a widening of secondary education and the raising of the school leaving age. This was expected, in turn, to produce a better educated work force.

By 1945 there was both a short-term need for extra university places, because of the backlog of deferments by wartime conscripts,[35] and a perceived permanent need for more places and wider access, to reflect the change in social expectations compared with pre-war days. Recognising this, the Universities Grants Committee recommended 'the expansion and improvement of facilities for university education which the public interest demands', pointing out that this could only be achieved 'with the aid of largely increased subventions from the Exchequer'.[36]

As deputy Prime Minister in the Coalition government, Clement Attlee had fully supported an expansion of at least 50 per cent after the war. When the universities expressed their reluctance to expand at this rate, he considered this 'a very serious matter, as we cannot hope to solve our post-war problems unless we can increase the supply of trained men and women in the various departments of our national life'.[37] This indicates that the main reason for the Labour government's expansionist policy for the universities was the country's perceived manpower requirements rather than greater social justice. It was within this framework, of human resource development, that the Government planned to extend the opportunities of higher education to a wider cross section of the population, and to make it more accessible by increasing the number of places and reducing the financial barriers.[38]

Within little more than six months of Labour's election victory, Hugh Dalton, the Chancellor of the Exchequer, had announced a near doubling of the previously agreed annual grant to the UGC to £9,450,000 in February 1946.[39] Meanwhile, Herbert Morrison, Lord President of the Council and Attlee's second-in-command, set up the Committee on Scientific Manpower, under the chairmanship of Sir Alan Barlow, with representatives from the various interests advocating university expansion.

In May 1946 the Committee recommended that the immediate aim should be 'to double the present output, giving us roughly 5,000 newly qualified scientists per annum at the earliest possible moment,' whilst also aiming at a substantial expansion in the number of humanities students.[40] The Report recommended that five university colleges should be upgraded to full university status and one new university and two or three institutes of technology should be founded to allow for this expansion. It also suggested that the Government should become more directly involved in the planning and development of higher education, and that the UGC should be empowered to 'concern itself more positively with university policy than it has done in the past'.[41]

In March 1946 Ellen Wilkinson wrote to Herbert Morrison suggesting that increased government funding for the universities justified greater co-ordination of responsibility to ensure a coherent and consistent government policy on higher education. She wondered whether they had 'adequate means for ensuring that the policy is implemented', and particularly whether the current arrangements for ministerial and collective government responsibility were satisfactory.[42]

Morrison prepared a memorandum for Cabinet which recommended that the expansion and government of the universities and the terms of reference and composition of the UGC should all be looked into. However he was at pains to stress that these steps would not involve 'any radical alteration of the existing relationship between the State and the Universities'.[43] Ellen Wilkinson's priorities were to press for maximum expansion over the next five years and increase the porportion of state school pupils entering higher education.[44] She urged the Cabinet to implement the Barlow Committee's recommendations and also to set up a similar committee to consider expansion in the humanities.[45]

The Minister also advised her cabinet colleagues that the relationship between the Government and the universities had been haphazard, and government policies had lacked coherence.

> There is no wish to change the character of University education, or to make the Universities into ... advanced vocational training schools ... but the need is daily becoming clearer for the Government to adopt a coherent policy for the Universities to plan their educational provision more consciously than they have done in the past in relation both to the output of ability from the schools and to the manpower requirements of the nation.

Both she and Morrison were inclined to put the universities under the control of the Ministry of Education but both the Ministry mandarins and the Treasury were opposed to this, and managed to bury the idea quietly.[46]

Nevertheless all the ministers concerned wanted higher education to be more directly controlled and planned by the Government, to meet the needs of post-war society. They did not trust the universities to introduce sufficiently substantial or speedy changes themselves. The notion of a more planned society was becoming widely accepted: this was a fundamental tenet of Labour's policies. Higher education could not expect to remain immune from this tendency. The universities' autonomy was still jealously guarded, but greater government influence over the nature and direction of higher education was exerted.[47] Robert Berdahl, in his survey of British universities and the State in 1959, regarded this as a 'dramatic transition to positive state leadership in higher education'.[48] Against this, one should consider Attlee's recollection:

> When I was in office, I steadily refused to try to increase the influence of the State on the Universities ... There are matters in which I think it is better to have trust and I think this is one of them.[49]

Despite Attlee's trust, there was an expectation after 1945 that the universities should be made to fulfil their allotted role in the planned economy and Welfare State, although it has already been pointed out that a 'radical alteration of the existing relationship between the State and the universities' was not intended.

One of the ways in which greater government control was exerted was through the UGC. Morrison, Dalton and Wilkinson, the Ministers directly concerned, all agreed that the UGC should be reformed.[50] It was given responsibility for ensuring financial accountability, dissemination of information, and planning to meet national needs. It had become 'in effect a small Department of Government in charge of the universities' which executed a policy of national priorities.[51]

Meanwhile, in January 1947, Hugh Dalton declared that the universities' needs, 'will rank high in any list of priorities, be they for men, materials or money', and that he was 'prepared to find the necessary funds to enable the universities to plan a vigorous development campaign'. 'I am in agreement with the main argument of the (Barlow) Report on the need for increased scientific manpower of university calibre', he affirmed. But he disputed some of the detailed forecasts and doubted whether the expansion could or should be as great as the Report advocated.[52]

In fact, during the period 1945-46 to 1950-51, government funding of the universities more than doubled, from £8 million to £16.6 million, and the universities became increasingly dependent on this source of funding. Quinquennial funding was introduced in 1947 to facilitate more effective planning. More direct intervention was achieved by earmarked funding. The UGC reluctantly accepted the earmarking of funds for special fields for reasons of national policy – to introduce new subjects or to secure rapid or large scale developments. Between 1947-52, 29 per cent of the recurrent grant was specially earmarked to encourage developments in science and technology, medicine, dentistry, agriculture and veterinary sciences, the social sciences, Oriental, African, Slavonic and East European studies, and for the newly established institutes of education. The national policy reasons for most of this earmarking were clearly manpower requirements. The social sciences were given special encouragement because economic and social issues were regarded as fundamental to the post-war planning of a more equitable welfare society. Oriental, African, Slavonic and East European studies were considered to be of national strategic importance.[53] The UGC was also 'invited' by the Cabinet Universities Committee to set up specialist sub-committees to exercise 'general surveillance' over subject areas of national importance.[54]

All this planning, surveillance and earmarking led to a 60 per cent expansion in total student numbers, from 51,600 in 1945-46 (virtually the same as 1938-39) to 85,400 in 1949-50. This increase was partly the result of the influx of ex-service men and women during this period, and there was in fact a small decline in numbers between 1949-53, because of the loss of 24,000 ex-service students, but most of the increased number of places were filled by school-leavers.[55]

One of the measures which was intended not merely to increase numbers, or boost special subject areas for reasons of manpower requirements or national strategic needs, but to change the social composition of the universities, was the removal of some of the financial barriers which made universities very inaccessible to the children of poorer, working-class families. Further Education and Training Grants had been available for ex-service personnel since 1943. By 1950 some 85,000 such awards had been made, half of which were taken up at universities and many others used for degree-level work at technical and further education colleges. But these awards did nothing to broaden the social intake from secondary schools. Indeed, they tended to make access more restricted for school-leavers, despite the expansion. University awards were highly competitive and many LEAs were grudging with their discretionary major awards. The Government could not force the LEAs to use their discretion more liberally, but in May 1946 the Ministry of Education issued a circular strongly encouraging them to be more generous.[56]

Ellen Wilkinson saw it as her Ministry's responsibility to ensure 'that no boy or girl who is qualified for a University education should be deprived of it through lack of money'.[57] She made a similar commitment at the Labour Party Conference in 1946.[58] She and her successor, George Tomlinson, did succeed in increasing the number of state scholarships and the amount of financial assistance for those winning scholarships to universities. By 1950 over 900 state scholarships were being awarded annually (treble the pre-war figure) and a further 10,000 new awards were being made by LEAs each year. About 75 per cent of students were by then in receipt of financial assistance from LEAs or other sources.[59] Nevertheless, LEA awards were still not mandatory and students remained at the mercy of the vagaries of LEA policies and practice.

What were the effects of the Government's higher education policies between 1945-51? Firstly, as has already been indicated, it is clear that the Government never intended any fundamental change in the nature of university education or the relationship between the universities and the State. There was no wish to destroy the universities as 'citadels of privilege'.[60] They continued to stand apart from the rest of education and were allowed to retain very considerable autonomy, despite the increased powers of the UGC.[61]

'The universities went into the 1950s still able to restrict expansion and growth to their own pace'.[62] The real expansion of the universities, after allowing for the post-1945 special provision for ex-service personnel, did not begin until the 1950s.[63] Their traditional curricula remained largely unchallenged and unchanged, at least until the establishment of the new university college at Keele in 1949.[64] They adapted only slowly to the technological needs of the post-war economy. Nor did the Labour government alter the social or gender composition of the universities in any significant way. As the Robbins Report later showed, the proportion of working-class students remained stubbornly unaltered at around 25 per cent.[65] The student body was still overwhelmingly drawn from the public schools and still predominantly male. It is hard to disagree with the view that 'higher education, especially at the older universities, in general changed scarcely at all in the years of Labour government, either in purpose or in character'.[66]

In all branches of education the Labour government failed to inject any real sense of urgency into the development of more or better vocational and technical education. Technical schools were the poor relation of the post-1944 tripartite system, and technical education remained the Cinderella of further education. The opportunity to introduce compulsory part-time education for all up to the age of eighteen was missed, as was the chance to develop higher technical education at the same level and status as university higher education. And although the universities themselves were considerably expanded, they were left very much as before, both in terms of social composition and subject orientation, with the notable exception of the effect of earmarked grants. It is a measure of the post-war Labour government's failure in this area, that within five years of its electoral defeat in 1951, a White Paper was calling for a rapid expansion of technical training opportunities at all levels, including a doubling of the numbers of workers given day-release by their employers.[67]

Notes

[1] R. Calder, 'The Application of Scientific Research to Scottish Industry', *The New Scotland*, The London Scots Self-Government Committee, Glasgow 1943.
[2] *Report of the Special Committee on Higher Technological Education (Percy Report)*, 1945; and the *Report of a Committee appointed by the Lord President of the Council on Scientific Manpower (Barlow Report)*, 1946.
[3] PRO, ED 136/819, exchange of notes between the Treasury and Ministry of Education, February–April 1946.
[4] PRO, ED 136/765, first meeting of Minister of Education's Standing (Advisory) Committee, 4.2.46; D.W. Dean, 'Planning for a Post-War Generation: Ellen Wilkinson and George Tomlinson at the Ministry of Education 1945-51', *History of Education*, vol. 15, no. 2, 1986, p157; B. Vernon, *Ellen Wilkinson 1891-1947*, Croom Helm, Beckenham 1984, p206.
[5] D.N. Pritt, *The Labour Government 1945-51*, Lawrence and Wishart, London 1963, p93.
[6] Vernon, *op cit*, p202; D. Rubenstein, 'Ellen Wilkinson Reconsidered', *History Workshop*, 7, 1979, pp161-2; F. Blackburn, *George Tomlinson*, 1954, pp169-70 and 175.
[7] P. Gosden, *Education in the Second World War*, Methuen, London 1976, pp411-7.

[8] N.A. Jepson, 'The Local Authorities and Adult Education', in S.G. Raybould (ed), *Trends in English Adult Education*, Heinemann, London 1959, p91; L.M. Cantour and I.F. Roberts, *Further Education in England and Wales*, Routledge and Kegan Paul, 2nd edn. London 1972, p1.

[9] Cantour and Roberts, *op cit*, p3.

[10] Public Record Office (PRO) ED 46/396 and 692; Ministry of Education Circular 133, *Schemes of Further Education and Plans for County Colleges*, 19 March 1947.

[11] *Ibid*; and Ministry of Education Pamphlet No. 8, *Further Education*, HMSO, 1947; PRO, ED 136/738.

[12] Cantour and Roberts, *op cit*, p3; Jepson, *op cit*, passim.

[13] Ministry of Education, *Further Education, op cit*, paras 10-11.

[14] *Ibid*, paras. 203-208.

[15] *Ibid*, paras. 22 and 27.

[16] *Ibid*, paras. 46-7 and 62.

[17] *Ibid*, para. 73.

[18] Jepson, *op cit*, p94.

[19] D.W. Dean, *op cit*, p108; B. Hughes, 'In Defence of Ellen Wilkinson', *History Workshop*, 7, 1979, p158; Vernon, *op cit*, p215.

[20] Ministry of Education, *Further Education, op cit*, paras. 14 and 202; PRO ED 34/26, 41, 92; ED 46/396, 692; ED 136/730, 738.

[21] Jepson, *op cit*, p98; H.C. Dent, *The Education Act 1944*, University of London Press, 4th edn, 1952, p51.

[22] Jepson, *op cit*, p97.

[23] Gosden, *op cit*, pp417-20; Cantour and Roberts, *op cit*, p3.

[24] *Ibid*, p4; Gosden, *op cit*, p420; R.O. Berdahl, *British Universities and the State*, University of California Press 1959, p98; W.A.C. Stewart, *Higher Education in Postwar Britain*, Macmillan, London 1989, p78.

[25] PRO ED 136/717, Hugh Dalton to Sir Wavell Wakefield, 29 January 1947. (One wonders what Dalton would think of the more recent conversion of the polytechnics into universities).

[26] PRO ED 136/717, HHB to Sir Robert Wood, 15 March 1946.

[27] E. Percy, *Some Memories*, Eyre and Spottiswood, London 1958, p213.

[28] Berdahl, *op cit*, p100.

[29] PRO, ED 165.,

[30] Gosden, *op cit*, pp420-22.

[31] L. Cantour, 'Public Sector Higher Education ', in W.A.C. Stewart, *op cit*, p297; R. Lowe, *Education in the Postwar Years*, Routledge, London 1988, p63.

[32] *Ibid*, pp63-5; Cantour, *op cit*, p297.

[33] Quoted in D.N. Pritt, *op cit*, p374.

[34] *Ibid*, p440.

[35] Gosden, *op cit*, p427.

[36] *Ibid*, pp428-30; Berdahl, *op cit*, p70; University Grants Committee, *University Development from 1935-47*, 1948, p76.

[37] PRO, ED 46/295, Attlee to Bevan, 29 January 1945; Gosden, *op cit*, p139.

[38] Berdahl, *op cit*, pp140 and 170.

[39] Gosden, *op cit*, p430.

[40] Barlow Committee, *Scientific Manpower*, HMSO Cmd 6824, May 1946, paras. 23 and 36.

[41] Berdahl, *op cit*, pp74-5; Gosden, *op cit*, 1944, p141; Lower, *op cit*, 59; Stewart, *op cit*, pp46-7.

[42] PRO, ED 136/716, Wilkinson to Morrison, 25 March 1946.

[43] *Ibid*, Memo from Lord President of the Council (Morrison), to Cabinet, July 1946.

[44] *Ibid*, Note by Minister of Education attached to the Lord President's memo.

[45] *Ibid*, Memo by Minister of Education to Cabinet, 9 July 1946.

[46] *Ibid*, and Minute paper by R.S. Wood, 13 March 1946, and correspondence between Humphrey Danes at the Treasury and John Maud and other officials at the Ministry of Education, July-September 1946.

[47] Berdahl, *op cit*, p71; Stewart, *op cit*, pp62-5.

[48] Berdahl, *op cit*, p68.

[49] *Parliamentary Debates*, House of Lords 5th ser., vol. 203 (1957), cols. 1125-6.

[50] PRO ED 136/716, Wood, Minute paper 13 March 1946 and ED 136/816, J. Maude's report of meeting between the Chancellor of the Exchequer and the Minister of Education, 3 June 1946.

[50] Berdahl, *op cit*, pp80 and 136.

[52] PRO ED 136/717, copy letter H. Dalton to W. Wakefield, 29 January 1947.

[53] PRO CAB 134/723, Minutes of first meeting of the Cabinet Official Committee on Universities, 22 May 1947 and ED 136/816, UGC memo, February 1947; Berdahl, *op cit*, pp143-4; Lowe, *op cit*, p60; Stewart, *op cit*, p61.

[54] PRO, CAB 134/723, Cabinet Official Committee on Universities, 22 May 1947; ED 136/716, Memo from Lord President, July 1946.

[55] Gosden, *op cit*, pp141-2.

[56] J. Lawson and H. Silver, *A Social History of Education in England*, Methuen, London 1973, pp419-20; Lowe, *op cit*, pp62-3; Vernon, *op cit*, pp215-6.

[57] PRO ED 136/716, Memo from Minister of Education to Cabinet, 9 July 1946.

[58] Hughes, *op cit*, p159.

[59] *Ibid*, p158; Lowe, *op cit*, p61; Pritt, *op cit*, p233.

[60] Berdahl, *op cit*, p170; Labour Party Annual Conference Reports, 1946, p192, 1947, p200.

[61] P. Gordon, R. Aldrich and D. Dean, *Education and Policy in England in the Twentieth Century*, Woburn Press, London 1991, p237.

[62] Dean, *op cit*, p107.

[63] Lawson and Silver, *op cit*, p430.

[64] Lowe, *op cit*, pp65-7.

[65] Lawson and Silver, *op cit*, p430.

[66] K.O. Morgan, *Labour in Power 1945-51*, O.U.P., Oxford 1985, p179

[67] *Technical Education*, H.M.S.O., 1955.

Part 2 – Foreign Policy and the Economy

In Search of Eldorado: Labour's Colonial Economic Policy

John Callaghan

If there is imperialism in the world today, by which I mean the subjection of other peoples by the political and economic domination of other nations, it is certainly not to be found in the British Commonwealth.

Clement Attlee, Lord Mayor's banquet, November 1947.

The organisation of Western Europe must be economically supported. That involves the closest possible collaboration with the Commonwealth, and with overseas territories, not only British but French, Belgian, Dutch and Portuguese. Those overseas territories are large primary producers ... They have raw materials, food and resources which can be turned to very great common advantage ...

If Western Europe is to achieve its balance of payments and get a world equilibrium, it is essential that these resources should be developed.

Ernest Bevin, House of Commons, 22 January 1948.

The Labour government's insistence on the obsolescence of imperialism and its promotion of the Commonwealth as an association based on freedom was matched only by the zeal with which its Ministers championed colonial 'economic development', especially after the summer of 1947. Colonial policy was a component of a broader foreign and defence policy; but it was also perceived as a critical part of the strategy for the economic restoration of Britain. As such, it was of concern to the

115

Government's most important figures and very far from being the preserve of the Colonial Office. During the course of 1948 Clement Attlee, Ernest Bevin, Sir Stafford Cripps, Harold Wilson, John Strachey, Hector McNeil and Arthur Creech Jones all added their voices to the cause of colonial development and loudly linked the economic future of Western Europe with the resources of Africa in particular. This thinking was not new, of course, and in this its most recent incarnation the policy is traceable to the war years. But it took the sharp deterioration in relations between the USA and the USSR during 1947, culminating in the Marshall Plan, before the British government was able to assert these schemes so confidently and frequently.

The principal reason for this was that, with the developing Cold War in mind, the American government abandoned its attempts to force the British to abandon the closed trading bloc of its Empire, and to adopt multilateral trade under the hegemony of the dollar. The acute dollar drain of 1947 and the convertibility crisis which brought Britain to the brink of bankruptcy underlined its economic weakness in spectacular fashion and the point was reinforced by the devaluation crisis of 1949. Once convinced that their own economic and political interests could be best served by massive aid to Western Europe, American policy-makers saw that the European colonial empires could assist in this economic restoration as well as in containing Communism. It was thus now possible for the British government to seek the restoration of the country's economic independence by using the Commonwealth as a protected trading bloc discriminating against dollar imports. The Report of the Marshall Plan Committee on 'European Economic Co-operation' published in 1947 had itself admitted that the pre-war dollar deficit of Western Europe was covered by the export of colonial raw materials to the USA. It followed that in post-war circumstances, which had massively widened the gap between American and European productivity, the dollar deficit – short-term injections of Marshall Aid apart – could be addressed in the long-run by the development of Western Europe's colonial assets.

Labour and Empire

Contrary to the myth assiduously cultivated by the Attlee government itself, there was nothing in Labour's record to suggest an anti-imperialist commitment when the party took office in 1945. The notion of planned economic development of the Empire had, however, surfaced from time to time but always on the margins of actual policy which, like that of the Conservative Party, supposed that the costs of any development of Britain's overseas possessions should be borne locally. This did not prevent socialist dreamers such as George Lansbury from imagining as early as 1925 the transformation of the Empire, under the beneficent central direction of future Labour governments, into 'a bloc against world capitalism'.[1] The practical policy prescriptions that might be derived from such an idea were never made clear, however. Few in the Labour Party were really interested in the colonies and of those that took a critical line the 'ethical-humanitarians' in the tradition of Gladstone were the more numerous. But even the advocates of 'trusteeship' exercised little, if any, influence upon the policies of the two minority Labour governments during the inter-war years.

What can be safely said is that these short-lived administrations emphasised continuity of policy; that Labour leaders for the most part were prisoners of a Victorian 'racial-cultural typology' which barred the way to clarity of thought on the Empire; and that they accepted the conventional notions of national interest and defence in relation to Britain's world role.[2] None of this was conducive to radical departures in imperial policy. Labour was nevertheless the reforming party in British politics and even contained radical impulses within its 'broad church'. The Independent Labour Party (ILP), for example, came out in favour of complete independence for India as early as 1926. But the Party as a whole remained cautious and studiously vague on this question – where it was not completley indifferent – throughout the 1930s, invariably talking in terms of 'progress towards self-government', rather than an unequivocal commitment to independence. When Labour colonial experts such as Creech Jones and Rita Hinden returned to the idea of colonial development during the war – as in the Colonial Charter considered by the Labour Party Conference in 1942 – circumstances made such schemes seem both necessary and feasible to broad sections of the business and political establishments.

Impact of War

The Second World War produced violent changes in many aspects of the imperial system. Much of the Asian empire was lost, and in a manner which dealt a fatal blow to European prestige. Local liberation fronts, many led by Communists, filled the gap left by the routed colonial authorities. In this way mighty movements of discontent would stand in the way of an inexpensive restoration of colonialism in 1945. But even where British rule was unbroken, as in much of Africa, some political instability was the unavoidable result of the demands of the war effort – increased production, rising taxes and import duties, military recruitment and greater central direction – even coercion – of the local populations. In Nigeria, Gold Coast, Kenya and North Rhodesia public revenue more than doubled during the war. In Tanganyika 86,000 men were recruited into the armed forces, in Nigeria 100,000 – in total about one million troops and carriers for the continent as a whole.

Africa also contributed manpower via increased production of crops such as palm oil, rubber and sisal. The loss of the Far East served only to increase the continent's economic important. But the growth in demand was not paid for in higher prices. Prices paid to farmers were controlled by colonial governments at levels well below the market price. Revenues extracted by these authorities were channelled into the war effort. But companies and their local representatives not only acquired cash crops cheaply; they also sold scarce manufactured imports at high prices, thus forcing farmers to produce more in order to buy them. In certain mines and plantations – where such methods were less efficacious – labour was directly coerced, as in Nigeria. Consumers meanwhile were faced with shortages, restrictions and inflation. If we add to this summary of disturbing influences the rhetoric of self-determination – notably in the Atlantic Charter of August 1941 – it is clear that by the end of the war there would be no easy return to 'business as usual' in the colonial system.

In India the imperial war effort led to a tenfold increase in the size of the Indian army, to two million men. Industry was expanded to meet war needs and yet the quantity of goods for the civilian population shrank, leading to a severe inflation and contributing to famine in Bengal where as many as three million people died. The practice of purchasing Indian goods with sterling credits held in London and frozen for the duration of the war (in effect, IOUs) transformed the country from a major debtor to Britain, with external sterling obligations of around £350 million in 1939, to become in 1945 the largest holder of sterling balances – credits measuring almost four times the earlier debt. The Government of India envisaged the use of these sterling balances for the purchase of capital goods for development purposes when the war was over. Cripps, who was to become Chancellor when Hugh Dalton resigned in 1947, was speculating on the political benefits for Britain of such modernisation as early as November 1942 when he wrote:

> If the British Government could enlist the sympathy of the workers and peasants by immediate action on their behalf, the struggle in India would no longer be between Indian and British on a nationalist basis, but between the classes in India on an economic basis. There would thus be a good opportunity to rally the mass of Indian opinion to our side.[3]

It was a prospect which beguiled Ministers and officials of both parties and which survived the war and the 'financial Dunkirk' that followed it; British political influence would remain predominant in the old Empire and within less formal spheres of influence such as the Middle East, if Britain emerged as the champion of development – or so it was thought. Clearly an underestimation of the strength of nationalism and an overestimation of Britain's economic resources figured in this reckoning. Even in 1942, as Cripps imagined British economic development of the subcontinent, the political reality in

India was moving rapidly beyond Britain's control.

Faced with the stubborn non-co-operation of the Indian National Congress, the war Cabinet had promised a future, federated dominion status for India in return for immediate collaboration in the prosecution of the struggle against Germany and Japan. When this offer – communicated by the Cripps Mission in March 1942 – was rejected, Congress turned to mass civil disobedience. The Viceroy talked of his own 'clear determination to crush that organisation as a whole'.[4] British policy, which has always nurtured reactionary elements, such as the Indian princes, on the subcontinent, now consciously built-up Jinnah's Muslim League as the sole legitimate, representative voice of a quarter of the population. In effect the Muslim League was encouraged to think of itself as possessing a veto against any constitutional change which conflicted with its recently formulated demand for Pakistan.

Although the political balance of forces was very different in the African colonies, similar economic pressures and devices to those described in relation to India were at work. Sterling had been declared non-convertible in 1939 and the dependencies exporting to Britain were paid in credits, usually Treasury Bills. War materials used in local theatres were paid for in the same way. The sterling bloc was accordingly transformed into a closely integrated monetary association, with the Bank of England possessing the power to prevent external payments unless permission was specifically granted. Fixed exchange rates were accepted within the sterling area and members' reserves were pooled in a common fund of gold and hard currencies entrusted to the British Exchange Equalisation Fund which held them as the reserve for the entire sterling area, and issued to each member such agreed sums as conformed to the needs of the centre, that is Britain. The sterling area thus became a financial union managed in London.[5] By these means Britain was able to pool and ration the hard currency resources of the Empire and buy essential war materials from the USA. This meant that a net dollar earner such as the Gold Coast received sterling credits in exchange for its hard currency which was spent by Britain. Joint Anglo-American control of shipping and the supply of war materials and food through a system of Combined Boards ensured the compliance of the sterling area countries with these arrangements. By the end of the war Britain had acquired debts of £3,700 million in this way – the vast bulk of them in the form of the sterling balances owned to the Empire countries.

American Economic Rivalry

It was never part of American intentions to permit this imperial system to survive into the peace. Roosevelt often surpassed Stalin in his criticisms of European colonialism, and American policy-makers saw the British Empire as it had functioned since the Ottawa Agreements of 1932 as a closed economic bloc – an impediment to the open global economy which they saw as a necessary prerequisite for the sustained prosperity of the USA. British officials and politicians could understandably see a link between Roosevelt's talk of timetables for colonial independence and a new UN system of trusteeship armed with powers of inspection of colonial territories, on the one hand, and pressures to dismantle the Ottawa system of imperial preference on the other. Yet the British knew they would need every assistance at the end of the war to emerge from economic dependency and financial insolvency. Britain had been forced virtually to liquidate its vast overseas assets in order to purchase American war materials under the 'cash-and-carry' policy inaugurated in 1939. After the war it could therefore expect massively reduced foreign earnings. But it was clear that there might be preconditions for any US assistance. The Americans were interested in eliminating imperial preference and made this abundantly clear from as early as May 1940 when Cordell Hull enunciated the goals of US policy.

A conflict of interests between the two nations was thus evident throughout the Lend-Lease negotiations during 1941. When the Americans took military bases, gold, and British secrets in return for war materials, Churchill commented that 'as far as I can see we are not only to be skinned but flayed to the bone'.[6] Since the combined trade of the pre-war sterling area and North America represented about one-half of the world total, the American determination to establish multilateral trade depended on agreement with Britain. Accordingly the USA made British commitment to multilateral trade a condition of the Mutual Aid Agreement of February 1942, and after bitter British resistance a formula was found in Article VII of the proposal which the Americans perceived as embodying this objective. Even before the war was over American officials used the new system as a wedge with which to get US firms into the imperial market and to restrict Britain's gold and dollar balances in order to circumscribe its room for manoeuvre.[7] The determination and apparent ability of the US to shape the world economy in its own interest was also exhibited at the Bretton Woods conference of July 1944 where institutions such as the International Monetary Fund (IMF) were created, dedicated to the 'harmonisation of national policies', the promotion of a 'multilateral system of payments' and the 'elimination of foreign exchange restrictions which hamper the growth of world trade'.[8]

Britain thus found itself economically dependent on a nation with economic and political interests antipathetic to its imperial system; one poll conducted in June 1942 found fixty-six per cent of Americans agreeing that the British could be described as 'oppressors', 'because of the unfair advantage ... they have taken of their colonial possessions'.[9] It is hard to believe, in this context, that the emerging watchword of colonial 'development' was unrelated to this public relations problem. The Colonial Development and Welfare Act of 1940, which made £55 million available in grants and loans over a ten year period when Britain itself was in dire financial straits, was certainly conceived with at least one eye on the 'series of labour revolts' which disturbed Trinidad and Jamaica in 1937 and 1938 and produced damaging publicity concerning the extent of poverty afflicting the West Indian working class.[10]

The economic neglect of the European colonies was one of Roosevelt's favourite themes during the war. As the conflict drew to a close Treasury officials acknowledged privately that there was still a need to 'justify ourselves before the world' as a colonial power;

and the Colonial Secretary, Oliver Stanley, informed the Chancellor that the right 'psychological moment' to announce 'a dynamic programme of Colonial development' would be at the war's end, when a clear call from London would reassure administrators of 'the permanence and adequacy of our policy'. The connection between economic development and the survival of Britain's world role was also spotted by colonial administrators.[11] Shortly after the general election of 1945 a further Colonial Development and Welfare Act, prepared by the Coalition, made £120 million available for investment over the next ten years.

Great Power Status

The point has been made before that, in spite of Britain's weakened position, there was no-one of significance in British public life who believed that Britain was anything less than a great power. A case could be made for arguing that the Foreign Secretary, Ernest Bevin, was a particularly pronounced victim of this delusion. He was given to public pronouncements which connected the maintenance of the Empire to the British standard of living. Thus he told the House of Commons on 21 February 1946:

> I am not prepared to sacrifice the British Empire, because I know that if the British Empire fell … it would mean that the standard of life of our constituents would fall considerably.

It was a point to which he returned on 16 May 1947, this time asserting that the standard of living depended on the safety of 'British interests in the Middle East'.[12] It was perfectly obvious that Britain's status as one of the 'Big Three' depended on the restoration of its global interests – a project that had been planned from the moment they were lost. Nor was Britain alone in this zeal for turning the clock back. The more enfeebled French, though allegedly faced with the threat of a Soviet attack, still found the money and manpower to fight a prolonged war in Vietnam, just as the malnourished Dutch summoned up the strength to oust Sukarno in Java. In both cases Britain assisted in the initial stages of repossession. It was an operation that was easily rationalised in terms of restoring political stability, stopping Communism and laying the foundations of international security. But as Bevin was at pains to point out, there were also crucial economic considerations at stake.

The Federation of British Industries recorded its own interest in this apsect of the matter in April 1942. One historian has observed in this connection that:

> The most common fear ... was that the Americans would sustain their drive towards multilateral trading arrangements, but would do so in ways which paid minimal heed to the adjustment needs of other industrial nationals. Thus the gains of post-war recovery would be overwhelmingly appropriated by US producers, leaving other western economies in a state of permanent subordination. One way out of this looming dependency was to enforce industrial efficiency at home; but under conditions of troop demobilisation this approach had severe limitations. It was in this context that British business opinion became deeply attracted to the thesis of colonial development, since the boosting of purchasing power in those underdeveloped areas where the UK enjoyed trade preferences and political control could make a vital contribution to the maintenance of the British market-share in international trade.[13]

But it was as commodity producers that the colonies met British post-war needs most of all, not just in foodstuffs and raw materials but also in dollars.

The abrupt termination of Lend-Lease within days of the defeat of Japan underlined Britain's precarious position, as did the harsh conditions which the USA attached to the Anglo-American loan of $3.75 billion negotiated at the end of 1945. This required that sterling be made fully convertible within twelve months of Congressional approval of the loan – a step that was guaranteed to exhaust Britain's reserves, as Keynes pointed out at the time. The US Secretary to the Treasury said of the loan 'its most important purpose from our point of view is to cause the removal of the emergency controls exercised by the United Kingdom over its international transactions far more speedily'.[14] Britain was also finally forced to agree to the abolition of discriminatory import quotas, and by the time the General Agreement on Tariffs and Trade (GATT) was signed in the spring of 1947, the UK had eliminated around 5 per cent of its trade formerly subject to imperial preference. The American pursuit of free trade also led to the collapse of the pre-war production and marketing arrangements for Middle Eastern oil between Britain and the US oil companies; the American share of oil output in the region, which had risen from 16 to 31 per cent between 1939 and 1946, jumped to 60 per cent by 1953.[15]

Thus the evidence from all sides highlighted Britain's economic weakness. But the scale of its foreign commitments had if anything expanded, as new overseas entanglements were added to the scores of territories, of every degree of dependency, of the Empire. When Labour entered office, the Empire was as extensive as ever and Bevin proposed to increase its size by adding Cyrenaica and Tripolitania (modern Libya) to it. Labour was already committed to the military occupation of Greece which the War Cabinet had begun in December 1944 in order to prevent a communist takeover, and it soon became clear that the military occupation of Germany was a long-term responsibility. In Palestine – regarded by the British military as an essential 'strategic reserve' – Labour inherited the problem of irreconcilable commitments and mounting violence between Arabs and Jews, before finally withdrawing in diplomatic disarray in May 1948. On the eve of this withdrawal, something like 270,000 British troops were stationed in various parts of the Middle East, including Iran, Iraq, Transjordan, Egypt, the Sudan, and the Horn of Africa.[16] A month after the British left Palestine, the so-called 'Emergency' began in Malaya and British forces became involved in a prolonged war against communist insurgents.[17] Thus, by the middle of Labour's term of office, the costs of Britain's global commitments exceeded those of the pre-war period, with four times as many men in uniform as there had been in 1939, despite the manpower shortage at home. The developing Cold War and the government's determination to maintain Britain's great power status – as revealed, for example, by the secret decision to develop a British nuclear bomb – ensured that the costs of its foreign policy would continue to rise.

Economic Development and Political Independence

It was the granting of independence to India in 1947 which established the Labour government's anti-imperialist credentials, but even this begins to look equivocal under closer scrutiny. The subcontinent had become ungovernable under the imperial regime by 1945, and Britain had not the force to prolong the Raj by means of massive coercion. Yet despite its weakened negotiating position, and past statements supportive of Indian self-government, the Government had in mind something akin to the Cripps offer of 1942: the creation of a federal India, with particular provinces and states able to opt for a separate independence, and an Anglo-Indian treaty to regulate mutual interests. Britain, it was hoped, would receive assistance in the defence of South East Asia from its new Commonwealth partner and strengthen its economic links with the subcontinent.[18] In November 1945, Bevin, Attlee, and Herbert Morrison could still envisage Britain championing the lower orders in India with schemes of economic development – the prospect of pre-empting the nationalists was not yet dead.[19] Britain's resources permitted no such thing, even had the political situation been more favourable, but it is significant that the thought could still be entertained.

Bevin and the Viceroy, General Wavell, even 'toyed with the idea of a further round of repression to force Congress into a reasonable frame of mind' – again despite the absence of the requisite resources, but providing more evidence that the complete independence of India was not the overriding goal of policy.[20] Constitutional concessions, it was hoped, would buy Britain continued influence where coercion was impractical or inadvisable. In Burma, the granting of independence was informed by the strength of Aung San's Anti-Fascist Peoples Freedom League; in Ceylon, by the need to keep the great naval base at Trincomalee and the knowledge that resistance to independence might have jeopardised everything. As for India, the Chiefs of Staff stressed, in March 1946, that Britain would rely in the future 'to an even greater extent upon reservoirs of manpower such as India can provide', and envisaged the provision of Indian troops 'for use in those British territories outside India the security of which is of direct importance to the defence of India'.[21] Mountbatten was accordingly given appropriate instructions concerning Britain's defence requirements when he became the last Viceroy, and departed at what was effectively the eleventh hour in an attempt to negotiate a settlement before the subcontinent was engulfed by communal violence.

The communist insurgency in Malaya after June 1948 was just the sort of problem the Chiefs of Staff had in mind when they talked of Indian assistance in the defence of the region. Malaya was the most important dollar earner in the sterling bloc and its rubber and tin were respectively the second and fifth most valuable sterling exports to the USA. Britain had spent £86 million pounds since the war in grants and loans designed to bring output of these commodities to their pre-war levels – a strategy that was succeeding until the double blow of the communist insurrection and the American recession of 1949. Fortunately for the Government's policy, the Cold War was well under way when the communist uprising began, and so it was possible for British policy-makers to alert the American government to the nature of their Malayan problem and elicit a sympathetic response. With France at war with the Vietnamese Communists, and China on the brink of a communist revolution, it was all the easier for British policy to be seen in a favourable light in Washington. The USA was thus prepared to increase its stockpiles of Malayan rubber and tin, and to accept strict limits on Britain's dollar imports, in order to help the British economy – and its ability to play a role in the global fight against Communism. The price of tin and rubber rose because of this policy and 'the dollar position of the entire sterling area improved markedly':

In the third quarter of 1949, the sterling area's dollar deficit had been $539 million. In the last quarter of the year, it had fallen to $31 million, and in early April Cripps reported that, in the first three months of 1950, the sterling area had earned a gold and dollar surplus of $40 million. Exports from Great Britain had almost nothing to do with the reversal, which was inspired primarily by increased sterling exports of cocoa, wool, tin and rubber. Of these, only the last two promised to remain attractive to dollar area buyers after the winter. By June Malaya had a trade surplus with the United States of $185.7 million, $142 million more than the next largest contributor to the sterling area dollar supply.[22]

The communist threat was invoked many times in these years. Bevin was convinced in September 1945, apparently, that the Soviet Union's demand for a Mediterranean port in Tripolitania 'was no less than a bid for the mineral resources of tropical Africa', and for uranium in particular.[23] Russian support for a Jewish state in Palestine was in Bevin's mind likewise informed by the ulterior motive of turning Palestine into a communist state. The Foreign Secretary seemed to believe that this was to be accomplished by the immigration of 'sufficient indoctrinated Jews'. But if it is true that 'the British believed they had good reason to warn the United States that the new state of Israel might become communist', as W.R. Louis maintains,[24] Bevin's personal shortcomings[25] will not do as an explanation. A variety of Foreign Office officials, politicians, and ambassadors drew attention to the threat of Communism in the Middle East. It was the danger of Communism which informed the policy of economic development in Cyprus, and it was the reason given by the British ambassador when he demanded such a programme in Iran. Communism, it was said, lurked in the background in Iraq waiting for the failure of the British-sponsored regime of Nuri Pasha.[26] In reality, the threat of Communism was potent in enough countries of the world (if not in the Middle East) for it to be a plausible bogey in others and – real or imagined – it was a useful device for galvanising the Americans.

Apart from the region's oil, the Middle East was of great strategic significance as a communications centre, in the defence of Africa and the Indian Ocean from the Russians, and as an offensive base against the USSR. With an independent India, the Labour government became convinced of the region's vital importance to Britain, and of the need to promote its economic development as a strategy for prolonging British influence. In some respects real resources were actually found to support this view.

Britain maintained a massive military presence in the region as we have seen. The so-called 'base' at Suez was a vast military arsenal, and the fact that the Egyptian government was determined to abrogate the Anglo-Egyptian treaty of 1936 only led the Labour government to increase the size of Britain's costly garrison in the country in 1948. But, military expenditures apart, the great resources required to finance and construct Bevin's grandiose schemes for the region – irrigation works, agricultural development and educational advance – were never found. The reality was that there was scarcity in virtually everything required to make these plans work in Britain itself. To make matters worse, 'partnership' in the region often meant a British alliance with just the sort of reactionaries who had no real interest in Labour's ideas of social progress. The Anglo-Iranian oil crisis, which led to the nationalisation in March 1951 of the world's largest refinery – the Anglo-Iranian at Abadan – illustrated all of these tensions in the British position. In London there was no real sympathy for the reforming, nationalist government of Mohammed Mussadiq, though its popular base was authentic, and the company, in which the British government had a fifty per cent stake, was ultimately lost, at least in part because American oil companies such as Aramco were offering far more generous profit-sharing deals in the region than Anglo-Iranian had been prepared to contemplate.

In Africa, where political independence appeared a distant prospect to colonial officials, the economic development begun during the war could be pursued without regard for the views of the Africans, but all the more confidently in the name of their future emancipation, which was now said to depend on a prior overcoming of 'backwardness'.[27] At the same time Cripps was able to tell an African Governors Conference in 1947 that, 'the whole future of the sterling group and its ability to survive depends ... upon a quick and extensive development of our African resources'.[28] Bevin was even more sanguine, telling Dalton in October 1948 that he envisaged the Americans 'eating out of our hands in four or five years', if Britain 'only pushed on and developed Africa'.[29] Similarly John Strachey, the Minister for Food, was convinced that 'by one means or another, by hook or by crook, the development of primary produce of all sorts in the colonial area ... is ... a life and death matter for the economy of the country'.[30]

Such thinking informed Strachey's enthusiasm for the groundnuts scheme, initially promoted by the Managing Director of the United Africa Company (a subsidiary of Unilever), whereby millions of acres of 'scrub' would be cleared in East Africa, mostly in Tanganyika, for the planting of groundnuts, in an effort to overcome the shortage of fats in Europe. This is chiefly remembered now as a spectacular folly which cost £40 million over five years and produced fewer groundnuts than were originally planted; but at the time it was described by the *Economist* as just 'the sort of economic planning which is needed to change the face of the colonial empire'.[31] Well before much-publicised, centrally-funded initiatives such as the Colonial Development Corporation and the Overseas Food Corporation – the two most important bodies created by Strachey's Overseas Resources Act of 1948 – were perceived to have failed, however, the African contribution to Britain's economic recovery had been substantial.

I have already shown that economic activity in the African colonies intensified during the war. In 1945 a system of marketing boards was created for the bulk buying of cash crops and the maintenance of artificially low prices paid to producers. The riots in the Buganda province of Uganda in 1949 were directly related to this exploitation of farmers. Processing industries – British owned and controlled – were given an effective monopoly and able to generate excessive profits. In Kenya, the production drive strengthened the hand of the white farmers who owned about twenty per cent of the best arable land, and produced nearly all the agricultural exports and taxable income. The Labour government actively encouraged emigration to Kenya with its economic goals in mind, and a further eight thousand whites were added to the population between 1945 and 1948. Even *Socialist Commentary* acknowledged the unrest which these development policies were causing throughout Africa, and African nationalists voiced their objections along these lines at a Fabian Colonial Bureau conference in London as early as 1946.[32] Economic considerations were later cited as important in the Government's appeasement of Dr Malan's racist regime in South Africa (uranium), and in the support it gave to the idea of a Central African Federation, opposed by every significant leader of black African opinion.

The intensification of the development drive in Africa in the late 1940s has been described as amounting to 'a second colonial occupation'.[33] Colonial administrations were reconstructed, experts arrived and schemes begun which 'often imposed additional labour on sceptical cultivators' while 'government-controlled marketing boards pocketed much of the proceeds of commodity sales'.[34] Net dollar earners such as Malaya and the Gold Coast were also involved in the system of compulsory lending to Britain which I described earlier. It only needs to be added that the sterling credits exchanged for dollars could not necessarily be used to purchase goods from Britain, since the Labour government gave priority to exports to dollar markets and rationed the amount and kind of exports to the colonies. Thus not only were funds that could have been used for colonial development given to Britain by these means, but the reduced proceeds from colonial exports which were actually earned could not purchase the many commodities in short supply. The resulting shortages and inflation were not the least cause of unrest everywhere from the Gold Coast to Tanganyika. Finally it should be mentioned that when the pound was devalued against the dollar in 1949, the system of fixed exchange rates between sterling and the colonial currencies enabled Britain to minimise the real value of its debts in the form of the sterling balances by devaluing these currencies to the same extent.

The amount of capital which flowed from Britain to the colonies under the Colonial Development and Welfare Act amounted to some £8 million per annum between 1946 and 1951 for the entire Commonwealth. In the same period the forced borrowing from the Commonwealth represented by the sterling balances held in London rose by £150 million, while the West African marketing boards alone held a further £93 million on deposit in London by 1951. D.K. Fieldhouse has concluded that 'the basic fact is that between 1945 and 1951 Britain exploited those dependencies that were politically unable to defend their own interests in more ways and with more serious consequences than at any time since overseas colonies were established'.[35] It is difficult to disagree with this verdict, and yet it should be noted that criticism of the Government's colonial policy was exceedingly muted within the

Labour Party during the relevant period. The Left in the party was divided and weakened by the Cold War after June 1947; it was also mostly patriotic, preoccupied with the domestic situation, informed by paternalism in relation to the colonies and generally anxious to see the Government succeed.

Tribune had been very critical of Labour's foreign policy in the first flush of post-war radicalism, but it rallied to the Government when the Marshall Aid programme was announced and Europe subsequently divided into two antagonistic camps. It became something of a coventional wisdom to argue that the Russians were determined to spoil the great social-democratic experiment in Britain, which they saw as a competitor in a global propaganda struggle between socialists. *Tribune* went along with this notion and soon adopted the official view of colonial policy; an editorial in August 1948, for example – entitled 'Let's Stay in Africa' – explained that this was the best way to overcome the backwardness of the colonies.[36] The Fabian Colonial Bureau and its like-minded friends – notably, Rita Hinden's *Socialist Commentary* – were even more zealous in their advocacy of 'development', while preserving a decorous silence on the question of exploitation. The overwhelming preoccupation of the party was of course its domestic programme and, with few exceptions, those who were interested in colonial policy subscribed to the new orthodoxy; economic development would pave the way to a successful (pro-Western) political independence.[37]

In fact the increased economic and political interference generated by these development schemes arguably hastened political independence by provoking opposition and providing it with a context of discontent. This goes some way to explain why the political reforms advanced in Africa during and immediately after the war were found to be inadequate almost as soon as they were enacted, even though they went further than anything hitherto anticipated by colonial nationalists.[38] Political progress, however, was not really the point. If there was a big idea which informed Government policy towards the colonies, it was surely that their economic development would put Britain – and indeed Western Europe – on an independent footing in relation to the USA. The other big idea of closer integration in Europe – which the Americans themselves favoured from June 1947 – was much less appealing. But that is another, related, story.[39]

Notes

[1] G. Lansbury, 'Empire Day', *Lansbury's Labour Weekly*, 23 May 1925.

[2] P.S. Gupta, *Imperialism and the British Labour Movement 1914-1964*, Macmillan, London 1975, p131.

[3] D.A. Low, 'The Mediator's Moment', in R.F. Holland and G. Rizvi (eds), *Perspectives on Imperialism and Decolonisation*, Cass, London 1984, p147.

[4] B.R. Tomlinson, *The Political Economy of the Raj*, Macmillan, London 1979, p142.

[5] S. Strange, *Sterling and Policy*, Oxford University Press, 1971, p57.

[6] C. Thorne, *Allies of a Kind*, Hamilton, London 1978, p105.

[7] S. Ambrose, *Rise to Globalism*, Penguin Books, fourth revised edition, Harmondsworth 1985, p9; See also G. Kolko, *The Politics of War: The World and United States Foreign Policy, 1943-1945*, Vintage Books, New York 1968, pp280-314.

[8] G. Kolko, *op cit*, p257.

[9] C. Thorne, *op cit*, p209.

[10] P. Weiler, *British Labour and the Cold War*, Stanford University Press, California 1988, p31.

[11] W.R. Louis, *Imperialism at Bay*, Clarendon, Oxford 1977, p102 and 51.

[12] Quoted in R. Palme Dutt, *The Crisis of Britain and the British Empire*, Lawrence and Wishart, London 1953, pp336-7.

[13] R.F. Holland, 'The Imperial Factor in British Strategies From Attlee to Macmillan', in R.F. Holland and G. Rizvi (eds), *op cit*, pp166-7.

[14] G. Kolko and J. Kolko, *The Limits of Power: The World and United States Foreign Policy*, Harper and Row, New York 1972, p66.

[15] P. Armstrong, A. Glyn and J. Harrison, *Capitalism Since World War Two*, Fontana, London 1984, p53.

[16] W.R. Louis, *The British Empire in the Middle East 1945-1951*, Clarendon, Oxford 1984, pp32-33.

[17] See A. Short, *Communist Insurrection in Malaya*, Muller, London 1975.

[18] J.G. Darwin, *Britain and Decolonisation*, Macmillan, London 1988, pp89-91.

[19] N. Owen, 'Responsibility Without Power: The Attlee governments and the end of British rule in India', in N. Tiratsoo (ed), *The Attlee Years*, Pinter, London 1991, p173.

[20] J.G. Darwin, 'British Decolonisation Since 1945', in Holland and Rizvi (eds), *op cit*, p192.

[21] B.R. Tomlinson, *The Political Economy of the Raj, op cit*, pp147-8.

[22] A.J. Rotter, 'The Triangular Route to Vietnam: The United States, Great Britain and South East Asia, 1945-50', *International Historical Review*, 6, 3, 1984, p419.

[23] W.R. Louis, *op cit*, p29.

[24] *Ibid*, p44.

[25] A. Bullock argues that Bevin was one of the best Foreign Secretaries that Britain ever had, in *Ernest Bevin: Foreign Secretary*, Oxford University Press, 1985.

[26] W.R. Louis, *op cit*, pp214-215; p307, p632, p640.

[27] A. Creech Jones, 'The Labour Party and Colonial Policy 1945-1951', in A. Creech Jones (ed), *New Fabian Colonial Essays*, Hogarth Press, London 1959, pp 25-26.

[28] D.A. Low and J.M. Lonsdale, 'Introduction: Towards the New Order 1945-1963', in D.A. Low and A. Smith (eds), *History of East Africa*, Volume 3, Clarendon, Oxford 1976, pp8-9.

[29] P.S. Gupta, *op cit*, p306.

[30] *Ibid*, p320.

[31] See H. Thomas, *John Strachey*, Eyre Methuen, London 1973, chapter 16; *The Economist* is quoted in Low and Lonsdale, *op cit*, p11.

[32] See the editorial for example, in *Socialist Commentary*, April 1949 and Rita Hinden, 'The Africans Don't Trust Us', in *Tribune* 27 February 1948.

[33] Low and Lonsdale, *op cit*, p13.

[34] J.G. Darwin, *The End of the British Empire*, Blackwell, Oxford, 1991, pp45-6.

[35] D.K. Fieldhouse, 'The Labour Governments and the Empire Commonwealth', in R. Ovendale (ed), *The Foreign Policy of the British Labour Governments 1945-51*, Leicester University Press, 1984, p95.

[36] *Tribune*, 20 August 1948.

[37] D. Goldsworthy, *Colonial Issues in British Politics 1945-61*, Clarendon, Oxford 1971, pp147-150.

[38] M. Crowder, 'The Second World war: Prelude to Decolonisation in Africa', in M. Crowder (ed), *The Cambridge History of Africa*, Volume 8, 1940-1975, Cambridge University Press 1984, p30.

[39] A. Schlaim, *Britain and the Origins of Unity*, University of Reading, 1978, pp134-42; See also M. Newman, *Socialism and European Unity*, Junction Books, Guildford 1983, pp129-31; and S. Newton, 'Britain, the Sterling Area and European Integration 1949-50', *Journal of Imperial and Commonwealth History*, 13, 3, May 1985, pp163-173.

Cold War:
The Economy and
Foreign Policy

Fergus Carr

> Whatever Britain's manifest economic weakness and the liabilities
> incurred by maintaining sterling as an international currency, her
> political and strategic influence, especially through the enduring
> presence of a world-wide Commonwealth, gave her importance
> beyond her physical means.
>
> Kenneth Morgan, *The People's Peace, British History 1945-1990.*

Economic factors played an important role in shaping the Labour
governments' foreign policy from 1945 to 1951. Britain emerged
from the war in severe economic difficulty and turned to the United
States for assistance. Vulnerability, and the perceived importance of
maintaining American support for British interests, determined the
development of foreign policy in the early Cold War. Here I
examine the interrelationship of economic factors and foreign
policy, and consider the economic consequences of foreign policy.

Britain's Insolvency

At the end of the Second World War Britain was financially
insolvent. The war effort had devastated the country's financial and
industrial position. It has been estimated that the war cost a quarter
of Britain's wealth, £7,300 million.[1] Debt to other countries had
grown from £476 million to £3,555 million in 1945.[2] Much of the

debt was to sterling area countries. Britain faced major difficulties in resolving this situation because of physical damage to its productive capacity and merchant marine. Obsolete plant, lack of investment, manpower shortages and the dislocation caused by war, all constrained exports. Invisible earnings had been cut by wartime sales of foreign assets valued at £4,200 million. Imports of food and raw materials were vital but foreign earnings scarcely paid half the cost.[3] Britain also faced continuing military costs from occupation roles as well as colonial policy.[4] Lend-Lease, the American provision of munitions, raw materials and food had been critical to the British war effort. Britain had received twenty-seven billion dollars in Lend-Lease aid.[5] With peace this line of supply was to end and Maynard Keynes feared a 'financial Dunkirk'.

On 21 August 1945, Lend-Lease was terminated without warning. Without American aid, plans for reconstruction would have to be significantly reduced, and austerity would prevail. As Hugh Dalton put it, Britain was now in an 'almost desperate plight.[6] The Cabinet sought further aid from America in the form of a grant of five billion dollars. The United States, however, would only consider a loan, of just 3,750 billion dollars.[7] Dalton described the British position as a slow retreat from, 'a free gift to an interest free loan, and from this again to a loan bearing interest; from a larger to a smaller total of aid and from the prospect of loose strings to the most unwilling acceptance of strings so tight that they might strangle our trade'.[8]

The strings were interest at two per cent, reduction of sterling balances, end of the sterling area dollar pool, non-discrimination against American imports, and the convertibility of sterling within one year of the loan becoming effective. Despite Aneurin Bevan's and Emmanuel Shinwell's opposition, the Cabinet approved the conditions; Clement Attlee could see 'no alternative'. The Labour government did not believe it could bargain; the Americans were in the dominant financial position.[9] However, it was another question whether Britain could honour the conditions.[10] Dalton, for example, believed, 'it is quite certain that the conditions will have to be revised ... and that even in the next year or two that this will require considerable variation which might even be unilateral.'[11]

On 15 July 1947, sterling was made convertible. But within five weeks convertibility was suspended. The sterling crisis exposed Britain's continuing financial weakness. The total outflow of gold and dollars increased from 900 million dollars in 1946 to 4,100 million dollars in 1947.[12] This quickly exhausted the loan. Treasury officials believed the crisis had been 'developing inexorably since the early years of the war and has been concealed successively by lend lease, borrowing for sterling and the United States and Canadian credits'.[13] The dollar drain reflected a massive dependence on the United States as a source of supply.

Exports could not offset the drain, as industry was deprived of labour because of government reluctance to cut manpower levels in the armed services.[14] Labour shortages also hit coal production, creating a fuel crisis in the bitter winter of 1947. The occupation of Germany also cost valuable reserves; some sixty million dollars were spent between January and March in 1947. Convertibility did not, on its own, cause the sterling crisis but it could hardly help when the country was in the midst of an acute dollar shortage. The Treasury was later to conclude that the crisis was caused by 'excessive overseas and defence spending and a lack of foreign confidence in a Labour Government.'[15]

Marshall Aid

The acute dollar shortage was not confined to Britain. The total European balance of payments deficit worsened from 5.8 billion dollars in 1946 to 7.6 billion in 1947.[16] General George Marshall, the American Secretary of State, believed that Europe 'must have substantial additional help or face economic, social and political deterioration of a very grave character.'[17] George Kennan was charged with developing the American response to the European crisis. Kennan's objective became the restoration of non-Soviet power in Europe through economic means, the European Recovery Programme (ERP).

Washington invited all Europeans to participate in the ERP. Neither Ernest Bevin nor President Truman would take responsibility for excluding the Soviet Union and making the final breach in Europe. The Soviet Foreign Minister, Molotov, however, rejected Anglo-French proposals for a joint European approach and withdrew, much to Bevin's relief and American satisfaction.

The United States now looked to Britain to play a leading role in the development of the ERP. The Truman administration, much to Bevin's dismay, sought an integrated economic community in Western Europe.[18] Bevin's ideas of Western Union outlined in early 1948 stressed consultation and co-operation, not federalism. The British tried to secure aid separate from the ERP but were refused.[19] Britain's dependence upon America forced acceptance of a European programme. Yet Britain's importance to the ERP forced America to accept that Britain would not take the lead role in European integration. Despite Marshall Aid, Britain's financial weakness persisted. In 1949 a short recession in the United States hit sterling area exports. With Britain responsible for managing the overall deficit of the sterling area, a dollar shortage once again resulted. The Labour government responded by cutting dollar imports, by public expenditure cuts and finally by devaluation in September 1949. The option of 'fortress sterling', of a closed discriminatory sterling area, was not pursued.[20] Financial strategy remained Atlanticist, reflecting the direction of foreign policy and strategy. Anglo-American co-operation had reached a high point during the war and British decision-makers assumed it would continue in peace. Keynes, for example, assumed America would grant aid or a gift to ease Britain's problems in 1945. Bevin suggested that Britain should be America's partner in the dispensation of aid to Europe in 1947. Washington saw this as an attempt to keep the wartime relationship, which was incompatible with their integrationist objective for the ERP.[21] Whilst Alan Bullock has suggested that this was a 'conflict between poverty and pride', it was equally an issue of perception and aspiration. The United States saw Britain as a power that could no longer play a world role.[22] Washington looked to Britain to play a European role in the development of containment of the Soviet Union. In contrast, the British saw their immediate dependence upon the USA as temporary. Bevin saw the American relationship as a means to retain a world role. Indeed he sought to exploit Britain's position as America's key European partner in order to secure support for British foreign policy in general. So whilst America saw the Anglo-American relationship as 'an instrument for American system building, Britain, belying the post war realities, saw it as the pillar of her own diametrically opposed design for reinstating herself as a major world power'.[23] The Atlantic orientation of British foreign policy was not simply induced by financial dependence, but by political and strategic aspiration. The Soviet Union would be of critical importance to the development of the Anglo-American relationship. The role, or rather perceived role, of the Soviet Union would determine the congruence of British and American interests. The Soviet 'threat' underpinned Marshall Aid and facilitated Bevin's efforts to secure the North Atlantic Treaty Organisation (NATO).

The Soviet 'Threat'

When Labour won the 1945 election, a reasonable expectation of the new government's foreign policy objectives would have been the development of the United Nations, reconstruction in Europe and the maintenance of friendly relations with the USA and the USSR. The Soviet Union was seen by much of the Labour Party and the general public as an ally that had suffered greatly in war. In official circles a different view was emerging. In senior military circles the USSR was seen as the long-term threat to the balance of power and, whilst the Foreign Office was less strident, it was turning to this perception in 1945. Attlee and Bevin were party to the development of official views in the wartime coalition. Bevin's foreign policy reflected this experience and was reinforced by his diplomatic encounters with Molotov, the Soviet Foreign Minister, and the pattern of Soviet policy in Eastern and Central Europe.

The Foreign Office saw Germany, South East Europe, Greece, Turkey, Persia and the Far East as areas in which Soviet policy was consistently opposed to British interests.[24] This view was complemented by Bevin's experience of negotiations with the Soviet Union in the Council of Foreign Ministers. The London Council meeting in September 1945 failed to secure any agreement. At the same time the Soviet Union called upon Turkey to cede the districts of Kars and Ardahan and for base rights in the Straits. In Iran, occupying Soviet troops were not withdrawn and supported the secession of Azerbaijan from Teheran. Britain had traditionally looked to Turkey as a block to Russian entry to the Mediterranean and to Persia also as buffer and a valuable oil rich asset. Greece was also seen as of strategic importance and in 1945 Britain was the occupying power. Bevin would not withdraw British troops, as he feared a third round of civil war and victory for the Greek Communist Liberation Front. He believed Stalin was following a policy of applying pressure at any point round Russia's borders where the weakness of the resistance might open the way to extending Russian power.[25] Bevin's response was based upon a traditional understanding of British interests, those of a global and imperial power.

Early in 1946 Attlee, within the Cabinet Defence Committee, questioned the rationale of Bevin's policy. In a radical analysis of Britain's external role, Attlee challenged the idea and cost of a Mediterranean and Middle Eastern strategy. He argued that, 'we cannot afford to provide the great sums of money for the large forces involved on the chance of being able to use the Mediterranean route in time of war.'[26] Attlee saw the strategy as outmoded, and suggested a reorientation in which Britain would be seen as 'an easterly extension of a strategic area, the centre of which is the American continent, rather than as a power looking eastwards through the Mediterranean to India and the East.'[27] Bevin opposed Attlee, and argued that if Britain withdrew from the Mediterranean, southern Europe would fall, like eastern Europe, 'under the totalitarian yoke' and key interests like Iraqi oil would be lost. The Chiefs of Staff strongly opposed Attlee, and Montgomery threatened a joint resignation.[28] In December 1946 Attlee again conveyed his concerns to Bevin and outlined them in a memorandum early in January 1947. Attlee doubted the validity of the military view that airpower stationed in the Middle East could be an effective deterrent to the Soviet Union. He pointed to the danger of provoking a Soviet counter-strategy of further expansion into Europe or the Middle East or both. He considered the Middle

Eastern states strategically weak and politically vulnerable. Bevin again countered by pointing to the economic potential of the Middle East and arguing that even if the Russians were not bent on world domination, they could not 'resist advancing into any vacuum we may leave'. He believed that 'a surrender of the type you suggest would only encourage the Russian leaders to believe they could get their ends without war.'[29]

In public and in the Labour Party Attlee supported Bevin and his foreign policy. Jonathan Schneer notes that 'in no respect was the contradiction between the Labour Left and the rest of the party sharper than with regard to foreign policy.'[30] The Labour Left resisted an anti-Soviet policy, was suspicious of the Americans and called for a 'third force' role for Britain. From the summer of 1946 criticism of Bevinism grew within the Labour Party. In October 1946 twenty-one Labour MPs sent Attlee a letter of protest against Bevin's policy, which was described as 'being infected by the anti-red virus cultivated in the United States'.[31] A critical resolution was placed before the TUC Congress and forty-three Labour Members tabled a critical amendment to the Address at the opening of Parliament in November. The amendment, moved by Dick Crossman, called for 'a democratic and constructive socialist alternative to an otherwise inevitable conflict between American capitalism and Soviet communism'.[32] With Bevin abroad, Attlee spoke for the Government and the amendment was defeated. The scale of disapproval was shown however in the number of Labour abstentions, which reached a hundred. In January 1947 the 'Keep Left' group was formed; its pamphlet *Keep Left* called for a British role independent of America and Russia but linked to a united Europe. The leadership hit back with its own pamphlet *Cards on the Table*, and Bevin's emotive assault on his critics at the Labour Party's Margate Conference in June 1947. Crossman recorded that Bevin 'carried the delegates with him in his demand that his policy should be condemned or accepted as a whole and in the implication which ran through his whole speech that criticism of it was an act of disloyalty'.[33] Marshall Aid and Moscow's rejection of the American offer broke the cohesion of the opposition to Bevinism. The 'Czech Coup' of 1948 had a great effect on the Labour Left and cold war tensions reduced support for Moscow. The majority of the Labour Left were slowly forced to take up anti-soviet attitudes essentially similar to those of Ernest Bevin.[34] The success of Bevinism in the Cabinet and the Parliamentary Party led inevitably to the pursuit of an Anglo-American alliance and the retention of a world role. As Elisabeth Barker notes, the need to secure American co-operation in the 'Middle East, the Pacific, Europe, and the atomic field was a driving force in British strategy so far as the Chiefs of Staff, Bevin and a less enthusiastic Attlee were concerned'.[35]

Anglo-American Differences

The Anglo-American relationship was not easily secured and where it failed economic constraints became more important. On the issue of atomic power wartime co-operation ceased. In August 1946, the US Congress prohibited atomic collaboration, with the passage of the Atomic Energy Act. In January 1947, in secret, Attlee authorised the development of a British atomic bomb. He was later to record that 'if we had decided not to have it, we would have put ourselves entirely in the hands of the Americans'.[36] Bevin agreed with Attlee and, as Peter Hennessy puts it, for 'the working class John Bull it was a matter of simple patriotism to put a Union Jack on the atomic bomb'.[37] The costs of the programme, some £100 million, were concealed from Parliament.

Palestine also revealed significant differences in the Anglo-American relationship. British policy had been set in the 1939 White Paper limiting Jewish immigration and providing for independence within ten years. In 1945 President Truman called upon Britain to lift restrictions on immigration and grant 100,000 Jews immigration certificates. Yet America refused to share either military or financial responsibility for Palestine. Bevin did not wish to antagonise Arab opinion, particularly as the region was integral to his overall strategy. But the Foreign Secretary was placed under considerable pressure by Truman's public support for Jewish immigration. At the same time Jewish terrorism against British forces grew and the prospect of a negotiated settlement receded. In February 1947

Britain abdicated responsibility and announced that the future of Palestine would be placed before the United Nations. Britain would withdraw from Palestine when its mandate expired on 15 May 1948.

Economic pressures led to further retreats in foreign policy. Hugh Dalton warned in 1946 that the overseas role could lead to economic disaster.[38] Dalton's concern was not just the direct costs of defence expenditure but the consequent manpower losses to British industry. Government hopes to secure Commonwealth support for the defence burden were not realised, and the 1947 economic crises forced the Cabinet to review its policy. The Defence Committee set defence expenditure at £600 million pounds per annum for 1948/49, instead of the £900 million planned.[39] The Chiefs of Staff failed to plan at this level and the Government had to call for a revised estimate. By the end of 1947 the Defence Minister, A.V. Alexander, submitted estimates amounting to £692.6 million for 1948, which were accepted by the Chancellor.[40]

Dalton had more success in securing a British withdrawal from Greece and Turkey. In February 1947 the United States was informed that Britain could no longer afford to support the Greek and Turkish governments. Although Marshall protested at the abrupt notice of British withdrawal, Truman sought Congressional aid for both countries. The resulting Truman Doctrine secured aid and established the general principles of American intervention as a global power. Bevin's policy was to encourage the growth of American commitments whilst seeking to retain Britain's importance to Washington. Britain's importance was in proportion to its external role and Bevin was reluctant to cut commitments unless under dire pressure as in the Greek and Turkish cases. In May 1947 Michael Foot urged that Britain withdraw from Germany and the Middle East. He warned against a foreign policy 'beyond our strength'. Bevin's retort was that he was 'not aware of any suggestion, seriously advanced, that, by a sudden stroke of fate, as it were, we have overnight ceased to be a great power'.[41] In the autumn of 1947 however the Foreign Secretary began secret talks with the United States over the Middle East.[42] The talks produced precisely the form of co-operation Bevin sought, recognition that both governments had to support each other and make sure their policies ran in parallel.[43] Britain was to maintain the necessary bases; the Americans to provide economic and political backing.[44]

NATO

Bevin's strategy of Anglo-American co-operation was crowned with the establishment of NATO in April 1949. He believed that an American military commitment to complement the ERP was essential. The difficulty of attaining such a commitment should not be underestimated. It would represent a radical change for the United States in peacetime, and 1948 was a presidential election year. Bevin began by following the logic of the ERP: creating a concerted European initiative and then seeking American support. In January 1948 he called for the creation of a 'Union' of Western Europe. He proposed that treaties be concluded with the Benelux countries (Belgium, Netherlands, Luxemburg) to form with the French treaty a 'nucleus' in western Europe.[45] The consequent Brussels Treaty was, in Elisabeth Barker's view, 'a sprat to catch a whale – a device to lure the Americans into giving Western Europe full military backing'.[46] The Berlin blockade facilitated events, encouraging the development of joint defence planning between the Brussels powers, Canada and the United States. When Truman was re-elected President in November, the way was clear for the Atlantic Pact. NATO cemented the Anglo-American relationship and became the framework for Britain's East–West relations.[47]

The Cost of the Cold War

In 1950 the economy began to show clear signs of recovery. Alec Cairncross reports that production continued to expand, the balance of payments swung into substantial surplus for the first time since the war, while the reserves doubled in a year and continued to climb well into 1951.[48] These positive trends were arrested by rearmament, following the outbreak of the Korean War in June 1950. Rearmament halted the rise in investment and reduced exports, turning a balance of payments surplus of £307 million in 1950 to a deficit of £369 million in 1951.[49] The long-term consequences are more difficult to gauge, but as Hennessy has observed 'there are powerful reasons for supposing our best hope for the kind of post-war economic miracle enjoyed by so many western European countries was scattered in fragments in the committee rooms of Whitehall, on the hills above Imjin in Korea and along the Rhine in Germany as British occupation forces were rearmed in readiness for a Stalinist assault'.[50]

British defence expenditure grew rapidly during the Korean War. In August 1950 a new three year programme was announced with planned expenditure of £3,400 million, an increase of £1,100 million on previous plans.[51] In January 1951 Attlee announced a further increase, bringing the programme to £4,700 million for the years 1951 to 1954.[52] This further increase was effectively a doubling of annual defence spending in the space of two years. Attlee admitted the programme 'must affect our standard of living: we shall all have to make sacrifices in the face of rising prices and shortages of consumer goods'.[53] In cabinet, Aneurin Bevan opposed the scale of rearmament and warned of its implications for the domestic economy. When Hugh Gaitskell, as Chancellor, proposed charges for the National Health Service, Bevan's opposition came to a head. He resigned from the government in April 1951 followed by Harold Wilson and John Freeman.

The Korean War illustrates the dilemmas of the Anglo-American relationship. In order to secure American co-operation Britain had to provide Washington with diplomatic and military support. The cost of the alliance was a level of defence expenditure that threatened recovery. Yet this was the inherent logic of Bevinism: the British had to display loyalty and pay a high price for the alliance. Indeed, to sustain Britain's importance the cost of alliance had to be high. In return London secured the American commitment to Europe and hoped to extend that to support for Britain's global role. The real cost however was that Bevin set the mould for post-war foreign policy and breaking it would prove very difficult.[54] The one post-war government that could have set a new course for Britain failed to do so.

Notes

[1] F.S. Northedge, *Descent from Power: British Foreign Policy 1945-1973*, George Allen and Unwin, London1974, p38.

[2] *Ibid*, p37.

[3] See S. Pollard, *The Development of the British Economy*, 4th edition, Edward Arnold, London 1992.

[4] D. Saunders, *Losing an Empire, Finding a Role*, Macmillan, London 1990, p50.

[5] A.P. Dobson, *U.S. Wartime Aid to Britain 1940-1946*, Croom Helm, Beckenham 1986, p1.

[6] K. Harris, *Attlee*, Weidenfeld and Nicolson, London 1984, p271.

[7] A. Cairncross, *Years of Recovery*, Methuen, London 1985, pp88-120. In addition Canada granted a credit of US $1159 million. See P. Burnham, 'Re-evaluating the Washington Loan Agreement: a Revisionist View of the Limits of Post-war American Power', *Review of International Studies*, Volume 18, Number 3, July 1992.

[8] H. Dalton, *High Tide and After, Memoirs 1945-1960*, Frederick Muller, London 1962, p74.

[9] See T. Brett, S. Gilliatt and A. Pople, 'Planned-Trade, Labour Party Policy and U.S. Intervention, the Successes and Failures of Post-War Reconstructuion', *History Workshop*, 13, 1982.

[10] See P. Burnham, *op cit*.

[11] A. Cairncross, *op cit*, p110.

[12] *Ibid*, p121.

[13] *Ibid*, p133.

[14] H. Pelling, *The Labour Governments, 1945-1951*, Macmillan, London 1984, p169.

[15] K. Middlemas, *Power, Competition and the State, Volume One: Britain in Search of Balance, 1940-1961*, Macmillan, London 1986, p155.

[16] J. Spero, *The Politics of International Economic Relations*, George Allen and Unwin, London 1980, p34.

[17] F.S. Northedge, *op cit*, p47.

[18] See S. Newton, 'The 1949 Sterling Crisis and British policy towards European Integration,' *Review of International Studies*, Volume 11, Number 3, 1985, pp169-182.

[19] See W.C. Cromwell, 'The Marshall Plan. Britain and the Cold War', *Review of International Studies*, Volume 8, Number 4, 1982, pp233-251.

[20] S. Newton, *op cit*, p175

[21] A. Bullock, *Ernest Bevin, Foreign Secretary, 1945-51*, Heinemann, London 1983, p535.

[22] See R.B. Manderson-Jones, *The Special Relationship, Anglo-American Relations and Western European Unity 1947-1956*, Weidenfeld and Nicolson, London 1972, p20.

[23] *Ibid*.

[24] See D.C. Watt, 'Britain, the United States and the Opening of the Cold War', in R. Ovendale, *The Foreign Policy of the British Labour Governments 1945-1951*, Leicester University Press 1984, p57.

[25] A. Bullock, *op cit*, p159.

[26] Cited in E. Barker, *The British Between the Superpowers 1945-50*, Macmillan, London 1983, p49.

[27] Cited in Barker, *op cit*.

[28] Cited in Barker, *op cit*.

[29] A. Bullock, *op cit*, p351.

[30] J. Schneer, *Labour's Conscience: the Labour Left 1945-51*, Unwin, Hyman, Boston 1988, p28.

[31] *Ibid*, p56.

[32] *Ibid*, p58.

[33] Cited in A. Howard, *Crossman, The Pursuit of Power*, Jonathan Cape, London 1990, p139.

[34] J. Schneer, *op cit*, p31.

[35] E. Barker, *op cit*, p53.

[36] Cited in K. Harris, *op cit*, p288.

[37] P. Hennessy, *Never Again, Britain 1945-1951*, Jonathan Cape, London 1992, p268.

[38] E. Barker, *op cit*, p56.

[39] A. Cairncross, *op cit*, p392.

[40] E. Barker, *op cit*, p102.

[41] House of Commons Debates, 16 May 1947, Col. 1973.

[42] Palestine was excluded from the talks.

[43] A. Bullock, *op cit*, p475.

[44] *Ibid*, p475.

[45] House of Commons Debates, 22 January 1948, Col. 399.

[46] E. Barker, *op cit*, p127.

[47] A. Bullock, *op cit*, p841.

[48] A. Cairncross, *op cit*, p22.

[49] See P. Hennessy, *op cit*, p415; A. Cairncross, *op cit*, pp212-233; M. Chalmers, *Paying for Defence, Military Spending and British Decline*, Pluto Press, London 1985, pp46-54.

[50] P. Hennessy, *op cit*, p415.

[51] M. Chalmers, *op cit*, p48.

[52] House of Commons Debates, 29 January 1951, Col.586.

[53] House of Commons, 29 Janaury 1951, Col.588.

[54] See R. Edmonds, *Setting the Mould, the United States and Britain 1945-1950*, Clarendon, Oxford 1986.

A Fateful Decision?:
Labour and the
Schuman Plan

John Grahl

Yet the prevailing mood while the decision was being made was more than natural anxiety. It was fear, and it is this which makes the contrast with French actions so striking and marks the event as more of a political than an economic turning point ... That the British reaction should have been both fearful and defensive may well have been of much more significance for the country's future than the decision not to join.

Alan S. Milward, *The Reconstruction of Western Europe.*

The European Coal and Steel Community (ECSC), established by the Treaty of Paris of 1951, was the first of the organisations out of which today's European Community (EC) developed. Although the subsequent European Economic Community (EEC), established in 1957, had a very different economic structure from the ECSC, it closely followed the institutional and political models which the ECSC had introduced.

Thus the same six countries, France, Germany, Italy and Benelux, were involved in the EEC and the ECSC. In both cases there was a clear supranational character to the agreement, expressed primarily by the executive (High Authority of the ECSC, then Commission of the EEC) which not only administered, but also proposed, common policies. National governments had an effective control over the executive through the Council of Ministers, but this control was collective in that majority decisions were taken on questions which had previously been agreed to be within the Community's competence. Other key institutions of the EEC followed the pattern of the ECSC and reinforced its supranational features – most importantly the Court of Justice, but also the Assembly out of which today's European Parliament grew. The Coal and Steel Community can thus be seen as initiating the European Community of today.

The proposals leading in May 1950 to the ECSC were contained in the Schuman Plan, so named after the French Foreign Secretary, Robert Schuman, in whose name it was published (although authorship was claimed by, and is usually more or less attributed to, Jean Monnet, head of the French national planning bureau and subsequently the first President of the EEC Commission). Although the Declaration which put forward the Plan referred explicitly to the coal and steel industries of France and Germany, it invited other European countries to participate.[1] After a few weeks deliberation, the British Labour government declined to do so. After the ECSC was set up, the Conservative government which took office in 1951 negotiated a limited British association with the Community.

It may be exaggerating to say that this rejection determined Britain's future relationship to the integration project. It did, however, set a pattern, of late, reluctant and minimal participation in the development of the Community, which has essentially continued ever since. The Conservative government of Harold Macmillan continued with British abstention when the Treaty of Rome brought the EEC into existence in 1957, and Britain set up the looser European Free Trade Area (EFTA) with smaller non-community countries as an attempted counterweight. (This was in spite of the fact that Macmillan himself was initially in favour of the Schuman Plan.) During the course of the 1960s, first Conservative then Labour administrations attempted to reverse the decision of the 1950s and to enter the Community, but were blocked by the France of General de Gaulle. When British entry was finally agreed in 1972, not only had institutional structures been set for twenty years, but key common policies, notably on agriculture, had been determined without reference to Britain, and in ways which were contrary to

British interests. Even within the Community, Britain has continued with minimalist policies towards it: increases in the Community's budget or in the range of its competence have been consistently opposed; the *momentum* of the Community, and the view held by most other members that it is not a fixed arrangement but an agreement to proceed towards closer economic and, especially, political union, has been stubbornly resisted. British views of the Maastricht Treaty show that in many respects there has been little change in attitudes over forty years: British negotiators first did all in their power to dilute the content of the Treaty: they then obtained British derogations from two of its main provisions; even then there was considerable parliamentary resistance to ratification of the Treaty. In all this British policy seems to be based on the same two negative concerns: on the one hand a reluctance to participate in integration and resentment of the costs and disciplines that Community membership requires; on the other, fear of exclusion and isolation if integration goes ahead without British participation.

It will not be suggested that Labour's rejection of the Schuman Plan in 1950 was the origin of this long and sorry record of indecision and ambivalence towards European integration. But it did determine that the integration process would begin without Britain, in the 'Little Europe' centred on France and Germany. And the rejection does illustrate the kind of consideration which made Britain, and in particular, the British Labour Movement, so sceptical of the Community as a political project. This chapter begins with a brief description of the Plan and then examines the motives behind Labour's policy. It is argued that the reflection was based on assumptions, such as Britain's continuing role as major world power, which proved unsustainable in the long run. At the time, however, these assumptions were at the worst, errors. To cling to them today, after their falsity has been repeatedly demonstrated by experience, seems more like delusion.

The Plan

The Schuman Plan was a brilliant political initiative. Although, as a French proposal, it expressed French interests, it was also influenced by the values of the European movement and was imaginative in the way it sought to achieve important national objectives within a new Federal structure. It also displayed a surprising generosity to France's traditional adversary, Germany.

The French position in the years immediately following the Second World War seemed fragile and isolated. Although France was an occupying power in Germany, its status as a 'victor' in the war was essentially honorary, not based on real military strength. As the Cold War intensified, the other two Western occupying powers, the US and Britain, increasingly adopted policies to promote Germany's recovery, and its political rehabilitation as a full member of the Western camp. France felt threatened by German recovery both in military and economic terms. Heavy industry, coal and steel, were central to those concerns since steel production was, at the time, the basis of military capacity. The institutional arrangements France had secured to guard against a resurgence of the German steel industry were increasingly precarious. An international Ruhr authority, controlled by the three Western occupying powers, supervised the key German industrial region and fixed ceilings to German coal and steel production. But the US and Britain were exercising pressure to raise these ceilings, and they had also made clear their intention to let the newly established Federal Republic of Germany decide on the question of the ownership of mines and steel mills. France had detached the Saarland from Germany after the war, thus in effect annexing an industrially significant area. But again this situation could not be expected to last. The same thing had happened after the First World War, but a plebiscite had clearly shown the desire of the Saarlanders to return to Germany. It would be difficult for France to prevent the same thing happening once the original allied proposal to dismember Germany had been abandoned. France's position as one of the occupying powers was thus a wasting asset.

151

Monnet's plan, adopted by Schuman after consulting the German Chancellor Adenauer, was to cut through the whole tangle of conflicting national interests by internationalising control over all western European coal and steel. There would be no restoration of German national control over its heavy industry – and thus the main strategic objective of the French would be secured. But this would not involve any kind of tutelage by other nations over Germany because all countries participating in the scheme would be on the same footing – they would all give up sovereignty equally. It would in fact appeal to the Germans as a means of rejoining the international community. French economic interests could not be completely guaranteed in advance, but an integrated Coal and Steel industry would at least make some low-cost Ruhr coal available to the Lorraine steel industry, thus limiting France's loss of competitiveness. The proposed Authority to manage the integrated industry would have wide powers to intervene if market forces threatened one set of interests. The French were bold enough to trust this federal authority to pay attention to their interests, even though they would have given up the possibility of unilateral action; and they also intended the Plan to transform existing interests through the process of integration itself.

Thus the Plan proposed a direct move to the supranational level and, on this basis, offered a clean solution to an otherwise intractable complex of military and industrial problems. At the same time it transformed the inherently weak diplomatic position of France, which was without either military or industrial strength to compare with the other powers, but now became the driving force of the emerging project for integration. London, until that moment unchallenged in its political leadership of post-war western Europe, was suddenly wrong-footed by this initiative from Paris.

Rejection

The immediate circumstances surrounding Britain's rejection have been frequently described.[2] Ernest Bevin, the Foreign Secretary, had been ill, and did not have very long to live. He had presided over a turbulent period in Britain's external relations, which began with the Potsdam summit and had seen both the independence of India and the division of Europe into increasingly hostile blocs. The Cold War became the central issue of his period in office, and Bevin had done much to define the successful Western response to the Soviet challenge through the Marshall Plan and the foundation of NATO. This experience did not predispose him to attach much importance to European integration as such. His view had been that Western Europe on its own lacked the means, and perhaps the will, to resist Communism.

The way in which Bevin learned of the Schuman Plan angered him. The US Secretary of State, Dean Acheson, had agreed to visit London for talks with the British before a formal conference involving Britain, France and the US. It became clear not only that the French had agreed the main lines of their initiative with Germany before it was published, but that Acheson had been informed about it while London was still in complete ignorance. Acheson, and Schuman himself after his arrival in London, had to smooth ruffled feathers. Cabinet discussion of the proposal also took place under unfortunate circumstances – both Prime Minister Attlee and the Chancellor Stafford Cripps were away from London, and Herbert Morrison presided at a thinly attended meeting which endorsed Bevin's decision not to participate in the forthcoming negotiations on the Plan. The actual sticking point in the intense exchange of views between London and Paris was supranationality – Britain would not participate in negotiations committed in advance to a federal structure, but wanted the negotiations to be without precommitment. France refused to move so far back from the declarations which had announced the Plan. It is difficult to see how the French could have given way on this point without undermining the strategic significance of their agreement with Germany. The British decision cannot, however, be attributed to the contingent factors surrounding the launch of the plan. Within the brief period during which British participation in the Coal and Steel negotiations was to be considered, the Government called for and obtained three position papers dealing with the military, diplomatic and economic aspects of the Schuman Plan.[3] Each of these gives a sober and balanced view of the Plan's implications and certainly does not make a case for summary rejection (although a dissenting paper from the War Office was extremely suspicious of Franco-German rapprochement). All the papers were, however, defensive in tone. None of them asked what Britain could contribute to the proposed Community. Rejection, in fact, was quite in the line of the British policy before and since. One can distinguish three main strands in Labour's rejection of the integration project and these will be examined in turn. In each case, it will be suggested, Labour's position involved a serious misreading of the issues involved.

Against Capitalist Europe?

The suggestion that the rejection of the Schuman Plan might have been based on ideological grounds is only considered here for formal completeness. No-one can seriously argue that foreign policy under Bevin, or indeed any other Labour Foreign Secretary, has been directed towards the promotion of Socialism. Labour had in fact adopted a quite traditional view of national interests throughout the post-war period. And economic agreements had been signed with the US, on monetary and trade questions, which went much further towards enthroning market competition in international economic life than anything involved in the Schuman Plan.

The Labour Party, as opposed to the Government, did issue a document on 'European Unity' in June 1950, which made public ownership and social welfare key issues in international co-operation, and this document might lend some weight to the argument that Socialist opposition to European Federal Structures was a factor in Labour's rejection of the proposal – but this was rather an embarrassment to the Government, which based its own rejection on much more orthodox diplomatic considerations. An article by the author of 'European Unity', Denis Healey, written in the same period, pointed out that socialists were certainly a minority within Western Europe (he assumed that they could be a majority in Britain) and that thus federalist structures might block the kind of internal policies which Labour wanted. But Healey's own argument rests much more on geopolitical considerations than on questions of public ownership.[4]

In fact the non-communist European Left as a whole tended to take a positive view of the Schuman proposals, although opinion was divided in both France and Germany. The leader of the German Social Democrats, Schumacher, condemned the Plan (although the prescient Willi Brandt welcomed it as a basis for Franco-German reconciliation). One can see on the Marxist Left the simultaneous birth of the myth that made first the ECSC then the EEC a tool of big European capital, and the logically inconsistent but emotionally reinforcing notion of European integration as an instrument of US military and political domination. The underlying reasons for opposition were that the communist Left in Western Europe still automatically aligned its position with that of the USSR, while much of the non-communist Left still tended to conceive its own political project very much in natioinal terms. What was, in fact, a strategic question, concerning the level and location of decision-making power, could then be represented as an ideological one, concerning fundamental issues of ownership. Certainly, in the British case, it was the transferral of decision-making power from Whitehall and Westminster to the Continent which was then, and since, the basis of Labour's objections.

What was misread in these responses was the social implication of Jean Monnet's thinking – the Schuman Plan, in fact, extended to Europe as a whole the kind of decision-making process which Monnet had previously promoted in the first French national economic plan.[5] (Adenauer was aware of this when he instructed the German representative at the Coal and Steel negotiations, Walter Hallstein, to resist French *dirigisme* in the structure of the ECSC.) The Monnet Plan in France, and the High Authority of the Coal and Steel Community, would never satisfy Marxists or other orthodox Socialists in that they accepted market processes and did not focus on questions of ownership. Nevertheless, both systems represented new and significant patterns of social control over economic activity, which attempted to make market competition more transparent and to organise public interventions according to coherent political priorities. In both cases there was full scope for the exercise of trade union influence. Morrison remarked when he learned of the Plan, 'It's no good, we can't do it. The Durham miners won't wear it.'[6] In view of the subsequent fate of both miners and steelworkers in Britain, this remark carries a degree of irony. In fact the Treaty of Paris accorded to the High Authority extensive powers to intervene in, and regulate, the industries concerned, although these powers were hardly used until the late 1970s, because in the long prosperity of the 1950s and 1960s they were not necessary. If British coal and steel employees did not benefit as much as others from the interventionist European regimes of the 1980s, it is because they fell victim to the dogmatism and malice of their own national government.

Atlanticism

A much more plausible explanation for the rejection is that the Labour government had made an atlanticist choice – that it had decided on a very close alignment with the United States, which precluded the type of European structure proposed in the Plan. Now it is certainly the case that the main foreign policy issues of the period concerned the Cold War, and the birth of the Atlantic alliance, the great geopolitical drama which pitted Britain and the USA against the Soviet Union. Nevertheless there had been a substantial shift in the nature of British-US relations. In the aftermath of victory there had seemed to be, on military grounds, a relationship of approximate equality, but increasingly Britain's economic weakness had tended to lead to dependence on the USA. Thus in 1947, a foreign exchange crisis had forced Britain to withdraw from the liberal foreign exchange regimes agreed at Bretton Woods, and for lack of resources Britain had not been able to continue the intervention against communism in Greece – the transfer of responsibility for this war to the USA became the occasion for the declaration of the Truman doctrine, which inaugurated the world-wide anti-communist crusade that followed over the next forty-five years.

If Britain was less and less an equal partner, it remained until quite late in the day the preferred European interlocutor of the Americans, and the country on which the USA relied to organise West European affairs. Thus Britain played a leading role in establishing NATO, and in setting up the OEEC as the recipient European organisation for the Marshall Plan. It was apparently the British assumption that the USA would continue to sustain this localised hegemony.

The fundamental error here was in the assumption that Britain could control the pattern of US intervention in Europe, and limit its impact on existing arrangements. In fact, US representatives became increasingly frustrated with the way Britain played its European leadership role. The US government was in favour of substantial European integration, which it perceived as the basis for both the strategic and the economic reorganisation of the West. Several efforts had been made to promote integration, notably at the inauguration of the Marshall Plan, where the Americans had tried to make aid conditional on substantial moves towards economic integration by the European countries. It was largely because of British resistance that this effort failed. It had become clear that Britain would not support any integration which compromised its own sovereignty. By 1949 the USA was contemplating a different approach, which paid much more attention to France as a leader in the integration process. In October Acheson had told US ambassadors in Europe that, 'By progress towards integration I have in mind the earliest possible decisions by the Europeans as to objectives and commitments among them on a timetable for the creation of supra-national institutions'. In November he wrote to Schuman on the German question, saying that 'the development of a German Government which can take its place in Western Europe, depends on the assumption by your country of leadership in Europe on these problem'.[7] There were difficulties for the USA in making this switch: France had a smaller sphere of influence, on the one hand; on the other, French economic traditions were *dirigiste* and protectionist, so that France was unlikely to sponsor the open and liberal form of integration which the Americans preferred. Even under Labour, Britain was more inclined to free trade than was

France. Nevertheless, France was ready for some moves towards integration (in fact, a willingness to pool aspects of sovereignty, on a reciprocal basis with other countries, had even been written into the Constitution of the Fourth Republic). Disappointment with Britain drove the US towards France so that one of the most disturbing aspects of the Schuman Plan to the British was the enthusiasm with which the USA received it. We can see here the beginning of a pattern. Throughout the post-war period France has been much more politically independent of the USA than has Britain, but France's commitment to its European partners, and to the European project, has made it, in the end, a more important interlocutor to the USA than Britain has been, in spite of the much closer alignment of British and US foreign policies.

Parliament and Sovereignty

The third, and easily the most important, motive for rejecting the Plan was the issue of national sovereignty. Bevin's position was completely consistent in the defence of full British sovereignty: repeatedly he blocked or diverted initiatives which had any suggestion of federalism or supranationality. The example of the Marshall Plan has already been referred to: Britain prevented the OEEC from obtaining any control over national economic policies and confined it to a role of communication and consultation. The same thing happened with the Council of Europe which was the most direct initiative of the European Movement. The Council of Europe brought together representatives from all the parliaments of Western Europe, but it never became more than a forum because the British refused from the start to give it any powers.

There was nothing idiosyncratic in Bevin's line on sovereignty, which was shared by the whole Parliamentary Labour Party and most of the Labour Movement. (Some writers and intellectuals had been attracted to the idea of a Federal Europe during the Second World War, but their ideas had never had any influence on policy.) Nor was there any serious difference between Labour and Conservative parties on the issue. Throughout the period 1945-51

Conservatives made lofty speeches on European unity, and they occasionally tried to embarrass the Government by portraying it as hostile to Europe, but there was never the least sign that they would be ready to take Britain into federal institutions.

At the time, and since, both parties were very reluctant to abandon any aspect of sovereignty, although the Tories have sometimes found it easier to make some of the necessary accommodations to the reality of integration. The position of Churchill does, however, stand out. During the period of Conservative opposition, his speeches in favour of European unity were particularly enthusiastic, but he had also been ready to act. In 1940, in a desperate attempt to keep France from surrendering to Germany, he offered the French government a complete and permanent union of Britain and France.

To return to Labour, there seems to be a clear connection between their reluctance to contemplate supranational institutions and their perennial tendency to see Parliament more as an end in itself than a means to social change. Of course, national sovereignty can be treated as an axiom: nations can be proclaimed independent, in the same way that individuals are declared to be free. But in both cases it is also possible to assess the substantial scope for genuinely autonomous action. Post-war Britain was still an immensely strong imperial power, but it was clear that the loss of Empire, which had started with Indian Independence, would continue, and that economic weakness would in fact constrain Britain's ability to pursue an independent role in the world. In particular, economic, military and diplomatic dependence on the United States had grown rapidly. In these circumstances, the collective exercise of sovereignty might increase the effective autonomy of nation states, just as state intervention and control can increase the actual range of choice of individuals in the market place. It is true, however, that it was impossible to anticipate the future economic significance of Western Europe.

There is an interesting contrast between British reactions to the Schuman Plan and those of the Netherlands. Dutch interests and attitudes were very similar to those of Britain. In particular, they were worried about Franco-German dominance of the emerging arrangements. As a small country, however, with no sea barrier against the big continental powers, the Netherlands was less inclined to exaggerate the value of independence. In fact Dutch presence at the Schuman Plan negotiations decisively affected the institutions of the Community. The Dutch delegation did not like the purely federal structure which Monnet had suggested for the ECSC, and wanted an intergovernmental component in its constitution. The resulting compromise was to establish a Council of Ministers, representing national governments, to approve or reject the proposals of the Authority. Although the Council usually proceeded by majority votes and not unanimity, so that national governments did not always have a veto on Authority proposals, it did substantially attenuate the federal character of the Community by giving nation states a direct voice in its affairs. Today, of course, the Council of Ministers is recognised as the most powerful community institution. The Dutch here give us an object lesson in the influence which can be exercised by participating in Community initiatives rather than by opting out.

Conclusion: The Lack of Investment

An economist is tempted to characterise Britain's relations with its EC partners as displaying the same lack of investment as is responsible for other acute problems in Britain today. Our manufacturing industry suffers from prolonged neglect and failure to modernise. Our urban environment and transport systems suffer from lack of infrastructure and public facilities. Our workforce is insufficiently educated and underqualified. Similarly, our international relations are impaired by lack of long-run commitment to our economic partners. The perspective we tend to choose is defensive and short term. As a result, calculations are dominated by immediate costs, and long-run benefits are systematically undervalued. When Britain obstructs a Comunity initiative, whether it be the European Monetary System, the Social Chapter or the Fund for Economic Convergence, it may minimise immediate costs. But at the same it antagonises partners, dissipates influence and reduces our long-term gains from Community membership. The resulting frustrations with the Community then become the grounds for refusing to participate fully in new undertakings so that the cycle is repeated.

It is not asserted that the ECSC was necessarily the right commitment. On the one hand the future growth of the EC was not foreseeable; on the other hand it would have been more imaginative, and perhaps in the very long run more advantageous, to have invested massively in Britain's relations with the countries of its former Empire. Nor is it asserted that the Labour governments of 1945-51 were primarily responsible for the failure to invest and re-equip. Rather, the contrary is the truth: as a whole, this period and the war years before it were the closest Britain ever came to the complete process of renewal which is needed. It is still true, however, that not enough was done.[8] Finding themselves in the leadership of an enormously rich and powerful state, Labour Ministers concentrated too much on managing the legacy of the past, not enough on building the future. So it was with the Schuman Plan – Labour's defence of existing interests was rational. It did not envisage, as the French dared to do, the new interests which could be brought into existence.

Notes

[1] The Declaration is reprinted in P. Fontaine, *Europe – A Fresh Start: The Schuman Declaration 1950-90*, EC, Luxmburg 1990.

[2] Alan Bullock, *Ernest Bevin, Foreign Secretary*, OUP, Oxford 1985, Chapter 21.

[3] Roger Bullen and M.E. Pelly (eds), *Documents on British Policy Overseas*, Series II, Volume 1, HMSO, London 1986, Chapter 1.

[4] Denis Healey, *When Shrimps Learn to Whistle*, Michael Joseph, London 1990.

[5] Jean Monnet, *Memoires*, Fayard, Paris 1976.

[6] W. Diebold, Jnr., *The Schuman Plan*, Praeger, New York 1959.

[7] Alan S. Milward, *The Reconstruction of Western Europe, 1945-51*, Methuen, London 1984.

[8] On investment in general see S. Pollard, *The Wasting of the British Economy*, Croom Helm, Beckenham 1982.

Part 3 – The Government, the Economy and the People

Praetorians and Proletarians: Unions and Industrial Relations

Richard Hyman

'This close co-operation with the Government is a golden opportunity for us,' a very wise union officer said, 'but it deprives us of independence, and you know what independence means to a movement like ours. It makes us have a double loyalty. The two loyalties clash all the time and no one has yet told us how to combine them.

Ferdynand Zweig, *The British Worker*, 1952.

Clement Attlee became Premier on 27 July 1945. Just over six weeks later, on 12 September, he travelled to Blackpool to deliver the first ever 'fraternal address' from a prime minister to the Trades Union Congress (TUC). This exercise (repeated in several of the following years) symbolised, as was intended, a 'special relationship' between the unions and the first majority Labour government. Such a relationship, celebrated at the time, has been the starting point for most historians of industrial relations during the Attlee years. But what was its nature, what was the balance of gains and sacrifices in the overt and implicit bargaining between ministers and union leaders, and how did the agenda of the corridors of power connect with experience and action on the ground? Here, of course, the controversies begin.[1]

Trade unions provided 120 of the 393 Labour MPs elected in 1945, and six members of Attlee's first Cabinet (by 1951 the number had fallen to four). They maintained their traditional dominance within the Party's National Executive Committee (NEC), and the numerical sway of their block votes at Conference was reinforced after 1946, when contracting in to unions' political funds was replaced by contracting out. Any potential challenge within the Party to the Government's policy decisions was firmly despatched by a 'praetorian guard' of major right-wing union leaders.[2] Their backing for the Cabinet on 'political' questions was complemented by the Government's commitment to the principle of 'voluntaryism'[3]: industrial relations issues should be left to unions and employers themselves to handle, with legal intervention only when the latter themselves agreed.

I do not attempt (except briefly in the conclusion) to discuss this broader role of trade unions in the formation and defence of Party and government policy.[4] My main focus is much more narrowly on developments within unions themselves: the reassertion of 'free collective bargaining', and its partial restriction in the period of explicit wage restraint; and the pattern of strikes and the supposed 'communist conspiracy'.

Union Organisation

The post-war years reinforced the pattern of trade union organisation inherited from the nineteenth century and given new institutional structure by the wave of amalgamations of 1913-24. While so many European labour movements were of necessity constructed anew after 1945, Britain remained uniquely characterised by a multiplicity of mainly tiny associations overshadowed by a handful of competing giants.

Between 1920 and 1940 the number of registered unions in Britain had fallen from 1,384 to 1,004; between 1945 and 1951 there was a negligible decline, from 781 to 735. TUC affiliates during these six years fell from 192 to 183. The only significant amalgamation during the period was that between the two main unions in the retail sector to form USDAW.[5] Numerically, the movement was dominated by the two massive general unions, the Transport and General Workers Union (TGWU) and National Union of General and Municipal

Workers (NUGMW); the Amalgamated Engineering Union (AEU), which had grown rapidly during the war but failed to share in the post-war union growth, caught uneasily between its traditional craft identity and the competition for a more heterogeneous constituency; the two major 'industrial unions', the National Union of Mineworkers (NUM) and of Railwaymen (NUR); and the Union of Shop, Distributive and Allied Workers (USDAW), which had many of the characteristics of a third general union. The big six accounted for almost half of total union membership, and the majority of the TUC – whose own representativeness was enhanced after 1946 with the repeal of the 1927 Trade Disputes Act and the re-affiliation of the civil service and postal unions.

Table 1: *Trade Union Membership 1945-51 (Thousands)*

	1945	1946	1947	1948	1949	1950	1951
TGWU	975	1230	1264	1271	1253	1242	1285
NUGMW	605	795	824	816	805	785	809
AEU	704	723	742	743	714	716	756
NUM	533	538	572	611	609	602	613
NUR	410	453	462	455	421	392	396
USDAW	376*	374	343	342	340	343	348
'Big 6'	3603	4113	4207	4238	4142	4080	4207
Female	*561*	*387*	*495*	*486*	*462*	*461*	*514*
TUC	6671	7540	7791	7937	7883	7828	8020
Female	*1242*	*1217*	*1220*	*1237*	*1217*	*1220*	*1318*
All Unions	7875	8803	9145	9319	9273	9242	9480
Female	*1638*	*1617*	*1662*	*1672*	*1661*	*1670*	*1775*

* Combined membership of the two component unions of USDAW

The wartime growth in union membership continued, despite the problems involved in the transition to peace-time employment, which caused a temporary fall in the membership of some unions. The buoyant labour market, and no doubt the existence of a pro-union government, presumably helped. It would be surprising if this did not encourage complacency; but how firmly rooted was the unions' organisational success? British trade unionism was still overwhelmingly a movement of male manual workers. In part this reflected the structure of the labour force, which had not changed radically since the early years of the century. Yet union density was also uneven: in 1951 it was 55 per cent for men, 25 per cent for women; 49 per cent for manual workers, 31 per cent for non-manual.[6] Aggregate union density was to slip gradually from the peak of 45 per cent achieved in 1948, as employment shifted to new growth areas where unionism was less well entrenched. The structure of the TUC – with its General Council based on 'trade groups' which reflected the balance of employment in former decades – helped ossify an organisational system whose inappropriateness was to increase in the post-war era.[7]

The full-time officer staff of British unions more than kept pace with the growing membership. In 1939, according to the estimates of Hugh Clegg, A.J. Killick and Rex Adams,[8] there were some 1500 union officials responsible on average for 4000 members each. During the war (when the job was a 'reserved occupation') the number rose to over two thousand, and it increased to more than 2500 by 1951 – reducing the officer-member ratio to 3600. Assuming that the same authors' survey (undertaken at the end of the 1950s) revealed a picture little altered in the intervening years, the typical official spent a quarter of his time (officials were overwhelmingly male) negotiating, another quarter on administration and correspondence, rather less time on union meetings and individual members' problems, and even less on recruitment. British unions, by comparison with those in most other developed countries, had rather rudimentary central bureaucracies;[9] mechanisms of control over the day-to-day activities of local officials were weak. Hence, for example, an official such as Jack Jones in Coventry, out of sympathy with the policies of the TGWU leadership, could nevertheless pursue his distinctive priorities within his own domain.[10]

For Jones, a key principle was to devolve responsibility and initiative to shop steward organisation – a policy inspired by the role of stewards in defending and extending union rights during the war. What is unclear is how substantial a position stewards held within British industrial relations more generally in the latter 1940s. Many later writers assumed a relatively smooth continuity between wartime shop steward organisation and the extensive workplace bargaining which was variously condemned and celebrated in the 1960s. GDH Cole, commenting at the time, wrote that,

> after 1945 many of the J.P.C.s [joint production committees] were wound up, though some remained; but the shop stewards' movement suffered no such major setback as after 1918 ... In practice shop stewards and works negotiating bodies have become of much more significance in determining the actual conditions of work than they used to be, or than they are even now recognised to be by the formal constitutions of many of the Trade Unions.[11]

Others have placed more stress on discontinuity, and the disruption temporarily involved in the switch from war production.

> During 1945-1946 the employers fought to re-establish [their prerogatives] and re-impose their will and authority on the workers in the workshops ... They welcomed the lifting of the Essential Work Order, as it was then easier to discharge shop stewards.[12]

Similarly, Steven Tolliday insists that,

> in the major motor firms the late 1940s were a difficult period for the unions. Despite the postwar boom, supply problems made production discontinuous and periodic layoffs facilitated the victimisation of activists and disrupted organisation.[13]

For Richard Price, 'workshop organisation and bargaining were in an essentially defensive posture until the mid- to late 1950s'.[14] Most recent researchers, while recognising the paucity of firm evidence, conclude that 'workplace organisation was rather less strong and stable in the years of the Labour government than it had been in wartime';[15] the pattern was uneven, but even in the 'advanced' sectors of manufacturing trade unionism it was often true that 'there remained a long hard slog in the post-war years before the unions achieved critical mass'.[16] Ironically, for many commentators it was the attempt by national union leaders to enforce wage restraint during 1948-50 – described below – which gave a powerful boost to shop-floor autonomy, to the dismay of many general secretaries a decade later.

'Free Collective Bargaining' in Peacetime

Under war conditions the formal processes of collective bargaining had altered little. Ernest Bevin, as Minister of Labour, relied primarily on the voluntary regulation of the labour market through union-employer negotiation – a policy which reflected the strong desires of most trade union leaders. Government initiatives were filtered through tripartite machinery, notably the Ministry of Labour's Joint Consultative Committee. It was along lines proposed by this body that Order 1305 was issued in 1940, in effect banning strikes and providing compulsory arbitration in the case of disputes. But the content of wage bargaining was not directly regulated; the Coalition government relied heavily on the self-restraint of union negotiators – not without success, for wages rose at less than half the rate of the first world war. (Ultimately, indeed, 'voluntary' adherence to government objectives was always encouraged by the fact that compulsion could be used if voluntaryism failed.)

Since the forms of 'free collective bargaining' had survived largely unscathed there was little to restore at the end of the war. The TUC's policy had been for Order 1305 to be rescinded, but majority feeling on the General Council when it came to the crunch was that the advantages of compulsory arbitration outweighed the restrictions on strikes, and the wartime machinery continued. Motions for the repeal of the Order were debated at Congress on several occasions between 1946 and 1950, but always defeated or remitted. Only in 1951 – when, as described below, events finally discredited the provisions – were the restrictions withdrawn.

Assessing the outcomes of collective bargaining is difficult. The calculation of trends in wage rates depends on weightings which vary between analysts; data on actual earnings are not particularly robust; the cost-of-living index up to 1947 was based on pre-1914 household budgets and bore a questionable relationship to actual expenditure patterns in the 1940s.[17] Hence it is impossible accurately to assess trends in the real value of wage rates and earnings.

Table 2: *Wages, Earnings, Hours and Cost-of-Living 1945-51*

	Wage Index	Male Earnings	Female Earnings	Normal Hours	Hours Worked	Price Index
1945	100	100	100	47.1	47.2	100
1946	108	100	103	46.2	46.0	99
1947	111	106	110	44.9	45.2	103
1948	117	114	117	44.8	45.4	110
1949	120	118	124	44.7	45.4	114
1950	122	124	130	44.7	45.9	116
1951	133	137	142	44.6	46.3	129

Note: Wage index = index of basic weekly rates, manual workers (July); earnings = weekly earnings of manual men (21 and over) and women (18 and over) (July 1945, October 1946-51); cost-of-living/retail price index (July) combines the old and new series (before and after June 1947)

In the immediate post-war years, workers did not take for granted an annual increase in pay; it would take another decade for this to become the normal expectation. After an upsurge of pay settlements in the first year of peace, the rate of wage increases had already settled back before the introduction of formal restraint. Real wage rates appear to have risen only marginally over the period of Labour government, and earnings slightly faster. Women's weekly earnings rose from 52 per cent of men's in 1945 to 54 per cent in 1951. The Government resisted the introduction of equal pay in teaching and the Civil Service, despite the formal policies of the Party and the TUC;[18] there is little sign that negotiators in the private sector took the issue particularly seriously. The tendency to agree flat-rate wage increases did indeed lead to some proportionate reduction in the gap between men's and women's rates (as well as narrowing craft differentials); but this was often counteracted by the greater opportunities for men to gain bonus payment and work overtime.

The most notable achievement in the period was the reduction in the standard working week. The normal week of forty-seven hours had been won in most industries in the aftermath of the First World War. In 1944 the TUC reaffirmed unions' traditional goal of the forty-hour week, but the General Council urged caution, and most union leaders accepted that initial hours' reductions would have to be more modest. Most negotiators were soon compromising on forty-four hours as the new standard, and by the end of 1947 this had become the predominant pattern. In most industries, the five-day week became established for the first time, with the disappearance of the Saturday half-day.

Wage Restraint

The deterioration in economic conditions in 1947 led the Government towards a far more interventionist role, culminating in March 1948 in the acceptance by a special TUC conference of union executives of a formal policy of wage restraint.[19] 'No Government in either peace or war had, in modern times, attempted to brake and steer the movement of wages so precisely as was now proposed.'[20] In the process, both left and right within trade unionism overturned their former policies towards wage regulation.

For many enthusiasts of 'socialist planning', a strengthened state role in the economic management of post-war Britain would necessarily extend to the systematic regulation of wage determination. Within the Attlee Cabinet, Emmanuel Shinwell and Aneurin Bevan were strong advocates of 'a new wages policy, including minimum wage rates in key industries, higher rates in unattractive industries, and an agreed policy of relating wage increases to acknowledged and proven increases in productivity'.[21] At the first post-war Congress of the TUC, the Electrical Trades Union (ETU) regretted that the General Council had not addressed the issue: 'there is a need for the Trade Union Movement to have an economic policy on the question of production, wages and prices'; subsequently it forwarded to the General Council its own proposals for such a policy. In 1946, the National Union of Vehicle Builders (NUVB) took up the theme, calling on the TUC to produce a report on a national wages policy, including a minimum wage and 'a more satisfactory lasting and equitable wage standard'.

Such ideas were rebuffed. In 1944, after Beveridge had called attention to the possible inflationary consequences of unrestricted pay bargaining in a context of full employment, the TUC had denied the need for government intervention or indeed for its own co-ordination of collective bargaining. In the framework of acceptable government economic strategy, the unions individually could be relied on to ensure 'that wage movements will not be such as to upset the system of price control'; self-discipline would suffice. 'The TUC has no intention of seeking adoption of any policy which would substantially modify the present position or impose limits upon the rights of the Unions to engage in collective bargaining,' was the official statement at the 1946 Congress. Even the notion of a minimum wage was unacceptable as an interference with 'free collective bargaining': in 1948, for example, a motion calling for such a minimum was successfully opposed on the grounds that 'implementation of the resolution would seriously interfere with the historic functions of our trade unions'. Within the Cabinet, Bevin remained a fervent supporter of 'voluntaryism', as was George Isaacs, the Minister of Labour and himself a former union official; their attitude easily predominated.

By the summer of 1946 the Government was already concerned about inflation and the more general economic situation. Following initial consultations on the question of wage stabilisation – when the TUC criticised 'undue emphasis on wages as a production cost' – a White Paper in January 1947 urged general co-operation in keeping down wages and prices. The fuel crisis at the start of 1947 intensified government concern, and led the General Council in February to appoint a Special Committee to formulate proposals on economic policy. This was to serve as the main mechanism through which the TUC became converted to wage restraint.

Towards the end of 1947 – particularly after Stafford Cripps replaced Hugh Dalton as Chancellor – majority opinion in the Cabinet moved towards intervention. Bevin remained implacably hostile: Hugh Gaitskell recorded a Cabinet meeting in November with 'Cripps and Morrison being calm and sensible, Ernie flying into a furious rage and accusing Cripps of leading us down the road to fascism'.[22] Arthur Deakin, Bevin's successor at TGWU leader and the dominant figure in the TUC, likewise insisted at the 1947 Party Conference that the 'question of incentives, the question of wages and conditions of employment, are questions for the trade unions, and the sooner some of our people on the political side appreciate that and leave the job to the unions the better for the battle for production'. But at the beginning of 1948 – in Bevin's absence[23] – the Cabinet approved a policy statement which was presented to Parliament by Attlee and published under the title *Personal Incomes, Costs and Prices*. To avoid 'a dangerous inflationary situation' there should be 'no further increase in the level of personal incomes without at least a corresponding increase in the volume of production'. 'Rises in wages and salaries should only be asked for and agreed upon' in 'exceptional circumstances' such as the need to attract labour to key industries. The government wished to avoid 'interference with the existing methods of free negotiation and contract', but could do so only if these principles were voluntarily observed.

The TUC General Council objected at the lack of consultation over this statement, but eventually agreed to support the policy in return for a government undertaking to restrain profits and prices as well as wages, and on the understanding that 'free collective bargaining' would remain 'unimpaired' and that wage increases would still be justifiable in terms of increased output, unreasonably low pay, labour shortages in essential industries, and the maintenance of 'essential' differentials. On this basis – which clearly left considerable scope for the ambitious negotiator – wage restraint won a substantial majority (5,421,000 – 2,032,000) at the conference of executives in March, and the policy was reaffirmed by a similar margin at Congress in September.

Deakin played a key role in the TUC's conversion to incomes policy. 'He claimed the right to have second thoughts about matters and to express them.'[24] No doubt part of the reason was the severity of the economic crisis, and the fact that wage restraint was flexible in definition and involved no statutory restrictions on collective bargaining. Also important was loyalty to a policy to which the Labour government was now committed, in a context of increasing Cold War polarisation. From now on, anti-communism helped cement the backing for wage restraint on the part of Deakin and many of his General Council colleagues. Conversely the Cold War turned British Communists from supporters of wages policy into vociferous opponents. The ETU in particular submitted critical motions to Congress in 1948 and each subsequent year.

The growth of opposition is a familiar story. Most writers agree that despite the lack of 'teeth', 'judged by any reasonable standard of governmental achievement in such matters, the policy of wage restraint was a success'.[25] Certainly the figures (see Table 2) indicate that wage increases were indeed restrained. Nevertheless, the impact was uneven. At the end of 1947 and beginning of 1948, as negotiators anticipated a possible wage freeze, there was an exceptional rush of pay increases.[26] Thereafter the impact was greater, but far from equitable. In the main, restraint was more tightly enforced in the public than the private sector. Some existing agreements contained cost-of-living sliding scales; others did not. The focus was on industry-level agreements; 'nothing was done about earnings in the plant, which continued to rise unevenly'.[27] Restrictions on national bargaining encouraged the introduction of 'merit money', production bonuses and other additions to basic pay; the effect was 'to undermine national agreements ... [and] the internal authority of trade union executives'.[28]

As prices continued to rise, particularly after sterling was devalued in September 1949, unions whose members felt disadvantaged by the policy – for example, because they could not benefit from workplace bargaining over piecework and bonus payments – began to object, precisely as the Government pressed for a tightening of the policy in the form of 'severe restraint'. Cripps and Bevin (who was by now wholeheartedly committed to wage restraint) persuaded the General Council to endorse more rigorous restrictions (including the suspension of cost-of-living sliding scales); but a special conference in January 1950 approved the arrangements by only 4,260,000 to 3,606,000. By September, a small majority at Congress rejected the policy. Even so, the TUC urged continued restraint. As the General Council insisted in 1951 – receiving substantial backing at Congress – 'the developing rearmament programme will, in the immediate future at any rate, mean a fall in the standard of living of the community as a whole' and it was therefore 'imperative that trade unionists should be guided by the reason and good sense which have generally prevailed'. But while Cold War priorities might sway block votes, the impact on union practice in collective bargaining was more elusive. 'The tenuous nature of union responsibility to the TUC carried the advantages of executive independence and wage policy flexibility, but also carried the disadvantage of giving individual unions the right to decide what degree of responsibility they owed to the TUC, and to what extent they would be bound by TUC decisions.'[29] As early as the summer of 1949 the left majority on the AEU national committee had approved a £1 wage claim, despite Jack Tanner's support for wage restraint.[30] This was untypical; but by the end of 1950, with the Korean War giving another twist to the inflationary spiral, 'the flood-gates were opened for a torrent of wage increases'.[31]

British Unions' Foreign Policy

Between 1945 and 1949 most major trade unions, both east and west, were represented in a single confederation, the World Federation of Trade Unions (WFTU). The TUC played a central role both in its creation and in its eventual break-up, and in the subsequent formation of the International Confederate of Free Trade Unions (ICFTU).[32]

At the height of wartime pro-Soviet enthusiasm in Britain, the TUC established a joint committee with the Russian unions and agreed reluctantly to support initiatives to create a new international trade union organisation. The plan provoked fierce resistance from the bitterly anti-communist American Federation of Labor (AFL), with which the TUC had enjoyed fraternal relations for almost half a century; but the Congress of Industrial Organizations (CIO), which had split from the AFL in 1938 on an initially left-wing programme, welcomed the plan as a potential boost to its own status. The TUC co-sponsored an international conference in London in February 1945, and in October of that year the WFTU was established in Paris.

From the outset, control of WFTU was balanced precariously between pro- and anti-communists. The General Secretary, Louis Saillant, who came from the French union confederation, 'denied that he was a member of the Communist Party, though he pressed its point of view sometimes more vociferously than the Communists did themselves'.[33] His opponents argued that the secretariat functioned under his administration as a vehicle for communist propaganda. The Presidency went to Walter Citrine; and when he left the TUC for the Coal Board in 1946, he was succeeded in the post by Deakin.

The uneasy existence of WFTU reflected an interplay of ideology and opportunism: all the main union movements involved were guided by the foreign policy goals of their respective governments, but were caught up in the rhetoric of international unity and reluctant to assume primary responsibility for a breakdown. The Foreign Office, both before and after the 1945 election, was hostile to trade union co-operation with the Russians. Bevin, fervently anti-communist throughout his term as Foreign Secretary, was opposed to TUC involvement in WFTU, and advised Deakin against assuming the Presidency.[34] The latter – like Citrine before him – shared Bevin's suspicion of the Russians, but believed that the TUC could best restrict their influence within international trade unionism as members of a common organisation.[35] Throughout his term of office he maintained close liaison with the Government; anti-communism shaped their common perspectives. For example, the TUC ensured that any WFTU protests at the suppression of Greek trade unionism by the ultra-right (and British-backed) government were low-key.[36] On colonial policy, the TUC – which under the wartime Coalition government had become 'part of the formal institutional structures for the oversight of colonial trade union movements'[37] – did its best to resist support for radical nationalism. Overall, the TUC and CIO – in intimate association with their governments – were effective in curbing the ability of the Russian unions to use WFTU as an instrument of Soviet foreign policy.

As Denis MacShane insists, a persistent underlying tension was the status of the International Trade Secretariats (ITSs), industry-level organisation which pre-dated WFTU and in some cases had existed since the turn of the century. The WFTU founding constitution envisaged that these should be integrated as industrial departments based at its own headquarters. Not surprisingly, the

ITSs were almost unanimous in wishing to maintain their autonomy and their existing locations; a view only reinforced by the fact that they were in most cases run by officials whose politics conflicted totally with those of the WFTU secretariat.

What precipitated breakdown, however, was the Marshall Plan (European Recovery Program), announced by the American government in the summer of 1947. After initial uncertainties, the Russians moved into vehement opposition, while western governments moved into equally forceful support. The confrontation inevitably affected WFTU, as each camp engaged in mutual acrimony. At the 1947 TUC Congress, a motion – pressed despite General Council pressure on the movers to withdraw – declaring continued support for WFTU was heavily defeated after Deakin gave a forceful denunciation of the Russians. Marshall Aid had evidently undermined the significant body of trade union opinion which had hitherto hoped for a non-aligned foreign and economic policy. MacShane has argued, plausibly, that the Marshall Plan appealed to a 'productionist-full employment vision' attractive to the Left, leaving the Communists isolated in their opposition.[38]

The realignment gave committed anti-communists, who had anticipated far stronger support for WFTU, a free hand. Deakin called for a meeting of the Executive Bureau to discuss Marshall Aid; when the secretariat prevaricated, the TUC convened a conference in March 1948 of national union movements which supported the Marshall Plan. Covertly the TUC leadership secured joint AFL and CIO support for a new, non-communist international. The Russian union leaders, apprehensive of a split, became conciliatory: but too late. The ITSs were offered new terms for integration which months earlier would almost certainly have been acceptable, but were now refused; and in October 1948 the TUC proposed that WFTU be suspended for a year. The final meeting of the Executive Bureau, in January 1949, ended in disorder, and Deakin led a walk-out of the key western representatives. At the end of the same year, they launched the ICFTU.

In the new organisation, the status of the TUC was reduced. Its proposal to base ICFTU in London was rejected; and on the insistence of the Americans, both leading officers were chosen from smaller countries. Only in 1951 did the TUC achieve a symbolic advance, when Vincent Tewson – who had succeeded Citrine as its secretary – became President of the new body. Given the hardening of Cold War divisions, the former brokerage role of the TUC had disappeared. And given an international commitment to 'productionist' capitalist reconstruction in Europe and the associated foreign and imperial policies, the possibility of more specifically socialist initiatives – which had inspired at least some of the original British supporters of WFTU – were foreclosed.

Strikes and the 'Red Peril'

It is conventional to view the maintenance of 'relative industrial peace' as one of the Labour government's successes; in contrast to the massive disputes which followed the First World War, strike losses in 1945-51 were light.[34] But writers have also emphasised the incidence of unofficial stoppages in the second half of this period, widely attributed to communist subversion; this in turn is commonly seen as a major reason for the anti-communist campaign by the TUC and many individual union leaderships. Such accounts are, however, misleading.

Strikes are conventionally measured in three dimensions: number recorded, workers involved, and 'days lost'.[40] These do not necessarily vary in parallel. In fact, a major watershed in the character of British strikes occurred after the 1920s: the numbers increased, but their average size and (particularly) duration declined, so that the figures for workers involved and days lost diminished. The years immediately after the First World War were notable not for the number of strikes but because so many were large and protracted – industry-wide stoppages driven first by workers' reaction to the escalating cost of living, then by employers' responses to a collapse in product markets. After the Second World War, relative price stability helped prevent major conflicts; but the actual number of stoppages (despite some decline from the peak of 1945) was at a record level. In this sense, the Attlee government presided over a period of exceptional conflict.

Table 3: *Strikes, Workers Involved and Days Lost 1933-51*

	Number of Stoppages	Mining	Metal Eng & Shipbldg	Transport	Workers (000)	Days (000)
1933-9 ave	735	293	130	42	295	1694
1940-4 ave	1491	712	480	98	499	1816
1945	2293	1319	591	156	531	2835
1946	2205	1339	449	105	526	2158
1947	1721	1066	291	119	620	2433
1948	1759	1125	266	111	424	1944
1949	1426	878	257	85	433	1807
1950	1339	861	227	68	302	1389
1951	1719	1067	318	91	379	1694

Strikes were remarkably concentrated industrially. In the early 1930s, coal-mining had accounted for over a third of all recorded disputes, and the figure had risen above 40 per cent by the outbreak of war; after 1945, the proportion was consistently over 60 per cent.[41] The three most strike prone industries – mining; metals, engineering and shipbuilding; and transport – together provided over 85 per cent of all recorded strikes through the years 1945-51.

The Labour government was as hostile towards strikes as any of its Conservative predecessors. The decision to retain Order 1305 was motivated in part by the belief that its penal provisions could serve as a deterrent against stoppages.[42] On two occasions, strike leaders were indeed prosecuted under the Order. In October 1950, ten gas maintenance workers were convicted of a breach of the Order and sentenced to a month's imprisonment (reduced on appeal to a fine); the result was a wave of protests, and calls for the repeal of the wartime restrictions. In February 1951 – when Bevan, the new Minister of Labour, was already considering replacing Order 1305 – members of the committee organising an unofficial national dock strike were also prosecuted. The outcome was a fiasco, for the action solidified a stoppage which was on the point of collapsing, and the jury – uncertain whether the strike was in fact a 'trade dispute' – failed to convict. In August 1941, Order 1305 was withdrawn.

One of the earliest decisions of the Attlee government

(displaying interesting parallels with MacDonald in 1924) was to resuscitate the emergency supply organisation which had been allowed to atrophy in the 1930s. The arrangements were kept secret (and not even discussed in the full Cabinet). On two occasions – in 1948 and 1949, both involving unofficial dock strikes – the Emergency Powers Act (which Attlee had renewed early in the life of the Government) was invoked. Much more frequently, though, the Government made use of wartime defence regulations in order to counteract the effect of strikes. Such intervention was at times designed to prevent the breakdown of supplies of gas, electricity or food. On occasions, however, there was no such 'emergency' justification: 'the Labour Government used troops for the deliberate purpose of breaking unofficial strikes'.[43]

Government hostility to strikes frequently stemmed – at least after 1947 – from a manichaean vision of industrial relations as a battleground between a national effort for economic survival and a systematic communist campaign of sabotage. According to Bevin in 1950, industrial conflict was the product of a 'Fifth Column ... led by the Cominform and instigated by Moscow to produce chaos, strikes, and difficulties of all kinds'.[44] The dominant union leaders shared this perspective. A rambling motion from the NUGMW to the 1948 TUC condemned 'the disloyal activities of small factions of the Movement which are ignoring constitutional trade union practice, and thereby undermining trade union solidarity and responsibility'. Two months later the General Council issued a statement, *Defend Democracy*, which urged unions to consider banning Communists from official positions. The hand of Deakin – who displayed something approaching paranoia towards Communists[45] – clearly lay behind this invitation (the NUGMW itself already operated such a ban); and the TGWU was the one significant union to act on the advice, at its 1949 biennial conference. Anti-communism also ensured that Arthur Horner, elected Secretary of the NUM in 1947, was consistently excluded from the third of the seats which the Miners traditionally occupied on the TUC General Council.

In fact the evidence of communist orchestration of strikes is remarkably slight.[46] Indeed the Communist Party opposed the biggest strike of the Attlee years, the unofficial docks dispute of 1945. As several writers have remarked, there were more strikes in the period when the Party still campaigned for national economic recovery, industrial peace and higher productivity than in the subsequent years when its industrial line became more militant. The one union which was firmly communist-dominated, the ETU, pursued relatively modest collective bargaining objectives despite its highly visible opposition to wage restraint. Its leaders insisted on 'trade union discipline' and gave 'no support for unofficial strikes'.[47] It would be surprising – indeed testimony to remarkable political inefficacy – if individual Communists were not active in the leadership of many of the strikes in the 1948-51 period, and if their national organisational network did not play a role in extending and generalising local conflicts. Nevertheless, it is notable that the Government – despite the resources of the secret police – failed to provide specific evidence of the Communist Party machinations which were so often denounced in general terms.

Conspiracy theories divert attention from material explanations of conflict: it is 'understandable that hardworking and harassed trade union officials, when their membership seems to be getting out of hand, should lay all the blame on agitators, *agents provocateurs*, Communists and the like'.[48] How then should post-war strikes be analysed? As has been seen, the figures were dominated by coal-mining. Here strikes were overwhelmingly small and short; those larger stoppages which occurred (such as the Grimethorpe strike of 1947, which eventually involved 50,000 workers and cost 300,000 working days) began over workplace issues and spread either through solidarity action at other pits, or because the involvement of strategic groups caused extensive lay-offs.[49]

Detailed analysis of the years up to 1940 by Roy Church and his colleagues shows that mining strikes were primarily concentrated in a small minority of pits.[50] This was almost certainly still true in the 1940s; indeed a detailed case study in Lancashire a decade later shows how local variations in geology, work traditions, management practice and union representation could result in radical contrasts in the texture of pit-level industrial relations.[51] Ferdynand Zweig provides vivid insight into the type of grievances which could generate conflict.[52] Many involved disruptions to production which reduced piecework earnings: conveyor breakdowns, faulty pneumatic equipment, bottlenecks on previous shifts, shortages of pit-props. Compensation for such contingencies was traditionally negotiated between workers and management as they arose; the consequence, as a later sociological investigation concluded, was 'that every detail of the production process has become affected by the balance of power between management and workers'.[53] With pay packets composed of a complex set of special payments, allegations of miscalculation were common, and could result in strikes. So could disputes over the allocation of labour to different faces which yielded unequal earnings opportunities. Striking was a rational pressure tactic: management was usually anxious to ensure uninterrupted production, and so would commonly offer concessions. Other sources of conflict were attempts by management to increase the required amount of production – the 'stint'; and efforts to reduce customary allowances of free coal.[54] Miners frequently complained that following nationalisation, managers failed to observe arrangements sanctified by 'custom and practice'; and that the new, bureaucratic managerial hierarchies obstructed the speedy settlement of grievances which was normal in the past.[55] With the centralisation of collective bargaining, and the firm NUM commitment to make nationalisation a success, there was also a feeling that union officials had become detached from the membership; unofficial action was a predictable consequence.[56]

In the metal industries, car production assumed a high profile as an arena of conflict. As indicated earlier, many disputes in the 1940s concerned redundancy, or management challenges to the status of shop stewards.[57] In addition, as in so much of engineering, the operation of payment by results made wage determination a constant focus of struggle. H.A. Turner, Garfield Clack and Geoffrey Roberts, in their analysis of the post-war pattern of car industry strikes, emphasise two factors: the 'pervasive irregularity of employment and earnings'; and 'anomalies or inequities between the pay of comparable groups of workers'. As workers gradually developed self-confidence in their collective strength – often at the immediate work-group level – so fragmented pressure tactics became part of the everyday reality of industrial relations in the car factories.[58]

Dock strikes assumed the greatest prominence in political debate and denunciation. The largest stoppage was in the autumn of 1945; Vic Allen, in his study of Deakin, insists that it 'defies analysis'.[59] In fact the stoppage, in support of an unofficial Dockers' Charter, obliged the TGWU to take up forcefully the strikers' pay demands and resulted in a substantial pay increase (from sixteen to nineteen shillings a day). Most disputes, however, concerned far more parochial issues; work allocation; compulsory overtime; and discipline. As in mining, large disputes were typically an outgrowth of such localised conflicts, often because management took an unusually firm line and dockers not directly involved reacted with traditional forms of solidarity.[60]

As in the pits, unofficial action on the docks also reflected a degree of disenchantment with both management and union. A sociological study of Manchester Docks in 1950-1 was overtaken by two unofficial strikes which were widely denounced as instances of communist conspiracy. The researchers' analysis was more prosaic. Most workers lived within walking distance of the docks, and formed part of a dense local community; the local TGWU officials lived in more distant (and presumably more salubrious) areas and were 'out of touch'. 'Deakin & Co.' were regarded as almost an alien force, dictating union policy; 'less than half the men interviewed were critical of their employers, nearly three-quarters were critical of their trade union'. Disciplinary procedures were regarded as legalistic, inordinately slow, and unfair; the union's reputation suffered by association.[61]

Noel Whiteside's study provides a broader context for assessing conflict on the docks: a struggle between a new 'rationalising' centralised management, firmly supported by the TGWU, and workers' long-standing principles of custom and solidarity. Traditional practices 'had been designed to share work, protect jobs and preserve local autonomy in determining pay and conditions'; against the background of these principles, day-to-day work arrangements reflected a constant process of give-and-take, and discipline itself was a negotiated issue. Under the National Dock

Labour Board, however, management sought to assert its prerogative to define efficient methods of work organisation, with grievances to be resolved through formal union-employer channels, ultimately at central level. Hence 'postwar dock strikes show that rank and file dockers resented the loss of local autonomy in industrial bargaining and rejected not only the introduction of stricter managerial discipline but also the objectives that management sought to achieve'.[62]

How far can one generalise this assessment? Whiteside makes the fascinating comment that the unofficial port workers' committees which sprang up in 1945, and helped co-ordinate national action in subsequent years, 'were similar in their objectives and their methods to local TGWU branches in the interwar period and, thanks to full employment, probably operated with considerably more success'.[63] G.D.H. Cole made a somewhat similar point in arguing that often a dispute which was 'now necessarily "unofficial" because of national agreements, would not so long ago have been normally an official strike, called by a District Committee of a Trade Union'.[64] More bureaucratic and centralised mechanisms of collective bargaining naturally generated unofficial disputes. But other factors also impinged. The Attlee government was committed to the development of more 'modern' management structures and techniques designed to maximise productivity; and in this it had the backing of the dominant trade union leaders.[65] As in the mines and on the docks, a workplace industrial relations rooted in the defence of custom and practice had quite contrary priorities and values. This disjuncture could, perhaps, be applied more generally to Labour's programme of social reform. The shape of post-war Britain was defined, in Paul Addison's terms, by 'three elites – the old governing class, the trade union oligarchy and the intellectual mandarins';[66] as Gareth Stedman Jones has put it, in a colourful turn of phrase, 'the post-war Labour government was the last and most glorious flowering of late Victorian liberal philanthrophy'.[67] It is at least plausible to doubt whether the final implementation of turn-of-the-century New Liberalism was received as uncritically on the shop floor as by the official representatives of the working class; unofficial militancy may betray an underlying alienation from the

185

norms and forms of social improvement institutionalised by Labour.[68]

Labour and the Unions: Power, Influence and Status

In the historiography of the Attlee government, the main 'facts' of its relationship with the unions are relatively uncontentious. But there are major differences of interpretation: were the unions a dominant influence on the formation of the Government's policy (at least in the domestic sphere); a key 'veto group' able to block initiative which might otherwise have been pursued; or a remarkably compliant accomplice in curbing the labour market power which full employment offered their members, and in accepting the sacrifices resulting from economic crisis and rearmament? Or can one indeed argue that all these assessments are in part correct?

The unions' positive and substantive demands on the Government may in retrospect appear modest. Its programme (shaped collaboratively in the 1930s and during the war) matched their own commitment to an economic system in which the role of the State was enhanced but closely bounded, guided by a process of 'democratic' (meaning indicative and non-directive) planning, and permitting trade unions to exercise their traditional role in 'free collective bargaining'. Union leaders (and no doubt most of their members) approached the post-war era with a 'depression mentality'[69] rooted in the traumatic experiences which followed the previous war. Their immediate priorities were to ensure a smooth and equitable process of demobilisation, and a painless return to peace-time production, avoiding labour market disruption; next, to repeal the vindictive 1927 Trade Disputes Act; finally, to achieve the specific measures of state intervention – limited nationalisation, the health service and the other social reforms – which were included in the 1945 manifesto. On all these commitments, the Attlee government delivered. Their achievements whetted no further ambitions; on the contrary, the TUC leadership showed absolute loyalty to the principle of 'consolidation'.

In addition, the unions had important *procedural* expectations. Their representation on tripartite consultative and administrative bodies, already highly developed during the war, should be sustained and extended; direct consultation with TUC leaders should precede government initiatives; intervention in industrial relations without TUC agreement was taboo. These demands were accepted by the Government in principle, even if not always satisfied in practice. The TUC frequently complained of inadequate consultation, leading Attlee at the end of 1946 (following Churchill's wartime example) to circulate a memorandum urging 'Ministers to be vigilant in ensuring that the TUC and, in suitable cases, individual trade unions, are fully taken into consultation wherever appropriate at the earliest possible stage'.[70] Breach of this protocol during the formulation of incomes policy in 1947-8 soured relations. Nevertheless, in general the Attlee government clearly confirmed union leaders' right of entry to the corridors of power. But did this give them a major influence in policy formation, or were they merely – in the words of a union leader of a later generation – 'loitering without intent'?

Some histories have treated the symbols of status as evidence of power.[71] Others have argued that, at least, union resistance (or the well-founded anticipation of opposition) prevented government intervention in the labour market which was necessary or desirable.[72] The problem with this argument, as Jim Tomlinson has insisted, is that Labour's political leaders for the most part were as unenthusiastic as the unionists towards such intervention.[73] Within the Government, wage restraint was regarded with similar misgivings to those expressed by the TUC. Once the decision was taken to intervene, the TUC 'made all the concessions', a reflection of its 'almost complete uncritical acceptance of the Government's main policy'.[74] As Attlee's biographer has commented, 'the unions may have theoretically preserved the principle of free collective bargaining: in practice, they yielded ... The amount of co-operation he did receive was nothing short of remarkable.'[75]

Certainly there is no basis for Samuel Beer's contention that trade union commitment to voluntaryism proved 'radically incompatible with the type of economic planning which was attempted by

187

Britain's Socialist government'.[76] As Kenneth Morgan concludes, 'planning, in any meaningful sense, played no prominent part in the government's economic strategy'.[77] What could more reasonably be asked is why the *shared* perspectives of Government and unions diverged so little from the principles of 'collective *laissez-faire*'; and here, what is at issue is the distinctive character of the British Labour Movement.

It might be argued that post-war trade unionism in industrialised countries has tended to reflect three alternative models: one of anti-capitalist struggle; a second, of political bargaining over macroeconomic policy; a third, commitment to 'pure-and-simple' negotiation with employers. British trade unions have been unique in their frequent efforts to adhere to all three models: combining anti-capitalist rhetoric with grudging collaboration with government and an underlying preoccupation with day-to-day collective bargaining. The institutional relationship between unions and the Labour Party, regularly reaffirmed in the half-century before Attlee's election victory, rested on acceptance of the primacy of business unionism whatever the formal approval of an alternative economic system.

After 1945, oppositional militancy was embraced only on the margins (though the actual practice of rank-and-file workers often seemed to display a more dogged, defensive and pessimistic variety of class antagonism). The ideal of consensual economic policy within a framework of socialist planning was part of the new Labour Movement rhetoric, but never pursued seriously (and was perhaps given most credence by marginal groups such as Communists and some on the Labour Left in the early years of the Government); multi-unionism and the limited powers of the TUC over its affiliates would in any event have made such an ideal unattainable. 'Free collective bargaining' remained the bottom line – at times qualified by political considerations, but never overridden.

In effect, the ideal of both Government and unions was less a 'New Jerusalem' than a modern housing estate within a more humane and more efficient capitalist economy. The reorganisation of production relations, or the creation of a new system of industrial relations, played no part in this objective. Dependence on the voluntary co-operation of private capital, in hostile economic circumstances and while seeking to maintain inflated military commitments, made even such modest social objectives eventually unsustainable. Whether a more radical attempt at socialist economic planning, mobilising popular support for encroachments on the workings of product, capital and labour markets, could have proved more successful is a question of hypothetical speculation. That this was not attempted is less a reflection of trade union conservatism after 1945 than of the inherited traditions of the whole British Labour Movement, consolidated, largely consensually, over many generations.

Notes

[1] Studies which examine the relationship in general terms and in some detail include: V.L. Allen, *Trade Union Leadership*, Longmans, London 1957, and *Trade Union and the Government*, Longmans, London 1960; Martin Harrison, *Trade Unions and the Labour Party Since 1945*, Allen and Unwin, London 1960; Ross M Martin, *TUC: the Growth of a Pressure Group 1868-1976*, Clarendon, Oxford 1980; Ken Coates, 'The Vagaries of Participation 1945-1960', in Ben Pimlott and Chris Cook (eds), *Trade Unions in British Politics*, Longman, London 1982; Lewis Minkin, *The Contentious Alliance: Trade Unions and the Labour Party*, Edinburgh University Press, Edinburgh 1991; Jim Tomlinson, 'The Labour Government and the Trade Unions, 1945-51; in Nick Tiratsoo (ed), *The Attlee Years*, Pinter, London 1991. There is also extensive treatment in Volume 3 of Hugh Clegg's *History of British Trade Unions Since 1889*, due to be published in late 1993; I am grateful for the opportunity to consult this in manuscript.

The fact that most general histories of the Attlee government give only limited attention to industrial relations is no doubt evidence of the extent to which, for most of the time, this was not a 'problem' area.

[2] 'A tight alliance between major Ministerial figures and major trade union leaders ... from 1949, organised and co-ordinated every major vote at the Conference' (Lewis Minkin, *The Labour Party Conference*, Manchester University Press, Manchester 1978, p24). The term 'praetorian guard' was first used, I think, by R.T. McKenzie, *British Political Parties*, Heinemann, London 1955; see 2nd edn, 1963, pp597-9.

[3] The phrase was Bevin's (Alan Bullock, *Life and Times of Ernest Bevin*, Vol 2, Heinemann, London 1967, p45); the principle underlay his reluctance to interfere directly with collective bargaining while wartime Minister of Labour, and was powerfully reasserted within the post-war Labour Cabinet.

[4] I also exclude from discussion the issue of the management and industrial relations machinery in the newly nationalised industries, and give only limited attention to the important topic of the international role of British unions.

[5] The NUM came into existence at the beginning of 1945, substantially reducing the number of independent unions. Its creation may best be regarded as transforming a

centralised federation of regional unions into a decentralised union of semi-autonomous regions.

[6] George Sayers Bain and Robert Price, *Profiles of Union Growth*, Blackwell, Oxford 1980.

[7] The TUC report on *Trade Union Structure and Closer Unity*, published in 1947 – in response to a resolution at Congress in 1943! – contained many worthy suggestions for encouraging inter-union co-operation, but showed no awareness of a need for new strategies for the recruitment and representation of a changing labour force.

[8] H.A. Clegg, A.J. Killick and Rex Adams, *Trade Union Officers*, Blackwell, Oxford 1961, p38.

[9] See, for example, J.D.M. Bell, 'Trade Unions', in Allan Flanders and H.A. Clegg (eds), *The System of Industrial Relations in Great Britain*, Blackwell, Oxford 1954.

[10] See Jack Jones, *Union Man*, Collins, London 1986; e.g. 'generally what happened in London had little impact on the Coventry district' (p133).

[11] G.D.H. Cole, *An Introduction to Trade Unionism*, Allen and Unwin, London 1953, pp54-5.

[12] Edmund Frow and Ruth Frow, *Engineering Struggles*, Working Class Movement Library, Manchester 1982, p220.

[13] Steven Tolliday, 'Government, Employers and Shop Floor Organisation', in Steven Tolliday and Jonathan Zeitlin (eds), *Shop Floor Bargaining and the State*, Cambridge UP, Cambridge 1985, p118.

[14] Richard Price, *Labour in British Society*, Croom Helm, Beckenham 1986, p201.

[15] Richard Croucher, *Engineers at War*, Merlin, London 1982, p344.

[16] Tolliday, 'High Tide and After: Coventry's Engineering Workers and Shopfloor Bargaining', in Bill Lancaster and Tony Mason (eds), *Life and Labour in a Twentieth Century City*, Cryfield Press, Coventry, n.d., p228. The case of Coventry shows that even within a single industry in a single city, the stability and effectiveness of shop steward organisation could vary markedly; see also Michael Terry and P.K. Edwards (eds), *Shopfloor Politics and Job Controls*, Blackwell, Oxford 1988.

[17] Throughout the war, the government had been able to restrain the index artificially through selective subsidies; see Clegg, op.cit.

[18] Pat Thane, 'Towards Equal Opportunities? Women in Britain Since 1945', in Terry Gourvish and Alan O'Day (eds), *Britain Since 1945*, Macmillan, London 1991.

[19] Accounts of the introduction of formal wage restraint include G.D.N. Worswick, 'Personal Income Policy', in G.D.N. Worswick and P.H. Ady, *The British Economy 1945-1950*, Clarendon Press, Oxford 1952; Barbara Wootton, *The Social Foundations of Wage Policy*, Allen and Unwin, London 1955; B.C. Roberts, *National Wages Policy in War and Peace*, Allen and Unwin, London 1958; John Corina, *The Labour Market*, Institute of Personnel Management, London 1966; Gerald A. Dorfman, *Wage Politics in Britain 1945-1967*, Charles Knight, London 1974; Leo Panitch, *Social Democracy and Industrial Militancy*, Cambridge University Press, Cambridge 1976.

[20] Roberts, *op cit* p58.

[21] Kenneth O Morgan, *Labour in Power 1945-1951*, Oxford University Press, Oxford 1984, p132.

[22] Philip M Williams (ed), *The Diary of Hugh Gaitskell 1945-56*, Cape, London 1983, p45.

[23] 'The government is at last going to do something about wages policy. In the absence of the Foreign Secretary – and only because of his absence – the Chancellor

and the Minister of Labour (the latter having been manoeuvred into it by some official conspiracy) got agreed in Cabinet a statement which marks an advance on everything else said before' (*ibid*, pp53-4). In his brief reference to the introduction of wage restraint, Bullock gives no hint of Bevin's opposition and indeed implies his support (*Ernest Bevin: Foreign Secretary 1945-1951*, Oxford University Press, Oxford 1985, p556).

24 Allen, 1947, *op cit*, p131.

25 Samuel Beer, *Modern British Politics*, Faber, London 1965, p208. Worswick ('Personal Income Policy', p329) speaks of 'quite considerable success': David Coates (*The Labour Party and the Struggle for Socialism*, Cambridge University Press, Cambridge 1975, p62) considers the Attlee government 'remarkably successful at incomes control'; Panitch (*Social Democracy and Industrial Militancy, op cit*, p26) adds that 'the policy's success with regard to wages was the direct result of the unions acting not as representatives but as agents of control over their members' demands'.

26 Clegg, *op cit*.

27 Hugh Clegg, *How To Run an Incomes Policy*, Heinemann, London 1971, p2.

28 Allan Flanders, 'Collective Bargaining', in Flanders and Clegg, *op cit*, p310.

29 Corina, *op cit*, p13.

30 The claim was endorsed by the Confederation of Shipbuilding and Engineering Unions – which the AEU had joined in 1946 – in September 1949. Negotiations stalled, with the employers calling for adherence to wage restraint. In March 1950 the CSEU agreed to hold a strike ballot, but the call was rejected by three to one. Finally in September – immediately after the TUC rejected continued restraint – an eleven shilling increase was offered. This was rejected, but in November was confirmed (with minor modifications) by the National Arbitration Tribunal.

31 Clegg, *op cit*.

32 The principal recent sources on these developments are Anthony Carew, 'The Schism Within the World Federation of Trade Unions', *International Review of Social History*, 24, 1984, and *Labour Under the Marshall Plan*, Manchester University Press, Manchester 1987; Peter Weiler, *British Labour and the Cold War*, Stanford University Press, Stanford 1988; and Denis MacShane, *International Labour and the Origins of the Cold War*, Clarendon Press, Oxford 1992. The two former authors emphasise the close relations between the TUC leadership and the Foreign Office, and their American counterparts, in the machinations which resulted in the WFTU split. MacShane, by contrast, stresses that the fundamental differences between communist and non-communist unions were never reconciled; that the original model of unification was not viable, because the International Trade Secretariats justifiably refused to submerge their identities in WFTU; and that western European unions had good reasons for supporting the Marshall Plan, irrespective of Cold War politics. Despite the obvious conflicts of emphasis, in my view the two positions are complementary as much as contradictory: MacShane explains the fragility of WFTU, Carew and Weiler why the break came at the time and in the manner that it did.

33 Allen, 1957 *op cit*, p291.

34 *Ibid*, p290; Bullock, *op cit*, pp741-2. In a revealing sentence, Bullock remarks (p108) that Bevin 'never ... visited New York as Foreign Secretary without arranging to meet the leaders of the American trade unions privately (George Meaney [*sic*], Sidney Hillman, Dave Dubinsky, William Green and Matt Woll)'. Hillman, the original CIO representative on the WFTU Executive Bureau, died in July 1946 (it is unclear how Bevin 'arranged to meet' him thereafter!); the other four were fervently anti-communist leaders of the AFL, with which Bevin had had

close contacts since his visit as fraternal delegate in 1915.

[35] Allen, 1957, *op cit*, p290; Weiler, *op cit*, pp62-4.

[36] MacShane, *op cit*, pp 126-7.

[37] Weiler, *op cit*, p27.

[38] MacShane, *op cit*, p186. MacShane examines in this context the case of Jack Tanner, formerly left-wing President of the AEU, who moved sharply to the right with the onset of the Cold War.

[39] Morgan, *op cit*, p499.

[40] The official criteria for recording strikes exclude the smallest and shortest stoppages; moreover, as more recent research has shown, many of the less substantial disputes which fall within the criteria are nevertheless not reported. In a period when strikes are often small and short – as in 1945-51 – this means that the official figures can considerably understate the actual pattern.

[41] In the 1950s, more than 70 per cent of recorded strikes were in mining. There is no way of telling whether this reflects a greater efficiency on the part of the Coal Board, by comparison with other employers, in reporting disputes.

[42] Justin Davis Smith, *The Attlee and Churchill Administrations and Industrial Unrest*, Pinter, London 1990, pp12-13. In this section I rely considerably on Smith's study.

[43] *Ibid*, p44. Bevan, who as Minister had doubts about the prudence of prosecuting strikers, nevertheless took 'as strong a line as any right-winger against dockers who struck against Cripps' wage freeze' and 'had no qualms about using troops against wreckers' (John Campbell, *Nye Bevan and the Mirage of British Socialism*, Weidenfeld and Nicolson, London 1987, p191.)

[44] Quoted in Smith, *op cit*, p94.

[45] Jones, *op cit*, p132. Roughly a quarter of the members of the TGWU executive were believed to be Communists, including Bert Papworth, the only 'lay' trade unionist to sit on the TUC General Council. David Howell comments (*British Social Democracy*, Croom Helm, Beckenham, 1976, p146) that 'Labour patriotism, with its suspicions of the Soviet Union as both foreign and Communist, formed a dominant element in the outlooks of many trade union leaders who drew a simple parallel between Soviet manoeuvres in Eastern Europe and Communist manoeuvres in their own organisations'.

[46] See, for example, Peter Welier, 'British Labour and the Cold War: the London Dock Strike of 1949', in James E. Cronin and Jonathan Schneer (eds), *Social Conflict and the Political Order in Modern Britain*, Croom Helm, Beckenham 1982.

[47] John Lloyd, *Light and Liberty*, Weidenfeld and Nicolson, London 1990, p323. Lloyd also suggests that one of the major power workers' strikes of the period – in London in December 1949 – was 'an embarrassment to the leadership' while another, involving installation workers in early 1951, was deliberately provoked by management and the general unions (pp315-8); the analysis is particularly interesting in view of the author's lack of sympathy for the union's former Communist leaders. Gaitskell, as Minister of Power, certainly regarded the ETU as an instrument of communist subversion; he wrote of the 1949 dispute that the Ministry of Labour 'were concerned almost wholly with ending the strike, whereas we were concerned with smashing the strikers' (Philip M. Williams, *Hugh Gaitskell*, Oxford University Press, Oxford 1982, p131). See also Morgan, *op cit*, p437.

[48] K.G.J.C. Knowles, *Strikes: a Study in Industrial Conflict*, Blackwell, Oxford 1952, p39.

[49] J.W. Durcan, W.E.J. McCarthy and G.P. Redman, *Strikes in Post-War Britain*,

Allen and Unwin, London 1983, p246. For Grimethorpe, see N. Fishman above pp68-70.

[50] Roy Church, Quentin Outram and David N. Smith, 'British Coal Mining Strikes 1893-1940', *British Journal of Industrial Relations*, 28, November 1990; and 'Towards a History of British Miners' Militancy', *SSLH Bulletin*, 54, Spring 1989.

[51] W.H. Scott, Enid Mumford, I.C. McGivering and J.M. Kirkby, *Coal and Conflict*, Liverpool University Press, Liverpool 1963.

[52] F. Zweig, *Men in the Pits*, Gollancz, London 1948 pp121-3.

[53] E.L. Trist, G.W. Higgin, H. Murray and A.B. Pollock, *Organisational Choice*, Tavistock, London 1963, p64.

[54] Zweig, *op cit* (p131), quotes managers arguing that the allowances were excessive, particularly at a time of national fuel shortage; but all the miners with whom he discussed this condemned any reduction 'on the ground that the right is based on old tradition and custom, besides being a part of a wage system'.

[55] *Ibid*, pp159-60.

[56] Zweig, *op cit* (pp164-5), quotes a Yorkshire miner who told him (in terms remarkably reminiscent of *The Miners' Next Step* of 1912) that 'the union officials regard themselves as our leaders who can commit us to whatever they think right, but working men need no leaders, but representatives'. Scott *et al*, *op cit*, report (p169) that in the branch studied in the late 1950s, the procedures adopted for branch meetings meant that pit grievances could normally be discussed only in the last ten minutes of a two-hour meeting – virtually guaranteeing that official channels were bypassed.

[57] The two issues were often combined. Henry Collins (*Trade Unions Today*, Muller, London 1950, pp118-9) commented that 'one of the main obstacles in the way of efficient and freely functioning shop stewards, is the hostility of some managements to them on principle, and the resulting fear of victimisation. A very large proportion of the unofficial strikes that have broken out since the war have arisen out of the dismissal of shop stewards, who tend to be among the first victims of "redundancy" '.

[58] H.A. Turner, Garfield Clack and Geoffrey Roberts, *Labour Relations in the Motor Industry*, Allen and Unwin, London 1967, pp333-6.

[59] Allen, 1957, *op cit*, p195: 'an excellent example of the inscrutability of dockers' behaviour'.

[60] This was the case with the 'zinc oxide' dispute of 1948, which led to the declaration of a state of emergency and a broadcast appeal by Attlee which brought the strike to an end (Attlee's text is given in G.G. Eastwood, *George Isaacs*, Odhams, London 1952, pp179-85). The major dispute attributed to 'communist subversion', which stemmed from the blacking of work on ships associated with a strike by the Canadian Seamen's Union in 1949, is discussed in detail by Weiler (*op cit*) and Smith (*op cit*). Here, management's tough line (backed by the government) helped escalate the stoppage. Other sources on the docks, in addition to works cited elsewhere, are Kenneth Knowles, 'The Post-War Dock Strikes', *Political Quarterly*, 22, July–September 1951; Jack Dash, *Good Morning, Brothers!*, Mayflower, London 1969; R.A. Leeson, *Strike*, Allen and Unwin, London 1973.

[61] Joan Woodward, *The Dock Worker*, Liverpool University Press, Liverpool 1954, pp45, 105, 127-8, 142.

[62] Noel Whiteside, 'Public Policy and Port Labour Reform' in Tolliday and Zeitlin, *op cit*, pp92, 98.

[63] *Ibid*, p100.

[64] Cole, *op cit*, p209. The development of a gulf between union leaders and officials is also identified by Ferdynand Zweig, *The British Worker*, Penguin,

Harmondsworth 1952, pp180-2: 'the unions have also changed their character. The times of struggle are over; theirs is the time of achievement and fruition. They have grown not only big but fat ... The unions are at present the bulwark of industrial peace and lawfulness. With the employers' federation and associations ... they have developed a whole code of industrial behaviour, in hundreds of rules, regulations, and standards which are kept by both sides ... In many industries there is very close co-operation between the union secretaries and the employers, as well as between their associations. This often breeds suspicion on the part of the workers. In Lancashire you can hear an uncensored expression about the bosses and the union secretaries: "They piss in the same pot" '.

[65] For example, the government sponsored the formation of the British Institute of Management and encouraged the creation of the Anglo-American Council on Productivity; see more generally N.H. Leyland, 'Productivity' in Worswick and Ady, *op cit*; A.A. Rogow [with Peter Shore] *op cit*; and Tomlinson, *op cit*. That rank-and-file response to the productivity drive may well have been hostile is suggested by the wartime study by Mass Observation, *People in Production* (Penguin, Harmondsworth 1942); in a patronising but significant comment the authors argued that 'less educated people' were 'most liable to assume that a process which goes on steadily is sound in terms of work, and they are most liable to react unfavourably to chops and changes which also revive those feelings of insecurity and irregularity of work which underlie the whole working-class attitude to working'.

[66] Paul Addison, 'The Road From 1945', in Peter Hennessy and Anthony Seldon (eds), *Ruling Performance*, Blackwell, Oxford 1987, p25.

[67] Gareth Stedman Jones, *Languages of Class*, Cambridge University Press, Cambridge 1983, p246.

[68] In his assessment of the Lloyd George social reforms before the first world war, Henry Pelling (*Popular Politics and Society in Late Victorian Britain*, Macmillan, London 1968) has identified considerable working-class ambivalence towards welfare imposed bureaucratically from above. This perspective is not however developed in his study of *The Labour Governments, 1945-51*, Macmillan, London 1984. Steve Fielding (' "Don't Know and Don't Care": Popular Political Attitudes in Labour's Britain', in Tiratsoo, *op cit*, offers a wide-ranging review of contemporary opinion research, and emphasises (p114) the prevalence of a 'popular political ennui' associated with an 'increasingly passive and conservative culture' and cynicism towards parties and politicians.

[69] James E. Cronin, *Industrial Conflict in Modern Britain*, Croom Helm, Beckenham 1979, p138.

[70] For details see Allen, 1960, *op cit*; Martin, *op cit*; and Minkin, *op cit*.

[71] For example, Beer, *op cit*; Keith Middlemas, *Politics in Industrial Society*, Deutsch, London 1979.

[72] Notably Roberts, *op cit*. See also Pelling, *op cit*, p265: 'the weakest aspect of the Government's management of the economy was its treatment of the trade unions. They were, of course, its allies, and for this very reason they had to be placated, rather than instructed'!

[73] Tomlinson, *op cit*.

[74] Allen, 1950, *op cit*, pp288-9.

[75] Trevor Burridge, *Clement Attlee*, Cape, London 1985, p194.

[76] Beer, *op cit*, p209.

[77] Morgan, *op cit*, p492.

Lessons From Scotland

Ken Alexander

Reason is, and ought only to be, the slave of the passions, and can never pretend to any other office than to serve and obey them.

David Hume, *A Treatise of Human Nature*, 1739-40.

An examination of the Labour government's policies for Scotland from 1945-51 would be brief and unexciting, for there was little distinctively Scottish about them. But perhaps aspects of the Scottish experience in this period can help us understand economic and political developments in Scotland and the UK since 1951. At the end of the twentieth century, politics in Scotland can exert powerful influences on British politics, and in particular the position of the Labour Party within these. It is even possible that different policies from the Attlee government could have resulted in a quite different shape to the politics of the 1990s. But for exploration of such matters an economic focus is too narrow; history, politics and culture must all play a part.

The Political Background

The Labour Party in Scotland emerged in the 1880s with a commitment to Home Rule, closely linked with the Land Question. The Highland Clearances stimulated both physical resistance and political activity, strengthened in the radical mind by the flow of royalties from the coalfields to landowners who had enforced the clearances. The influence of Irish politics, with the formation of the Irish National Land League in 1874 and Gladstone's Home Rule Bill of 1885, and the Scottish speaking tours by Henry George in

1882 and Michael Davitt in 1885 combined to build a strong link between agrarian reform and socialist theory.[1]

With the growth of socialist organisation, particularly that of the Independent Labour Party (ILP), in Scotland the demand for Irish Home Rule merged with that for Scottish Home Rule. John Wheatley, a miner and the most effective politician in the ILP, drew his strength from Irish immigrants and other Catholics in Glasgow. His friend James Connolly, who had worked as a miner in Scotland, effectively linked nationalism and socialism in his teaching. His execution by the British government in Dublin in 1916 had a dramatic effect on his many friends and followers in Scotland. The crucial marxist influence in Scotland was that of John Mclean, whose family had been cleared from their crofts in Mull and Inverness-shire. He greatly influenced working-class militants such as Willie Gallacher, James Maxton and Manny Shinwell, during the Great War. By 1919, when the Secretary for Scotland told the War Cabinet that the Clydeside strike for an eight-hour day was a 'Bolshevist rising', the link between socialism and nationalism was established.[2]

In 1924 Ramsay Macdonald, Prime Minister of the short-lived minority Labour government, introduced a Home Rule Bill for Scotland, but it was talked out at its second reading. Although Labour had the largest group of Scottish MPs and Scottish Liberals depended on Home Rule votes, the failure emphasises the problems of a party which depends on Scottish support, when Home Rule is of little interest, or even thought dangerous, in the rest of Great Britain.

Another, more radical, Home Rule Bill was introduced in 1927 and again lost in 1928. In that year the Labour Party restated its intention 'to support the creation of separate legislative assemblies in Scotland, Wales and England, with autonomous powers in matters of local concern'. Later that year was formed the National Party of Scotland. The flow of the tide was shown by the election of the novelist and Scottish Nationalist, Compton Mackenzie, as Rector of Glasgow University in 1931, and the formation in 1935 of the Scottish (Self-Government) Party, campaigning for devolution, as distinct from separation. The economic distress of the 1930s at first stimulated interest in both independence and Home Rule, but as the crisis deepened and the Left focused on the issues of unemployment and inadequate social benefits, interest in distinctive solutions for Scotland waned. Scottish trade unions were mostly linked to British unions, and solidarity became the dominant theme. The Communist Party view, widely influential in the unions, was that demands for immediate autonomy should not divert the working class from consolidating all democratic forces against war and Fascism.[3] The lifting of the depression might have been expected to stimulate interest in change, but in 1938 and 1939 the feeling that war was inevitable seems to have had the opposite effect – enthusiasm for Home Rule declined.

From 1923 to 1939 Scotland had a higher percentage rate of unemployment than Britain as a whole, although some regions of Britain had levels even higher than Scotland's [see Table 1]. By the end of the 1930s, the Government had introduced a range of measures to deal with the 'depressed areas', but the benefits to those areas were small. Forty per cent of all new factory building in Britain between 1932 and 1938 was in the Greater London area, to which unemployed workers in the regions were encouraged to move.

Table 1
Percentage of Insured Workers Unemployed

	July 1937	Dec 1945	June 1947	Dec 1949
S. Wales	21	11	7	4.5
N. Wales	18	10.5	5	4
S. Lancs.	19	4.5	4	2.5
Merseyside	19.5	3.5	5	4.5
W. Cumberland	26	6	4	2
N. East England	15	5.5	3.5	3
Scotland	18	4.5	4.5	3.5
Gt. Britain	10	2	2	1.5

Source: M.P. Fogarty, 'The Location of Industry', G. Worswick and P. Ady (eds), *The British Economy, 1945-50*, Clarendon Press, Oxford 1952.

In 1940 a Royal Commission (Barlow) on the *Distribution of Industrial Population* reported that the objective should be 'the decentralisation of industry and population and a regionally diversified industry'. The Coalition government's response was the Distribution of Industry Act (1945), introduced by Hugh Dalton as the President of the Board of Trade. The most important new power – reinforced in 1947 – was the licensing of new factory building, which was used to discourage expansion outside the Development (formerly 'depressed') Areas. Meanwhile the 1944 White Paper on Employment Policy had laid the foundation for a Keynesian consensus, reinforced by the commitment to a redistribution of industry.

The Interaction of the Arts and Politics

Culture is no less important than politics and economics in Scottish affairs. Although since the 1707 Treaty of Union the influences flowing north have been massively greater than those flowing south, the more remarkable fact is the extent to which Scots have maintained, and indeed developed, distinctive cultural elements. Separate legal and religious, and to a lesser extent educational, systems have contributed to this achievement, but it is mainly the free-spirited work of musicians, poets, writers and, more recently, historians, with substantial encouragement from the media, who have provided the threads with which Scots have sustained and extended their distinct cultural elements.

Walter Scott's influence was immense but ambiguous, raising national consciousness and pride, but not speaking to the problems of a developing industrial society. Robert Burns reinforced both the sense of nation and the egalitarian temperament of the Scots. But it was the writers of the early 1930s who broke the inherited mould of 'tartanry and kailyardism', by linking literature with social issues and politics, mainly nationalist and/or socialist. Although motivated by the Scottish circumstances of the time, this 'renaissance' was not a unified cultural movement. The political journeyings of its initiating genius, C.M. Grieve ('Hugh MacDiarmid'), in and out of the Fabian Society, the Independent Labour Party, the Scottish Nationalist Party (twice), the Social Credit Movement and the

Communist Party (twice), were not such as to encourage followers. But a network of links between musicians, artists, writers and others, and the establishment in 1936 of the Saltire Society to promote Scottish culture, manifested a new life and direction to the arts in Scotland, despite linguistic and political differences among those involved. Such differences are illustrated by Leslie Mitchell ('Lewis Grassic Gibbon') writing in a book jointly edited by himself and MacDiarmid:

> I am a nationalist only in the sense that the sane Heptarchian was a Wessex man or a Mercian: temporarily, opportunistically ... If it came ... to some fantastic choice between a free and independent Scotland, a centre of culture, a bright flame of artistic and scientific achievement, and providing elementary decencies of food and shelter to the submerged proletariat of Glasgow and Scotland, I at least have no doubt as to which side of the battle I would range myself.[4]

In spite of frictions, the movement gathered pace and stimulated interest, spilling over into education and the media. Although set back by the war it has influenced Scottish life from that time on.

Planning for Post-War

Throughout the war, commentators feared that the economic circumstances of the inter-war years would return to Scotland with re-deployment into peaceful production. The Secretary of State for Scotland in Churchill's government was Tom Johnston, who had served as Parliamentary Under-Secretary in the Scottish Office in the 1929 Labour government. He was strong for Home Rule and had an ILP background; his Cabinet position probably reflected anxiety that Scotland should not be so alienated from the war effort as it had appeared to be from 1914 to 1918. Johnston demonstrated how effective a limited form of devolution could be. He developed a Council of Industry in which industrial leaders could advise him, and a Scottish Council of State, with four previous Secretaries of State for Scotland as members. The official history of the Scottish Office designates the war years as 'Years of Opportunity', and describes this Council as 'a sort of political jemmy to prise out of Whitehall the concessions that Scotland sorely needed.'[5] Although war production reduced unemployment, it also required substantial movement of Scottish workers to England. The Board of Trade instructed that five hundred Scottish women be recruited each week for war factories in the Midlands, and Johnston made it clear that this was unacceptable. More factories and war orders came to Scotland and the flood south was reduced. However unemployment, though greatly reduced, remained a Scottish problem. The percentage of U.K. war production based in Scotland had risen from 3.5 per cent to 13 per cent in 1943, but in January 1944 Scottish unemployment accounted for 22 per cent of the British total.

Johnston's most important successes were in post-war planning. Many of his own aims related to possibilities of Highland development – hydro-electricity, fishing, hill farming. In 1943 a bill establishing a North of Scotland Hydro-Electricity Board, essentially a public utility with an explicit social and economic remit, was passed unanimously in the Commons and accepted by the Lords, despite earlier opposition from the powerful landlord interest in that place.

At the party political level, the Labour Party Scottish Council in 1941 produced a Post-War Plan for Scotland. Powers to locate factories and plants to assist population dispersal and the avoidance of over-dependence on particular industries were featured. Independence or 'separation' was rejected,

> but with equal emphasis we advocate the establishment of an executive authority in Scotland with legislative and administrative power to deal (a) with all matters that have solely public importance and (b) with the Scottish aspects of social and industrial legislation.

On the Highlands, 'the first essential condition to the development of this half of the country is the elimination of the private ownership of land.' The Party at UK level was careful to emphasise that this was a suggestion which would be examined in the course of wider policy making. The Scottish Conference of 1944 called for an inquiry into the issue of a Scottish legislative assembly.

Interestingly, the London Scots Self Government Committee, a body with twelve MPs amongst its officers, several of them political colleagues of Tom Johnston, published a book in 1942 emphasising the potential contribution of science to prosperity. Ritchie Calder, later Lord Ritchie Calder, warned, 'Scotland's war-time prosperity must deceive no one; it has little relation to its permanent peace-time prosperity.' He advocated a Department of Scientific Research in Scotland, with special emphasis on the creation of new industries and 'pilot factories' on a near commercial scale. He foresaw the limited period of prosperity for the heavy industries, and therefore urged the need for Britain to become a 'kind of vast research laboratory'.[6] The 1990s formulation of these ideas would mean linking the appropriate knowledge base into the development work of science parks: Ritchie Calder was a quarter of a century ahead of informed thinking. Also interesting is a booklet on *Highland Power* published by the Scottish Committee of the Association of Scientific Workers in 1944, in response to Johnston's Highland Development Act, making detailed proposals for economic development in five industries.

A Report on Infant Mortality in Scotland by Sir John Boyd Orr in 1943 was cited by the *Economist* as 'further proof of the poverty of Scotland. Its infant mortality rate is a true indication of its position as Britain's biggest depressed area'. In 1944 a Labour candidate standing for the Coalition government in a by-election in Fife had only a narrow majority over the then Chairman of the Scottish National Party, Douglas Young, who had gained notoriety for resisting call-up on the grounds that conscription of a Scot was a violation of the Treaty of Union. At the Annual Congress of the Scottish TUC Tom Johnston, as Secretary of State, argued that it was 'impossible to apply compulsory measures in the location of industry as long as business was privately owned'. This was to become a recurrent issue at Scottish TUCs when Labour was in government. In April *Forward* referred favourably in an editorial to a Nationalist pamphlet, *Scotlandshire – England's Worst Governed Province*. Two weeks later Dr Robert MacIntyre won a by-election for the SNP in a strongly Labour constituency, Motherwell, though Labour regained the seat at the 1945 General Election. Labour's

Scottish *Speakers' Notes for Constituencies* stated: 'The Rt. Hon Tom Johnston has transformed the Scottish Office from a graveyard of dead hopes to a centre of objective activity'. It specified the Hydro-Electricity Act for Northern Scotland (1943), the re-establishment of a Herring Industry Board in 1944 and the appointment of a team of entomologists to see if midges and mosquitos could be exterminated. 'A British Parliament for British Affairs and a Scottish Parliament for Scottish Affairs' was suggested as a slogan. The 1945 anti-Conservative swing was less in Scotland than in England (9.8 per cent compared to 12.2 per cent). Labour won forty of the Scottish seats, Conservatives and allies thirty, Communists one, Liberals none and Independents three. The Scottish National Party, with eight candidates, lost five deposits, won no seats and only 1.2 per cent of the total votes cast in Scotland. [See Table II for the political trends from 1935-1992.]

Table 2
Votes and Seats, Political Outcomes, Scotland 1935-1992.

	Con & Allies		Labour		Liberal		SNP	
	% votes	MPs	% votes	MPs	% votes	MPs	% Votes	MPs
1935*	41.6	45	36.7	24	14.1	3	1.3	0
1945*	36.3	30	47.4	40	9.1	0	1.2	0
1950*	44.8	32	46.2	37	6.6	2	0.4	0
1951*	48.6	35	47.9	35	2.8	1	0.3	0
1955	50.1	36	46.7	34	1.9	1	0.5	0
1959	47.3	31	46.7	38	4.1	1	0.8	0
1964	40.6	24	48.7	43	7.6	4	2.4	0
1966	37.6	20	50.0	46	6.8	5	5.0	0
1970	38.0	23	44.5	44	5.5	3	11.4	0
1974	32.9	21	36.6	40	8.0	3	21.9	7
1974	24.7	16	36.3	41	8.3	3	30.4	11
1979	31.4	22	41.5	44	9.0	3	17.3	2
1983	28.4	21	35.1	41	24.5	8	11.6	2
1987	24.0	10	42.4	50	19.2	9	14.0	3
1992	25.7	11	39.0	49	13.1	9	21.5	3

* In 1935 and 1945 the Nat Libs contributed 7 and 5 seats respectively to the Conservatives total, the ILP contributed 4 and 3 to the Labour total, and the Communist Party held one seat. The yearly percentage totals do not add up to 100, because of the small number of votes going to Independents and others.

Sources: J.P. Cornford and J.A. Brand, 'Scottish Voting Behaviour', in J.N. Wolfe (ed), *Government and Nationalism in Scotland*, Edinburgh University Press, 1969, pp17-37; David McCrone, *ibid*, pp148-9; John Bochel and David Denver, 'The 1992 General Election in Scotland', *Scottish Affairs*, No 1, 1992, pp14-26.

The Labour Government

Two thirds of the Scottish Labour MPs elected in 1945 had pledged support to 'some measure of legislative devolution'. In August *Forward* carried a lengthy article by Douglas Young recalling Labour's long-term commitment to Home Rule and Attlee's personal declaration of support in 1937, and suggested that the economic problems now facing Scotland strengthened the case for devolution. In October the Thirtieth Annual Conference of the Scottish Council of the Labour Party voted ninety-seven to sixty-seven for a resolution stating: 'the time has come to consider whether the setting up of a Scottish legislative assembly, with adequate powers to deal with domestic affairs, would best secure the increased well-being of Scotland'. The resolution called on government to appoint a representative committee to examine this issue and to report.

Tom Johnston had not stood for re-election in 1945, but the emphasis he had placed on post-war planning was now bearing fruit. In 1946 the Clyde Valley Plan was published, with new insights and recommendations. The overcrowding of Central Glasgow was to be reduced by a policy for new towns (East Kilbride, established in 1946, was Britain's first). The prosperity of ship-building would be short-lived, and the productive coal seams in Lanarkshire would soon run out. Steel production would be relocated to an appropriate port. A key recommendation was a shift of some of the powers of the existing local authorities to a new regional authority. In the face of opposition from vested interests – both political and industrial – the Report was not implemented and its warnings left unanswered. In terms of economic policy this was the greatest mistake and failure of Scottish Labour.

The Hydro-Board, now chaired by Johnston, was a success, expanding rapidly and laying a basis for an economical and environmentally friendly power supply. There was also a limited success in attracting new companies to Scotland, some of which would have preferred to stay in England but were redirected under the 1947 powers for the redistribution of industry. Inward investment, mainly from the USA, was also being targeted, and the greatest success was the 1950 decision of IBM to locate near Greenock a plant which, unlike many other inward investments, is still operating successfully in the 1990s.

In December 1945 Sir Stafford Cripps, President of the Board of Trade, indicated that the target was to create employment for 143,000 men and women in Scotland. A White Paper in 1947 increased this target to 150,000, while recognising that the cuts in investment would delay its achievement. By mid-1948, 55,000 of this target had been achieved, reflecting the very high proportion of new factory building which had gone to the Development Areas – over 50 per cent compared to a population share of 20 per cent. The magnitude of the total public investment was, however, modest. But what fears there were for the future were calmed by the very low level of unemployment, and the Labour view that nationalisation was the proper response to the structural problems arising from the preponderance of heavy industry. Thus, when the Government response to the balance of payments difficulties in 1947 was a sharp curtailment of expenditure and of advanced factory building under the Distribution of Industry Acts, and a reduction in the rigour with which the powers to influence the location of industry were applied, Labour Movement concern focused on the case for more public ownership. The other emphasis of the Labour Movement at this time was on social advance – health and housing – rather than on the longer term issue of unemployment.

The national question was not entirely quiescent, though given little prominence in the Labour Movement. George Orwell wrote in *Tribune* in February 1947:

> The Scottish Nationalist movement seems to have gone almost unnoticed in England. I don't remember having seen it mentioned in *Tribune*, except in book reviews. It is ... a small movement, but it could grow because there is a basis for it. Many Scottish people, often quite moderate in outlook, are beginning to think about autonomy and to feel that they are pushed into an inferior position. They have a good deal of reason. You have an English or anglicised upper class and a Scottish working class which speaks with a markedly different accent.[7]

This was an interesting view, combining the feelings of the people, class and linguistics in a way which remains central to Scottish politics.

In 1947 the Scottish Council of the Labour Party returned to the issue it had raised in 1945 and stressed the urgent necessity of an inquiry into Home Rule. In 1948 it re-affirmed that policy, but agreed to wait until the promised White Paper was available. Later that year this White Paper proposed changes which could speed the progress of Scottish bills through the Westminster Parliament, and the formation of an advisory body, a Scottish Economic Conference, on which all the established bodies with economic interests would be represented. The 1948 Scottish TUC described these proposals as 'far short of the needs and expectations of the Scottish people'. In contrast the Annual Conference of the Labour Party in Scotland accepted the White Paper, and the Scottish Executive's report, *Forward Scotland*, stated, 'Every opportunity must be taken to improve the mechanics of Scotland's government, and to give the maximum amount of Scottish control consistent with full membership of the British Parliament.'

On the economy, this Report claimed that Labour's policies had created 43,000 new jobs in Scotland since 1945 and planned to increase this to 100,000. This target was coupled with a strongly *dirigiste* declaration that, 'The Labour Party reserves the right to the State itself to create industries where social and human considerations require it, to take action where private industry fails.'[8]

At this time the Communist Party produced a substantial and realistic analysis of the economic problems ahead for Scotland, linking its policy-proposals with the case for self-government, and arguing strongly against the run-down of the heavy industries and the reliance being placed on the expansion of light industry. The policy emphasis was on more public ownership. Support for Home Rule included two reservations, which reflect the problems of trade unions at the UK level, and the worries of Scots:

The provision should be written into the Constitution of any Scottish Parliament that industrial standards legislated by a

Scottish Parliament and levels of social security and unemployment insurance, food subsidies etc., should not be less than those prevailing in the U.K. as a whole.[9]

An indication that Nationalist and Home Rule sentiment was rising came from the Unionist (Conservative) party in Scotland in 1949 when they referred to the need to attain, 'effective Scottish control of Scottish affairs' and to develop policies to this end for the forthcoming general election.[10]

In the same year the Scottish Convention, a devolutionary body, launched a Scottish Covenant which in time claimed nearly two million signatures. In the 1950 general election there was a 2.6 per cent swing to the Conservatives in Scotland. Labour lost three seats, the Liberals regained two and the three Nationalist candidates all forfeited their deposits. But young nationalist raiders made the headlines across the UK when they removed the Stone of Scone from Westminster Abbey at Christmas 1950 and returned it to Scotland. The political significance of the act lay not in itself but in the impact on the young, through comic irreverence considerably ahead in time of the satirical 'revolution' of the late 1950s and 1960s.

In 1951 Labour activists in Scotland concentrated on social and foreign policy issues, especially on the health service cuts and the rearmament programme which led to the resignation from the government of Aneurin Bevan and Harold Wilson. A makeshift survey of questions being raised at Labour meetings over nine months, published in August 1951, showed fifty-seven on wages and profits, forty-two on the compensation terms and appointments to recently nationalised Boards, thirty-eight on prices and the cost of living, twenty on foreign policy and seventeen on rationing and controls. No questions had been raised on regional issues or employment. Only three of the motions proposed by Scottish constituency parties to the UK Labour Conference in 1951 touched on regional economic matters, all on controls of the distribution of industry. This is not surprising. Although Scotland's share of unemployment was rising, the level did not rise above 3 per cent until the late 1950s. Gross Domestic Product (GDP) per head was 91.8 per cent of the UK level, but it was not until later that this gap was to widen, to 87.5 per cent in 1961. Income from employment (1951) was 94.6 per cent of the UK level. The range of Scottish statistics we now have were not available in 1951. Indeed it was left to an academic to provide the first comprehensive picture, with many statistics for 1951 not becoming available until 1964.[11]

Two motions proposed to the Scottish Labour Conference were regionally orientated, one asking for a Socialist Plan for Scotland, and the other for the control of nationalised industries to be decentralised. This last issue grew in importance, as the draining of control of what had been independent Scottish companies, to England and abroad, as a result of take-overs, attracted concern. In 1951 Jean Mann MP was reported as saying that Socialism and Home Rule should be seen as alternative goals. Labour's Scottish Conference in 1951 passed a resolution proposing a Royal Commission on the future role of a Scottish Parliament.

The consensual structure introduced by Tom Johnston in wartime had been adapted, but still functioned well. The Labour Party in *Campaign Notes* for Scotland in the 1951 general election included this endorsement (of the policy if not of the Party) from Lord Bilsland, a highly respected banker:

> The events of the last five years had constituted a minor revolution in Scotland and ... gone far to restore the balance of the economy. There was no parallel in her history to the surge of activity and regeneration in progress in Scotland today.

In the general election Labour attracted 48.8 per cent of the Scottish votes, and the Conservatives and their allies 48 per cent. There were thirty-five Conservatives and allied MPs, thirty-five Labour and one Liberal. The new Conservative government lost no time in establishing a Royal Commission on Scottish Affairs (the Balfour Commission) which reported in 1954.

Assessment

The achievements of the Attlee governments in 'regional policy' should be judged without benefit of hindsight. At that time the major problem to be tackled was the absorption into a peacetime labour force of the eight million men and women who had been in the services or in war production. Correcting pre-war regional imbalances was recognised as desirable, but the raft of economic policies which has been deployed since to deal with such imbalances had yet to be developed.[12]

From 1945 to 1950 the Development Areas, with 19 per cent of Britain's population, had 34 per cent of all industrial building. The consequent employment was considerably less than had been assumed, creating jobs for approximately 5 per cent of the insured population of the Development Areas. It would not be reasonable to describe this as a failure when put alongside the great success made of the transition from war to peace, with British unemployment at an all-time low, and regional differences broadly the same as pre-war [see Table 1]. But the Government can be criticised for lack of attention to the structural problems and the acute difficulties these presented. In Scotland the neglect of the Clyde Valley Plan is the clearest illustration of that failure. During the fifteen years from 1950 employment in Scotland grew by only 3.6 per cent, while the UK growth was 14.6 per cent. Any possibility of righting regional imbalance was lost. In 1950 and 1951, however, there was little pressure on the Government to develop an active policy of industrial restructuring. It was not until the recession of 1958-59 that regional policies began to be given greater emphasis.

Faced with the actual circumstances, and theoretical and policy inadequacies of the time, could Labour have done any better? Greater emphasis on the need for structural change, the price being higher unemployment in the short-run, would not have been an easy policy for a Labour government to follow. Linking public ownership with a policy explicitly aimed at redressing regional imbalances could have brought some benefits. Training to provide the skills which can attract investment, now an important element in Labour's economic policy, could have been deployed with some success in a period of great labour scarcity, and although the number would have been small this would have been more productive than training with no greater purpose than to increase mobility. Greater emphasis on process innovation (possibly 'copy-cat'), and less on crude productivity improvement, might have helped reduce the worrying deficit in Scotland's private fixed investment in manufacturing industry, only 8.2 per cent of the UK total in 1951. Apart from these possibilities, there is little useful that could have been done without anticipating methodologies which had not yet been invented or tried elsewhere.

Had the empirical data on company profitability been available for analysis on a regional basis, enabling a comparison of like with like, the tight controls on location could have been used to strengthen the Development Areas on a more permanent basis. The use of input-output analysis could have made some contribution both to an awareness of the consequences of the decline of heavy industry and the types of inward investment likely to do business with existing plants. The specific encouragement of versatility and flexibility within networks of medium-sized plants which can quickly respond to new opportunities within a chosen area is now seen as an effective policy option. Concurrently, the encouragement of managerial innovation and entrepreneurship, in a commercial climate in which family influence and rigidities played an unfortunately large part, could have been fruitful. It is worth remembering that it was a Labour government, some years later, which first paid serious attention to the importance of understanding and encouraging the growth of the small and medium sized company sector.[13] A recognition that clusters of small and medium sized firms are a necessary prerequisite for self-generated innovation and regional development would have produced a markedly different and more effective response to the threatened industrial contraction. The expanding public sector could have been used to encourage and strengthen small and medium sized private enterprises, an improbable application of the 'commanding heights' concept!

It is easy enough now to select from such possibilities, and others, a package of measures which would have provided an industrial strategy with a built-in regional bias. But the knowledge base was not available, even if the foresight had been. That was the failure, without which some of the more painful adjustments of later years could have been achieved with less human waste and social disruption.

The other failure was a political one, not to recognise that the demand for Home Rule was growing, driven by a combination of pragmatic and democratic attitudes and ingrained cultural differences which rather than being habituated were evolving.

What Next?

Labour in office has consistently failed to deliver the Home Rule aspirations of a majority of its Scottish members and voters. As Labour has not been in power since 1979 this particular failure may be of diminishing significance. However many Scottish voters see the difficulty of winning a majority at Westminster as signalling that Labour is even less likely than before to be able to establish a Parliament in Edinburgh, given the increased obstacle which would be created if Scottish representation at Westminster had to be reduced as part of Home Rule package.

Why is it reasonable to assert that nationalism, or 'nation-ness', will increase in importance in Scottish politics? There are three factors at work, each likely to become more powerful.

Firstly, there is the weakening of the UK economy, coupled with the as yet unwavering belief that economic success depends upon government policies and that Europe will before long take over many of the key policy instruments.

Secondly, and clearly related to the first point, there is a conviction that as powers accumulate in Brussels, democratic pressures will be increasingly important to establish the geographical 'fine-tuning' necessary if policies are to be designed to meet the needs of the regions, and especially the peripheral ones. A Europe of the regions and smaller nations has an additional and powerful attraction, providing a political mechanism which could curb the dominance within Europe of one or more of the largest nations. This idea is not new; it was argued by Andrew Fletcher at the beginning of the eighteenth century.[14]

Thirdly, there are complex cultural factors at work. Intrusive mid-Atlanticism provides the most obvious example of the forces undermining the close links, determined by history and religion, which exist between a nation state and the culture of the people who live within its boundaries. Small countries with a distinctive cultural tradition may feel particularly under threat, and the self-generation of home-grown culture is a natural response. The strengthening of the interaction between cultural output and social and economic problems in the 1930s has continued since, with powerful cross-referencing in the media, both 'mass' and 'opinion-forming'. The view that 'there is no direct connection between (the arts) and the waxing and waning of political nationalism' forgets that the arts take some time to deliver their effects. More to the point is the same author's comment: 'cultural concerns provide some raw material for nationalism, but are rarely its *raison d'etre*.'[15] The influence of folk-song provides an illustration of this, effectively linking tradition and radical political comment.[16]

Many Scottish intellectuals are concerned, sometimes it seems to the point of despair, about what they see as the country's cultural deficiencies. They do not seem to take into account what may be expected from a small nation which has suffered very serious demographic loss, due to its failure to be able to compete with the absolute and relative advantage of a larger and richer neighbour in attracting talent and fruitfully employing it. Just as in the quasi-cultural area of sport, supporters take pleasure not only in the stars who currently play for their team but also in those stars who were nurtured and trained in it, so small nations in particular may, without self-deception, take pride in their country's contribution to world culture, no matter how geographically dispersed that may be. Our troubled intellectuals also take the 'tartanry tradition' far too seriously, apparently failing to see the new forms and interests developing in the cultural lives of the Scots. Popular culture is a difficult concept, but essential if we are to understand the factors which over time influence political behaviour.

The present response of the Labour Party to nationalism is to support Home Rule in a loose alliance with the Liberals within the Constitutional Convention. Labour has agreed that some form of proportional representation would apply in elections to a Scottish Parliament, a recognition that re-creating Scotland as a political community requires the forfeiture of an accustomed advantage. A similar agreement for future Westminster elections would almost certainly depend on political objectives much wider than Home Rule for Scotland. A growing recognition that the politics of the twenty-first century will differ so significantly from those of the twentieth that adjustments are necessary to the style and content of political behaviour may provide the incentive for wider change. A commitment to proportional representation for Westminster elections, and an agreement to short-term alliances to elect a Parliament which would bring about a number of constitutional changes, including regional Home Rule where this is supported, appears the most hopeful solution to a number of related issues which currently hobble our democracy and postpone the economic and social policies which are required for Great Britain, and for the nations and regions which make it up.

If present political frustrations continue, my expectation is that there will be further inroads into the Labour vote, partly from Militant but mainly from successive surges in the SNP vote. The Home Rule vision will be overtaken, either by the break-up of the presently United Kingdom or by a growing political apathy. A review of data from the polls and from surveys of political attitudes suggest that 70 per cent of voters in Scotland want a Scottish Parliament with 'home rule' powers within a United Kingdom. Labour governments have missed earlier opportunities to meet this wish. In late twentieth century politics in Scotland it is the particular responsibility of Labour politicians to find a way of overcoming this democratic deficit.

Notes

[1] Michael Fry, *Patronage and Principle*, Aberdeen University Press, Aberdeen 1987, pp91-103.
[2] John S. Gibson, *The Thistle and the Crown: A History of the Scottish Office*, HMSO, Edinburgh 1985, p65.
[3] Edgell Rickword, 'Stalin on the National Question', *The Left Review*, Vol.2, T.H. Wintringham, London 1937, p749.
[4] Lewis Grassic Gibbon, 'Glasgow', L.G. Gibbon and H. MacDiarmid (eds), *Scottish Scene*, Jarrolds, London 1934, pp136-147.
[5] John S. Gibson, *op cit*, pp93-110.
[6] Ritchie Calder, 'The Application of Scientific Research to Scottish Industry', *The*

New Scotland, The London Scots Self-Government Committee, Glasgow 1943, pp26-37.

[7] George Orwell, *Tribune*, 14 February 1947, M.S. Orwell and I. Angus (eds), *In Front of Your Nose*, Harcourt Brace Jovanovich, New York 1968.

[8] M. Keating and D. Bleiman, *Labour and Scottish Nationalism*, Macmillan, London 1979, p254.

[9] John Gollan, *Scottish Prospect*, Caledonian Books, Glasgow 1948, p225.

[10] James Mitchell, *Conservatives and the Union*, Edinburgh University Press, Edinburgh 1990, p27.

[11] Gavin McCrone, *Scotland's Economic Progress, 1951-1960*, George Allen and Unwin, 1965.

[12] A comprehensive bibliography on regional studies, published in the 1970s, listed one item in the 1930s, two in the 1940s, nine in the 1950s and twenty-five in the 1960s. A Regional Science Association was established in the USA in the 1950s, E.M. Hoover having published *The Location of Economic Activity* in 1948. In Britain there was S.R. Dennison's *The Location of Industry and the Depressed Areas* (1939), and a P.E.P. *Report on the Location of Industry*, also 1939. Sargent Florence's *The Selection of Industries for Dispersal into Rural Areas* was published in 1944. The first major regional study was *The Scottish Economy* (1954) edited by A.K. Cairncross, and the major British study by W.F. Luttrell was published by the National Institute of Economic and Social Research in 1961.

[13] *Report of the Committee of Inquiry on Small Firms*, (Bolton), HMSO, London, 1971.

[14] John Robertson, 'The Political Intelligence of Andrew Salter of Saltoun', *Chapman*, No.61-2, Edinburgh 1990.

[15] David McCrone, *Understanding Scotland: The Sociology of a Stateless Nation*, Routledge, London 1992, p212.

[16] Jack Brand, *The National Movement in Scotland*, Routledge and Kegan Paul, London 1978, pp112-126 covers the importance of the folk-song movement. Readers interested in this particular aspect of popular culture will find much of value in Hamish Henderson, *Alias MacAlias*, Polygon, Edinburgh 1992.

The Best of Both Worlds?: Women's Employment in Post-War Britain

Catherine Blackford

> The best of both worlds has come within their grasp, if only they reach out for it.
>
> Alva Myrdal and Viola Klein, *Women's Two Roles*, 1956.

The most striking feature of women's paid employment in the post-war period is that, despite notable changes in patterns of women's work, fundamental inequalities between men and women in the workforce remained intact. Although more women, particularly older married women, entered a wider range of jobs after 1947 (compared with the pre-war period) women's work was still overwhelmingly low paid, semi or unskilled and different from men's. The aims of this work are to explore the changes in patterns of women's work after the war, and to consider how the policy of the Labour governments from 1945-51 contributed to maintaining sexual inequality by reinforcing the sexual division of labour in the home and workplace.

Before assessing the policy of the Labour governments towards women's employment however, it is important to set it alongside the attitudes of women's groups and feminist organisations during the late 1940s and 1950s.[1] Although feminists called for equal pay and a woman's right to work, they were not demanding absolute

214

equality with men. Alva Myrdal and Viola Klein wanted women to have the opportunity to combine two roles, believing this ideal might give women the 'best of both worlds'.[2] The Married Women's Association, arguably the most prominent feminist organisation of the period, concentrated its efforts on improving the legal and economic position of women in the home. It used the language of equal rights, but applied it to an area of sexual difference, promoting marriage and motherhood as a vocation in the process. Thus it could be argued that socialists and feminists conceived of sexual equality in rather narrow terms, which did not involve any challenge to women's primary responsibility for raising children and looking after the home.

Growing Numbers at Work

Although the number of women working immediately after the war declined, the economic and industrial policy of the first Labour government led to a huge demand for women's labour from 1947 onwards. If one compares the figures for this period with the pre-war years, it is quite clear that more women were working outside the home in the 1940s and 1950s, and that the age and marital status of women workers had changed to a considerable extent. During the inter-war years most working women were young and single, the largest number employed in domestic service before they married. The textile and some other industries had a tradition of employing older married women, but these appear to have been regional exceptions. Even new job opportunities for women in developing manufacturing industries such as food and drink, chemicals and electrical engineering were overwhelmingly the preserve of young single women in their late teens and early twenties;[3] whilst in white collar jobs and professions, to which the 1919 Sex Disqualification Removal Act had granted women entry, marriage-bars effectively limited the workforce to young unmarried women and older single women.

During the Second World War, the conscription of male workers to the armed services led to a demand for female labour in a much wider range of jobs and on a larger scale than previously. Since a majority of the adult female population was composed of married women, the Government came increasingly to rely on their labour. Other demographic factors also played a part in determining the marital and age profile of the female workforce. The use of 'older' married women in their thirties, forties and fifties was inevitable, given that there were more women in these age groups as a result of the declining birth rate. Added to this, women's longer life expectancy and the declining average size of families meant that they often had more time, energy and perhaps incentive to return to paid work. Richard Titmuss compares the average of two or three pregnancies in the 1950s with the average of ten in the 1890s.[4] Not surprisingly then, the Attlee government's demand for labour after the war resulted in further appeals to older married women to return to work. By 1951, 21 per cent of married women worked, compared to 10 per cent in 1931; by 1961 this figure had reached 32 per cent. Married women's percentage of the female workforce also increased from 16 per cent in 1931 to 43 per cent in 1951 and 50 per cent in 1958.[5] According to Kelsall and Mitchell in *Population Studies*, the majority of women who worked in the 1950s were between twenty and thirty years old, although women aged forty to fifty-nine years were in a slight majority by the 1960s.[6]

Changing Patterns of Work

As has already been mentioned, the greatest number of women working before the war were employed in domestic service or the textile industry, with a smaller number taking up jobs in new manufacturing industry, and related areas such as shops and offices boosted by the expansion of distribution and commerce. These 'new' industries differed from the old staple industries both in terms of what they produced – consumer goods for the domestic market – and how they produced it. Instead of skilled male workers, semi or unskilled female operatives were employed on new mass-production processes. These often involved a conveyor belt and always involved repetitive and monotonous work.[7] Why women's labour was used almost exclusively for this type of low paid, low status work both before and after the war has been the subject of considerable socialist feminist debate.[8] These efforts to understand how patriarchy and capitalism interact to use women's labour in particular types and areas of work, usually defined as low skilled, has helped some historians to begin to analyse women's position in the workforce, rather than simply to describe it.

After the war, the number of women in manufacturing industry increased considerably, both in industries in which small numbers of women had worked before the war, and in new areas of industry which women entered for the first time during the war. At the same time, the expansion of manufacturing industries producing consumer goods led to more job opportunities for women in new department stores, shops and offices. Women's share of the metal manufacturing industry increased from 6 per cent in 1939 to 12 per cent in 1950, and in engineering from 10 per cent to 21 per cent during the same period.[9]

Questioning Official Figures

Figures relating to women's employment after the war need some qualification however. As Jane Lewis has pointed out, comparisons between women's paid work before and after the war, derived from census returns, may not reflect accurately the extent of women's economic activity in the inter-war years.[10] Since census forms defined 'work' rather narrowly, many women may not have included temporary or casual work in their own homes, or those of other women, under the category of employment. It is possible therefore, that whilst, for many married women, employment in factories, offices and shops was a new experience, engaging in paid work was probably not. However, one byproduct of women's closer association with the 'official' workforce was the increase in women trade unionists. By 1945 the total number of women in trade unions had passed the one million mark for the first time in peacetime since 1918; one working woman in four was a member of a trade union.[11]

217

Home or Industry? The Government's 'Juggling Feat'

Another important factor in relations to post-war women's work, which is not reflected in figures showing an increase in women's employment, is that many women worked part-time. The number who did so is difficult to determine since the official figure of 12 per cent derived from the 1951 Census has been considered an underestimation.[12] However, along with the employment of older married women, the practice of part-time and shift work was another legacy of the war which the Labour government revived. Although this practice was clearly designed to increase the number of women available for work in periods of acute labour shortage, it also benefited employers, who could boost profits by keeping production processes going longer. In addition, it made women's labour available to capital '... on terms which did not threaten to upset the status quo in the household, since a married woman working part-time could still perform the full range of domestic tasks'.[13] Kelsall and Mitchell's analysis of figures relating to women's work supports this argument showing that although women in the 'family phase', 20-39 years old, formed the most numerous sector of the female workforce, most worked when children were of school age and thus slightly less dependent.[14]

Also hidden in figures for women's work are the differences between women who worked, as well as between women who did and did not work, in terms of class and race. According to Kelsall and Mitchell the majority of married women who worked were working-class.[15] Myrdal and Klein's assertion that the number of married middle-class women who worked was 'too small to warrant social investigation',[16] and Judith Hubback's discovery that many educated middle-class women committed themselves to marriage and motherhood as a career backs this up.[17] This may go some way to explaining why middle-class feminists in the 1940s and 1950s focused predominantly on issues affecting women in the home. Of those married middle-class women who did work, most tended to be in routine white collar jobs, as opposed to 86 per cent of working-class women who did manual jobs and 72 per cent semi or unskilled work.[18]

Given that many married Afro-Caribbean women came to Britain after the war as workers, and that racism often restricted their husbands to low paid jobs, it is likely that a higher percentage of black married women worked. Once at work black women also tended to be concentrated in the lowest paid and least skilled sectors of 'women's work'.[19] Hazel Carby makes the valid point therefore, that generalisations about both women's experience of paid work and attitudes towards married women working, may be very different if they take black women into account. She argues that the employment of married Afro-Caribbean workers outside the home did not cause the same controversy or concern as that of indigenous white women, for whom marriage and family and paid work were still seen as alternatives, even though increasing numbers of working-class women engaged in both.[20]

In 1945 the Labour government inherited an economy ravaged by war. Half the country's wealth and two-thirds of its export trade had been lost, with the result that Britain was unable to pay for more than one-third of its imports.[21] To rebuild the economy the Government aimed to increase production in export industries especially. In so doing, it created a great demand for labour. At first efforts were made to meet this demand by employing ex-prisoners-of-war and European 'guest workers', but within a year there was an estimated shortfall of over one million workers. To meet this demand the Government decided to follow wartime practice and make use of its largest remaining reserve of labour – women. Although the war effort had been wound down more slowly than in 1918, and some women were still working, many were concentrated in areas of work considered unessential to economic and industrial expansion. The Government's aims were therefore twofold: to get women back into the workforce on a large scale and into particular jobs and industries. They were confronted with a dilemma similar to that of the Coalition government during the war, which Penny Summerfield has usefully characterised as a conflict between patriarchy and capitalism.[22] This conflict also shaped the Attlee government's policy towards women's paid employment after the war, involving it in what Elizabeth Wilson has termed a 'weird juggling feat'.[23]

Both during and after the war the respective governments' need for women's labour was set against the ideological belief that women's primary role lay within the home, and that the tasks women performed there should remain in the private sphere. To increase women's participation in the workforce during the war, the Coalition government had gradually and reluctantly introduced measures to conscript women's labour. Its legislation allowed exemptions for women with children under fourteen (the school leaving age) and even for married women without dependent children, but with other domestic responsibilities. Towards the end of the war many in the latter category were persuaded to take up part-time work. Significantly, the Government was reluctant to provide any support for women workers whose primary responsibility for domestic work in the home meant that they worked a double shift, even though a number of factories, often under union pressure, supplied supporting facilities. That this affected women's availablity for work and their performance if they did work, appears to have been something the Government was slow to accept, or at least act upon. Its own committees urged it to take more responsibility for childcare, feeding and long working hours. Although the number of nurseries for children of working mothers appears to have increased dramatically from fourteen in 1940 to 1345 in 1943, Penny Summerfield maintains that this level of support was still inadequate.[24] Although more part-time work was introduced, thirty-hour shifts were still physically draining for women performing two roles.

The Attlee government's efforts to recruit women's labour from 1947 were bounded by the same ideological belief in women's primary responsibility for the home. It was also anxious to restore social stability and order after the disruption of war by rebuilding the family and traditional gender roles within it. An added impetus was its belief in the need to raise the birth rate; this was to be accomplished by encouraging women to increase the size of their families. The Beveridge Report (1942), which formed the basis of the Labour government's welfare legislation after 1945, also had this consideration in mind. It praised the value of women's work in the home as housewives and mothers on the grounds that this work of national importance would raise the birth rate and ensure the continuation of British values in the world.[25] However, the Labour government was not prepared to support this work of 'national importance' whether it was in the home or in both the home and workplace, by expanding services to relieve women's domestic responsibilities. In 1946 the Government grant to local authorities for nursery places was cut, thus leading to prohibitive increases in fees. Although Denise Riley has argued that the subsequent closure of nurseries was not entirely due to Government economic policy,[26] Labour did not consider the funding of nursery provision as part of its policy for increasing women's employment. Instead, women were encouraged to make their own arrangements with members of the family or minders. W. Crofts, writing in *History Today*, does point out however that in textile and woollen areas, where a desperate demand for women's labour was not being met, collective arrangements for child care and other domestic work were eventually organised.[27]

Labour's recruitment campaign launched in June 1947 was therefore carefully calculated in an attempt to meet the needs of post-war reconstruction without undermining patriarchal power within either the home or workplace. The appeal was targeted at women aged between thirty five to fifty, who it was assumed would not have dependent children. However, a Government recruitment advertisement detailing how a mother of six children, with three of school age, found time to help the export drive in the textile industry, suggests the Government was prepared to welcome any women into the workforce, regardless of the extra burden of work this might place upon them. Thus, rather cynically, it applauded Mrs Kate Vickers, who managed her shopping and housework during the day and helped the country 'pull through' by working an evening shift in the textile industry.[28] Other important aspects of the Government's recruitment campaign were the stress on the temporary nature of women's return to work in a time of national emergency, and their return to 'women's' jobs rather than 'men's'.

Women were therefore encouraged to enter particular jobs in industries and areas of work where there were shortages of labour – chemicals, electrical engineering, domestic service and transport, for example. To ensure women remained in these 'essential' areas of work, the Government passed a Control of Engagement Order in October 1947. This prevented women aged between eighteen and forty years, who had no dependent children and who worked full time, from leaving work in essential industries. In general however, the Government preferred persuasion to compulsion, and spent considerable sums on propaganda designed to get women back to work. Advertisements appeared in cinemas, newspapers, on radio and on large public hoardings, and were backed up in the hard pressed textile and woollen districts by Royal visits. The images of women these advertisements projected soon changed from the sleeves-up approach of wartime to pictures and stories about part-time women workers who wore 'pretty dresses and hats and knew the value of a "bit of extra brass" '.[29] In framing its appeal to women therefore, the Government reinforced the sexual division of labour in the home and workplace. Creating greater sexual equality was simply not on its agenda. Indeed, in 1948 when demand for women's labour was at a peak, women's wages as a percentage of men's actually declined from 53 per cent to 45 per cent.[30]

Failure to Implement Equal Pay

The only issue on which the Labour government might have been expected to increase women's equality with men in the workplace was on the issue of equal pay. The Labour Party had supported the principle for many years, but once in office was resolutely opposed to its implementation. In 1946 the Royal Commission on Equal Pay recommended in its majority report that women in the common classes of public services should be given equal pay. This right was not to be extended to women in industry, whose work was not considered of equal value to men's – a point with which all three women on the Royal Commission disagreed. Support for the implementation of equal pay during the years of post-war Labour government was also strong and organised within the Labour and Women's Movements. Against the wishes of the National Executive, the Labour Party Conference had voted for implementation of equal pay by over two million votes. Meanwhile, women trade unionists and women's groups working through the Equal Pay Campaign Committee and the Equal Pay Coordinating Committee, launched a high profile public campaign. Like the Labour Party, the Trades Union Congress also supported the principle of equal pay, but its support for the Labour government's statement, *Personal Incomes, Costs and Prices*, from 1948 to 1950 effectively committed it to a policy of wage restraint which compromised its support for the implementation of equal pay. Even Florence Hancock's presidency of the Trades Union Congress General Council from 1947 to 1948 (a 'first' for women trade unionists) did not influence TUC policy, since she used her position as Chair of the National Advisory Women's Committee to persuade women activists to support Government policy. For its own part, the Government's arguments against implementation included the claim that it would lead to male workers demanding an increase in family allowances (given that men earned a 'family wage') and that increased spending power would lead to inflation. However, the fact that the issue of equal pay was left out of the Labour Party programme in 1953 (apparently by mistake) suggests that the issue was not a priority for the Party either in office or opposition.[31] No doubt strong support among many male trade unionists for a 'family wage' to maintain male wage differentials played some part in determining Labour Party policy.

The 'Double Shift' and Women's Secondary Status

It can be concluded, then, that the Labour government's economic policy contributed towards changing patterns of women's work after the war, raising in particular the number of working-class married women engaged in paid work within the 'official' workforce. However, the Government recruitment campaign did not aim to bring women into the workforce on the same terms as men. This was essentially because it believed that women's primary role lay within the home, looking after the family. It considered their entry into the workforce a temporary affair. It also believed

223

that sexual difference, resulting in distinct roles for men and women in the home, gave men and women particular skills and qualities which were appropriate for different types of paid work outside the home. However, women's secondary or 'reserve' status in relation to paid work, combined with their subordinate social status as women, meant that what was considered 'women's' work was overwhelmingly low-paid and unskilled. Thus in appealing to women to enter the workforce, the Government reinforced the sexual division of labour at work, and in the process encouraged the concentration of women in low-paid sectors of the economy.

Significantly, most feminists did not recognise this development as contributing to women's inequality at work. Myrdal and Klein saw the increasing rate of married women's work as 'the second stage of the social revolution'.[32] In accepting women's primary responsibility for the home and family, they maintained that women had a different relationship to the labour market. Women's working lives were seemingly divided into three phases: education and training before marriage, marriage and family, and thirdly, retraining and return to paid work. Although they asserted women's equal right to work, they acknowledged that taking a break to have a family meant that jobs requiring constant development of skills might not be realistic choices for women.[33] Yet the types of work they considered 'next to ideal' were those already considered 'women's work'. Thus whilst they saw a connection between women's role in the home and their opportunities at work, they did not see the sexual division of labour in the workplace as problematic. Women's position at work, just as in the home, was interpreted as different rather than unequal.

It is clear then that the widespread ideological belief in women's primary domestic responsibility was embodied in the Labour government's appeal to women to return to work. To balance its urgent need for women's labour outside the home with its belief in the importance of women's work within it, the Government focused its appeal on married women assumed to have the least domestic responsibilities. The failure to provide any support services for working married women, except in exceptional circumstances[34] reinforced the message that domestic work, and especially childcare, were to remain within the home, and that in taking up a new role outside the home, women were not going to lose their old one within it. Instead they were to be praised for performing two roles.

Special thanks to Sue Mew for her encouragement, comments and insights during the writing of this work.

Notes

[1] The distinction between 'feminist' organisations and women's groups during this period is difficult to determine, given that few groups explicitly used the term. The Married Women's Association for example, involved women identifying themselves as feminist, but decided not to use the term to describe the organisation, in case it deterred women from joining.

[2] Myrdal, A. & Klein, V., *Women's Two Roles*, Routledge & Kegan Paul, London 1956, pxvi.

[3] Glucksmann, M., 'In a Class of Their Own? Women Workers in the New Industries in Inter War Britain', *Feminist Review*, 24, 1986, p27.

[4] Titmuss, R., 'The Position of Women: Some Vital Statistics' in Flinn, M.W. & Smart, T. *Essays in Social History*, Oxford, Clarendon Press 1963.

[5] Summerfield, P., *Women Workers in the Second World War*, Croom Helm, Beckenham 1984.

[6] Kelsall, & Mitchell, 'Married Women and Employment', *Population Studies*, 13, 1959.

[7] Glucksmann, *op cit*.

[8] Feminist Review (ed) *Waged Work: A Reader*, Virago, London 1986.

[9] Summerfield, *op cit*, p187.

[10] Lewis, J., *Women in Britain Since 1945*, Blackwell, Oxford 1992, p66.

[11] Soldon, N., *Women in British Trade Unions: 1874-1976*, Gill & Macmillan, Dublin 1978, p148; R. Hyman, above, p167.

[12] Lewis, *op cit*, p72.

[13] Walby, S., *Patriarchy at Work*, Polity Press, Cambridge 1986, p207.

[14] Kelsall & Mitchell, *op cit*.

[15] *Ibid*. They define a woman's social class according to the manual or non manual status of her husband and father.

[16] Myrdal & Klein, *op cit*, p85.

[17] Hubback, J., *Wives Who Went To College*, Heinemann, London 1957.

[18] Kelsall & Mitchell, *op cit*.

[19] Bryan, B. *et al.*, *The Heart of the Race*, Virago, London 1986, p25.

[20] Carby, H., 'White Women Listen! Black feminism and the Boundaries of Sisterhood', in Centre for Contemporary Cultural Studies (ed) *The Empire Strikes Back*, Hutchinson, London 1984.

[21] Crofts, W., 'The Attlee Government's Pursuit Of Women'. *History Today*, 36, p30.

[22] Summerfield, *op cit*.

[23] Wilson, E., *Only Halfway to Paradise*, Tavistock, London 1980, p43.

[24] Summerfield, *op cit*.
[25] Beveridge, W., *Social Insurance and Allied Services*, HMSO, London 1942.
[26] Riley, D., 'War in the Nursery', *Feminist Review*, 2, 1979.
[27] Crofts, *op cit*, p35.
[28] *Ibid*, pp34-5.
[29] *Ibid*.
[30] Soldon, *op cit*, p60.
[31] Lewnhak, S., *Women and Trade Unions*, Benn, London 1977.
[32] Myrdal & Klein, *op cit*.
[33] *Ibid*, pp155-6.
[34] Crofts, *op cit*.

'Race' and Immigration: Labour's Hidden History 1945-51

Kenneth Lunn

> I do not know who has put the wind up the Home Office and destroyed the reputation of the Labour Party for non-racialism by suggesting that we would not absorb 26,000 people this year into a humane and reasonable society ... I feel humiliated to have to stand here and make this speech.
>
> John Mackintosh, 1968.[1]

Thus John Mackintosh, Labour MP, spoke out in the Commons against James Callaghan's decision in 1968 to restrict the entry of Kenyan Asians into Britain. This has often been quoted, particularly by those on the Left, as signifying the emergence of a 'racist' stand in Labour's immigration policy. However, it can be argued that the reputation of the Labour Party for 'non-racialism' up until this date was something of a sham, as an analysis of its period in office between 1945 and 1951 indicates. The racist dimensions of this period may not have been apparent to contemporary observers nor to subsequent historical studies of those years. However, a closer examination of the Attlee governments suggests that the concessions to racist pressures usually attributed to Callaghan's actions can be detected in the ideological and policy debates of the immediate post-war years.

Racism and the Historians

Many of the standard texts do not concern themselves with issues of 'race' and immigration, content to see these themes as products of the 1950s and 60s. Thus, for example, Henry Pelling's study of the Labour governments does not refer to these issues.[2] Kenneth Morgan's 1984 volume offers only a brief reference to 'the problems encountered by West Indian immigrants over jobs, housing, and racial discrimination', as discussed by a March 1950 Cabinet, and suggests that the failure to anticipate subsequent 'difficulties' and to offer a more positive and interventionist policy at this point was indicative of the overall lack of radicalism of the Attlee governments.[3] Most other studies have been content to plough a similar furrow to that marked out by Pelling and Morgan.

Even Partha Gupta's study of imperialism and the Labour Movement suggests that little concern was focused on the issue of racial discrimination during the period of the Labour govern-ments.[4] In some senses, it would appear to be the case that 'race' was not a significant political issue for the 1945-51 governments. Apart from the 1948 Nationality Act, which is often identified as having avoided any genuine focus on 'racial' connotations, there was no significant legislation. Nor, it could be claimed, was 'race' a major focus of political debate, in the way that nationalisation or welfare provision was.[5] Some sources have attributed this lack of attention to a particular insularity which encompassed the British Labour Party, not simply in the 1945-51 period, but from its very inception, and thus hindered its perception of 'race' as a likely political issue.[6]

However, even if this is a sustainable argument, it should not obscure the realities of the situation faced by the post-war Labour governments, and to suggest that lack of legislation or major policy decisions is tantamount to an absence of political significance is surely too limited a perspective on what constitutes 'politics'. There were a number of issues around which significant discussions took place, in which possible policy and theoretical implications were identified and in which political choices became more clearly articulated. Responses to those West Indians who arrived in Britain in 1948-9 are one indicator of such processes, but other dimensions – the settlement of Poles and European Volunteer Workers, recruitment of Irish workers, discussions about the future of 'The Empire' – all helped to focus what might be seen as a very important political culture around the notion of 'race', one which could then be articulated more powerfully in the 1950s and 60s.

Since most texts make little or nothing of the issues and debates surrounding 'race' and immigration, it is important to identify those studies which at least focus on the question of black Commonwealth migration into Britain and on Labour attitudes to such population movements. S. Joshi and B. Carter, some ten years ago, noted the significance of such issues:

> Contrary to the commonly held view ... 'race' as a 'problem' had already been essentially structured by 1951. This was as apparent with the Labour Party as with the Conservatives. The Labour Party, in fact, was not merely a passive reactor to Conservative initiatives, but undertook policies and propounded ideas which significantly influenced the creation of a racist Britain.[7]

This conclusion was arrived at through a consideration of a number of different interventions and events. Joshi and Carter note the centrality of the arrival of the *Empire Windrush* in 1948 and the parliamentary debates around the implications of the 492 Jamaicans on mainland Britain. They also focus on the so-called 'riots' of 1948-9, on the Nationality Bill of 1948 and the special Cabinet committee set up in 1950 to consider the implications of increased migration, particularly from the Caribbean. Around all the events, they detect the formulation of an ideological position which, if it rejected any immediate action, set in place the likelihood of immigration controls, based on a racist framework. Thus, for example, in considering the 1948-9 disturbances, Joshi and Carter note that 'problems' of 'race' were identified and discussed,

> ... but, in view of the pressing need for labour, were ignored by the Labour government as a political issue (although confidentially at Cabinet and senior civil service levels, they were used as an argument for immigration control).[8]

More detailed consideration of available evidence came in a study by D.W. Dean, which arrived at very similar conclusions to those of Joshi and Carter. Fundamentally, it identified the ways in which 'race' and immigration became significant issues for the Labour government and the ways in which Labour sought to defuse issues and postpone decisions.[9]

Dean identifies a possible shift in the dominant thought of the party – from a vague general adherence to a liberal policy of an 'open door' to Commonwealth immigrants, who were British citizens, to one which highlighted the possibility of immigration controls for the sake of 'racial harmony'. This change in thought is typified by Attlee's 1948 speech, which appeared to reinforce the centrality of a liberal 'open door' policy:

> The tradition ... is not to be lightly discarded, particularly at a time when we are importing foreign labour in large measure. It would be fiercely resented in the colonies themselves and it would be a great mistake to take any action which would tend to weaken the loyalty and goodwill of the colonies to Great Britain.[10]

However, there was a postscript to this statement which indicated the essentially pragmatic rather than moral basis to such a strategy – and hinted that it could be overturned if the 'open door' were too inviting: '... if our policy were to result in a great influx of undesirables we might, however unwillingly, have to consider modifying it.'[11] It is evidence such as that uncovered by Joshi and Carter and Dean which requires a more thoughtful appraisal of Labour attitudes towards black immigration and 'race' and an evaluation of the possible theoretical and policy implications of these years.

Peter Hennessey's recent work has encapsulated the outline issues very neatly. He sees the arrival of the *Empire Windrush* as a 'turning-point in British history',[12] a point which might be debated but is an understandable sentiment. For example, he speculates on whether the British Nationality Act would have offered such a liberal definition of citizenship if the *Windrush* had arrived a month or so earlier and publicised the possibility of 'mass' immigration into the British Isles. By 1950, despite the very limited numbers of

West Indian immigrants (less than 6000 by 1951), the Cabinet had begun a detailed consideration of the 'problems' created by the additional numbers. By June 1950, Cabinet discussions had focused on the possibility of controls. Between July 1950 and January 1951, a special Cabinet Committee, GEN 325, chaired by Chuter Ede, the Home Secretary, discussed the question at some length. Its advice, accepted by Cabinet, was that the 'unrestricted access' for Commonwealth and colonial subjects (and for Irish citizens) should continue, in the interests of harmony, but that close attention should be paid to any significant growth in immigration numbers. Legislation to limit numbers could be considered if it was felt appropriate.[13] It is evidence such as this which supports the argument for seeing the post-war years as a significant element in the process of defining 'race' and 'immigration' as political 'problems' for the British State and for society.

Yet such discussions say little about how the Labour Party and its constituent elements came to identify the 'problems' which were constituted by 'race' and how it was that it became a significant Cabinet focus by 1950. What has yet to be fully researched, despite the pioneering work by Joshi and Carter and others, are the processes whereby the issues were 'racialised'. A closer examination of some aspects of Labour thinking and policy-making can identify the lack of significant consideration of these issues within the party generally. Most debates within the NEC were initiated from the Advisory Committee on Imperial Questions, a somewhat obscure and marginalised group which seemed to have very little influence within the massed ranks of Labour. It did, however, identify the likelihood of migration following the Second World War,[14] and discuss ways of dealing with the population pressures which would occur particularly in the Caribbean. By 1949, the committee title had been changed to the Commonwealth Sub-Committee and it produced a memo on 'The Colour Problem in Britain and its Treatment'.[15] This was a detailed document, attempting to identify those blacks and Asians present in Britain and to establish what difficulties confronted them. The fact that this was a 'colour problem' was raised without any comment! Its conclusions were undramatic but noteworthy. Discrimination in housing and accommodation were noted as everyday occurrences; the suggestion was made that half of those letting accommodation discriminated against 'a coloured guest':[16]

> Socially speaking, also, there is a fairly widespread attitude of combined shyness, aloofness and snobbishness, which a coloured person often has to encounter in nearly every walk of English life.[17]

Problems in obtaining employment were also noted. 'Prejudice' was deemed to be endemic in British culture; reference was made to the 'extensive legacy of popular tradition and stories, true as well as untrue, about their (the 'foreigner's') indigenous habits and customs.'[18]

Thus, the main focus of any 'solution' was education of the white population – through school, cinema, radio and official action.[19] Whilst it was felt that a 'general attempt at legislation on racial or colour grounds' was 'probably neither desirable nor practicable in this country', there were possible areas to explore. The licence laws might be used to penalise discrimination in pubs, clubs, dance-halls and the like. Discriminatory clauses in leases might be seen as legally invalid and removed. The 'colour bar' should continue to be condemned by Government spokespersons and others in order to influence public opinion against its workings.[20] The memo ended with a note of praise: 'The pronouncements of certain Ministers against the colour bar have been admirable and the recent survey by the Colonial Office Information Department of public interest in colonial affairs is to be commended.[21] Here, at least, was evidence of some wider interest not noted in many of the standard texts, but, in overall terms, the exception rather than the rule.

Fascism and Anti-Semitism

Outside of the NEC, there appeared to be a similar lack of concern. As a recent study of the debates around the arrival of the *Empire Windrush* has shown,[22] the arrival of the West Indians was very quickly forgotten and produced little public statement from Labour and government sources.[23] On a more general basis, discussion of 'race' issues was limited. In the early years of the Labour governments, attention was much more firmly focused on the threat of British Fascism and on its associated anti-semitism. The General Secretary's papers for early 1946 show very clearly the local concerns of Labour Party branches with the rebirth of British Fascism and a number of resolutions calling for legislation making 'racial persecution'[24] an offence. Reference was, by implication, towards the anti-semitism of Fascism. It has been argued that it was this preoccupation with fascism and anti-semitism which helped to obscure the implications of the *Empire Windrush* in 1948.[25] However, even in this lobbying, the question of a wider racism was not totally ignored. At the 1946 conference, following a general motion calling on the government to take drastic action against the re-birth of Fascism, a much more specific resolution, demanding precise legislation to declare fascist organisations illegal, was moved. This reflected the growing concern of local parties and the consistent calls on the NEC to consider such action. However, in addition, it called for similar laws 'making action or propaganda calculated to lead to any form of anti-semitism, racial or colour discrimination an offence'.[26] Moved by Harold Lever, MP for Manchester Exchange, it was an attempt to make a more effective intervention against the perceived fascist threat and to include groups other than Jews. The speeches at the conference, however, make it clear that, in spite of the broader working of the motion, it was anti-semitism which was seen as the issue related to the rise of fascist rhetoric. Alice Bacon, MP, replying for the NEC, dismissed the likelihood of a significant fascist revival and the 'safe' resolution calling only for 'drastic action' was won; the Manchester resolution was defeated.

Subsequent conferences revealed little futher interest in the topic. The 1948 conference did have a number of resolutions dealing specifically with racial discrimination against 'coloured people', but only one (from Moss Side, Manchester, Labour Party) was specifically in favour of integration and full opportunity.[27] A composited resolution focused again on the fascist threat, and called on the Government,

(a) to render criminal the publication by writing or from a political or public platform defamatory statements concerning groups identifiable by race, creed or colour;
(b) to render illegal any organisation or association which propagates racial or religious hatred or discrimination.[28]

Moved by Bernard Finley, Harrow West District Labour Party, the debate was again essentially structured around Fascism and anti-semitism, until the intervention of E.C. Smith, Tottenham North. He began his speech: 'My Party feels that the colour bar is a disgrace. We have seen negroes banned from taking part in sports and we have seen them barred from certain restaurants in London.'[29] He then also turned to Fascism and supported the call for interventionist legislation. Harold Laski, on behalf of the NEC, was thus able to devote his response entirely to the fascist threat and, as a result of his promise of constant vigilance, was able to have the mover and the seconder of the resolution remit it to the NEC. As the NEC minutes record, the notion of 'Discrimination against Coloured People' was simply 'Noted'.[30] Thus, any concern at a local level about attitudes to other ethnic minorities in Britain was subsumed within the general approach to the revival of fascist groups, mainly in London.

In effect, the only significant area where some positive action was taken was over the presence of 'coloured' students in Britain. By 1950, the Party was expressing great concern about the possible isolation of colonial students in London and elsewhere and the International Department made vigorous efforts to remedy the situation, organising social activities, conferences and delegations to the House of Commons.[31] The question had been previously addressed in 1948, when a report of the International Department had identified its lack of contact with these students and the relative lack of success by the Fabian Colonial Bureau in providing support (indeed, it was noted that the Bureau would not formally represent the Labour Party in any contact).[32] The report, however, explains the anxiety very clearly. It had little to do with any social concern for such students, far away from home and likely to face prejudice in an unwelcoming Britain. The worry was about the more successful organisation and involvement of the Communist Party, with its active Colonial Department, free African News Sheet and social relations through such contacts. Thus, it was the concern over political influence and control which was the main focus of the Party and behind the call for the appointment of a Colonial Assistant within the Department, whose immediate task would be to deal with students and colonial deputations and put them in touch with local Labour Parties, an appointment agreed in July 1948.[33] A 1949 Report gave three aims to the overall strategy: first to help break down student isolation; second, to inform them of politics, particularly those of the Labour Party, and third, 'to help counteract the effects of communists, British and Colonial, to exploit the awakening political consciousness of colonial people for their own ends.'[34] Thus, despite, the apparent diversity of concerns, it does seem that the major preoccupation of the International Department and the Party officials was the desire for ideological and political control of colonial students and paid little attention to any concerns about the impact of 'racism'.

Race and the Colonial Empire

In addition to debates on racism in Britain and on the nature of immigration in these years, there were other circumstances which contributed to the racialisation process under these Labour governments. For example, in many of the debates about colonial development and the drive to self-government, the question of the 'colour bar' was raised. Thus, in the 1947 annual Labour Party Conference, James Callaghan very forcibly reminded delegates that 'the colour bar must go' if the African was to have 'the reasonable and decent standard which Socialists have always demanded for themselves.'[35] Various pressure groups within the Labour Movement also began to focus on the 'evils' of the South African State, with a powerful debate on the issue being generated at the 1951 conference.[36] It is difficult not to see these attitudes developed and/or reflected in the discussions about discrimination in Britain discussed above.

It is also the case that the debates around colonial matters helped to shape general attitudes towards the 'coloured race'. For most Labour politicians, this was their major point of contact, direct or indirect, with other ethnic groups and it does appear that many of them could not escape the condescension of previous years, or avoid an increasingly paternalistic view of other 'races'.

Despite the many statements of good intent and expressions of equality with 'coloured people', many of which were totally in keeping with a dominant public rhetoric of the period, it is difficult not to recognise the processes whereby 'race' was being continually contructed as 'a problem'. Not everyone operated in the same framework as Hugh Dalton, however, who, when offered the Secretaryship of the Colonies following the 1950 election victory, recorded in his diary:

> I had a horrid vision of pullulating, poverty-stricken, diseased nigger communities, for whom one can do nothing in the short run, and now, the more one tries to help them, are querulous and ungrateful ...[37]

He rejected Attlee's offer. Most other figures took a less strident view, but pursued a line which identified first and foremost a tone which was conciliatory towards white opposition to, and intolerance of, blacks,[38] a position which was often constructed out of colonial strategies but which then became applied to the domestic situation in Britain. Thus, Arthur Creech Jones, in discussing the question of land settlement in Kenya in 1947, suggested that the Highlands could not be opened up to unrestricted settlement by 'the natives'. This would raise racial tensions and encourage the solidarity of whites throughout Africa to resist liberal policies. A strategy of gradualism, particularly where whites had had previously exclusive rights, was needed. This strategy was seen as 'more effective in advancing the interests of the blacks than general declarations which were were not backed by practical planning.'[39] It seems likely that such a view shaped general strategy towards the issues raised by the settlement of blacks in Britain during the 1945-51 period, and the likelihood of additional immigration in subsequent years.

'European Volunteer Workers'

In addition, there were other ethnic groups whose presence in post-war Britain contributed to the racialisation process. Attention has recently been drawn to the numbers of Irish citizens who entered Britain during the period 1946-1950, intending to stay for more than one year. There was a net influx of between 100,000 and 150,000. Specific recruitment schemes were introduced: the newly-nationalised mining industry took over 2000 Irish workers in 1946. In 1947, 29,000 men and women were recruited for essential industries and services – agriculture, mining and nursing being the main occupations.[40] There is ample evidence of trade union resistance and negotiation about such recruitment and of discrimination and prejudice which confronted many of those Irish who came to live and work in Britain during these years. The status of Irish citizens was consistently questioned and the racial stereotyping which had become part and parcel of British culture by the nineteenth century continued to 'problematise' the influx of these workers at national and local level.[41]

Other European groups also added to the 'racial' question. Those who are generally classed as 'European Volunteer Workers' (EVWs) and the Polish Resettlement Corps, ex-servicemen who remained in Britain at the end of the hostilities, were the most significant groups. The Labour Movement had certain misgivings about the employment of such workers and contested quite vigorously the basis of such schemes. There were disputes about the levels of unemployment said to exist at the end of the war, and hence the need for 'foreign' workers. Pay and conditions of work also raised significant discussions. There still existed a stereotypical view about 'immigrant labour' and the potential for undermining hard-won gains, which could draw on a popular and populist racism. In this particular situation, the possibilities of non-union 'foreigners' being employed at below union rates of pay, or in inferior conditions, appeared a distinct possibility, as various incidents were brought to the attention of union executives and local offices of the Ministry of Labour. Whilst these responses could draw upon a racist discourse, it should also be noted that the objections to these workers was often part of a much wider debate about control at the point of production and thus was concerned with issues wider than a straightforward objection to 'foreigners'.

There were also tensions based on the alleged 'fascist' tendencies of the newcomers, a fear which corresponded to the concern with the re-emergence of a domestic strand of the ideology. There had been well-publicised incidents of anti-semitism among the Polish forces in Scotland during the war years and sometimes vehement anti-Soviet views expressed by Poles and other East Europeans were taken as indicators of fascist sympathies.

To allay these fears as far as possible, the employment of Poles and EVWs was eventually carried out by careful agreement between the Ministry of Labour and the unions concerned in particular industries. Employment, particularly of EVWs, was confined to a few sectors of the economy. Seventy per cent of the men worked in agriculture or coal-mining; ninety-five per cent of the women in textiles and domestic work. Most agreements, particularly those concerned with Polish workers who were likely to become permanent members of the labour force, and perhaps naturalised British citizens, required full union rates of pay, union membership and a clause which stated that foreigners would only be employed in the absence of suitable British labour. These agreements were negotiated at a national level but attempts to implement them locally often created difficulties. Disagreements and disputes, often provoked by the insensitivity of local employment officials and employers, who failed to consult union branches or check that the agreed conditions were being enforced, frequently made the headlines. Many local confrontations over apparently 'racial' objections were, in fact, part and parcel of a broader industrial relations framework, sometimes racialised but often based on other economic and/or political issues.[42]

The contrast between these workers and those incomers from the Caribbean was notable. Europeans were recruited on very specific and controlled terms of employment, whereas the West Indians were 'free' to operate within the capitalist market, at least in theory. In reality, the British State, and Labour politicians, were ultimately far more inclined to the employment of European labour, which could constitute the classic 'reserve army of labour' in a very legalistic sense. The perceived threat of large-scale immigration from the West Indies, which was as yet uncontrolled by legislation, created, as has been shown, far more tension within the Party and the bureaucracy generally. In such a situation, a perceived hierarchy of races became more clearly defined. Europeans could provide sound racial stock; West Indians created, or added to, the 'colour problem'. It was not even necessary to make such a contrast for 'race' to become an issue. As Diana Kay and Robert Miles have shown, discussions on the EVWs focused quite clearly on this theme:

> The EVWs were ... racialised in the course of assessing their suitability as suppliers of labour power and therefore as migrants. But, this was a racialisation which often resulted in a positive rather than a negative evaluation ... the EVWs ... were considered to be of 'good stock', to have 'vigorous blood', and to possess other qualities that promised the possibility that they would become or could be made into 'good Britons'.[43]

Whilst Kay and Miles do note the unevenness of this process ('Slavs' were particularly singled out as 'unhealthy stock'), their point is that racism was not crucial to determine the status of such workers. Their 'alien' status was clear cut and legally defined. Thus, as they argue, the British State 'had no reason to legitimate any racism expressed from below'[44] towards the EVWs, whereas migrants from the Caribbean were not legally 'aliens' and thus racism was an essential element in any control or exclusion process.[45] Without wishing to challenge the essential arguments here, it would be important to stress that the mere existence of a racial discourse surrounding the Poles and EVWs, whether legitimated by the State or not, could only serve to heighten a general awareness of 'race' issues and thus contribute to the general process highlighted in this study.

A Shadow on the Future

Overall, then, it can be argued that the 1945-51 Labour governments presided over a significant period in the history of 'race' in Britain. This may not have been an obvious process, or one which was apparent to many of the participants at the time and to many subsequent commentators, but it is one which is now clearly identifiable. This is not to say, however, that the process is clearly delineated. We still know little about the way in which racial discourses developed at a local level. It is also important to stress that many Labour activists were not part and parcel of this process and contributed to a counter-culture, albeit one which had much less impact than its opposing views. It may also be the case that the racialisation process was an uneven one, one still in the process of formulation, with dissonant voices still drawing upon more liberal views and perspectives at particular moments. As has been suggested, whilst racialised control of immigration was directly avoided before 1951, the basis was being constructed during these years, slowly but inexorably. More significantly, ways in which 'race' was being identified as a 'problem' helped to construct the unhappy history of 'race relations' in Britain in subsequent years.

Notes

[1] *Hansard*, Parl. Debates 1967-8, vol 759, col 1591 – quoted in Foote, *The Labour Party's Political Thought: A History*, Croom Helm, Beckenham 1985, p240.
[2] H. Pelling, *The Labour Governments, 1945-51*, Macmillan, London 1984.
[3] K. Morgan, *Labour in Power, 1945-51*, Oxford University Press, Oxford 1984, p56.
[4] P.S. Gupta, *Imperialism and the British Labour Movement, 1914-1964*, Macmillan, London 1975, p338.
[5] *Ibid*, pp275-348.
[6] D.W. Dean, 'Coping with Colonial Immigration, the Cold War and Colonial Policy: the Labour Government and Black Communities in Great Britain, 1945-51', *Immigrants and Minorities*, vol 6, no 3 (1987), p313.
[7] S. Joshi and B. Carter, 'The role of Labour in the creation of a racist Britain', *Race and Class*, vol xxv, no 3 (1984), pp69-70.
[8] *Ibid*, p61.
[9] See Dean, *op cit*. For a more detailed consideration of the 'official mind', see M. Smith, 'Windrushers and Orbiters: Towards an Understanding of the "Official

Mind" and Colonial Immigration to Britain 1945-51', *Immigrants and Minorities*, vol 10, no 3 (November 1991), pp3-17.

[10] Quoted in Dean, *op cit*, p316.

[11] Quoted in *Ibid*, p317.

[12] P. Hennessy, *Never Again: Britain 1945-51*, Jonathan Cape, London 1993, p440.

[13] *Ibid*, pp442-3.

[14] See NEC minutes, 26/2/47, Labour Party Archives, National Museum of Labour History.

[15] See NEC minutes, 23/2/49.

[16] NEC minutes, 23/3/49.

[17] *Ibid*.

[18] *Ibid*.

[19] Significant concrete proposals for such an educative programme were put forward – naive perhaps in the context of 1990s 'race relations' but indicative of some positive intervention in this area by at least one group within the party.

[20] NEC Minutes, 23/3/49.,

[21] *Ibid*.

[22] K. Lunn, 'The British State and Immigration, 1945-51: New Light on the Empire Windrush', in T. Kushner & K. Lunn (eds), *The Politics of Marginality: Race, the Radical Right and Minorities in Twentieth-Century Britain*, Frank Cass, London 1990.

[23] This interpretation challenges the view of Hennessy, who ascribes particular significance to the Windrush's voyage, the 'tizzy' created for central Government and generally sees the event as a 'turning-point' in British history (*op cit*, p440).

[24] Motion of Acton Labour Party and Trades Council, 10/1/46, General Secretary papers, GS/RAC/39, Labour Party Archieves.

[25] See Lunn, *op cit*, pp169-70.

[26] *Report of the 45th Annual Conference of the Labour Party, 1946*, p112.

[27] See Gupta, *op cit*, p338.

[28] *Report of the 47th Annual Conference of the Labour Party, 1948*, p179.

[29] *Ibid*, p181.

[30] NEC minutes, 23/6/48.

[31] See Commonwealth Sub-Committee of NEC, correspondence, File 2 'Colonial Students in Britain 1950', Labour Party Archives.

[32] See report of International Sub-Committee of NEC, July 1948, in NEC minutes, 28/7/48.

[33] *Ibid*.

[34] NEC minues, 26/10/49, 'Report to Commonwealth Sub-Committee on Colonial Students'.

[35] *Report on the 46th Annual Conference of the Labour Party, 1947*, p115.

[36] Gupta, *op cit*, p338.

[37] Dalton's Diaries, 28 February 1950, quoted in Gupta, p336.

[38] This is not to say that there were no positive voices. Somewhat ironically, in the light of the opening quotation of this article, see James Callaghan's speech to the 1947 conference, in which he called for an end to the exploitation of Africans and for the elimination of the 'colour bar', as quoted above (no 35).

[39] Commonwealth and Imperial Affairs Sub-Committee, 21/3/47, in NEC minutes, 26/3/47.

[40] D. Kay and R. Miles, *Refugees or Migrant Workers? European Volunteer Workers in Britain 1946-1951*, Routledge, London 1992, p30.

[41] See K. Lunn, 'Irish labour recruitment schemes, 1937-48', *Labour History Review*, vol 57, part 3 (1992).

[42] K. Lunn, 'The Employment of Polish and European Volunteer Workers in the Scottish Coalfields, 1945-1950', in K. Tenfelde (ed), *Towards a Social History of Mining in the 19th and 20th Centuries*, C.H. Beck, Munich 1992, pp584-5.

[43] Kay and Miles, *op cit*, p175.

[44] For details, see Kay and Miles, *op cit*; R. Miles and D. Kay, 'The TUC, Foreign Labour and the Labour Government 1945-51', *Immigrants and Minorities*, vol 9, no 1 (1990).

[45] Kay and Miles, *op cit*, p176.

The Changing Mood of Working People

Jim Mortimer

> In 1945 both the conditions in Westminster and Whitehall and
> the political climate in the country outside were extremely well
> suited for a big and sustained advance towards a socialist planned
> economy ... In the history of the British Left, there can seldom
> have been an administration so conservative in its solicitude for
> the stuffier constitutional conventions, so instinctively suspicious
> of all suggestions for popular participation in decision-making
> and workers' control, and so determined to damp down the fiery
> demands for a new social order that had won them the election.
>
> Richard Crossman, 'The Lessons of 1945',
> *New Statesman*, 19 April 1963.

My main memory of the second half of the 1940s is of the change of
political mood among working people, and among active trade
unionists in particular, between 1945 and 1951. This change was not
measured in the votes cast for the principal political parties. Indeed,
Labour secured a higher proportion of the total votes cast in the
1951 General Election, which it lost, than in 1945 when it secured an
overwhelming parliamentary majority. In 1945 Labour's share of
the total vote was 47.8 per cent. In 1951 it was 48.8 per cent.

This increase in Labour's share of the votes cast owed much more
to a persistent distrust of the Tories among millions of working
people than to any enthusiasm for Labour's 1951 election
programme. A view widely held among active rank-and-file
supporters of the Labour Movement, and one which I shared, was
that the Labour government, though it had introduced many good
social changes during its period of office, had 'run out of steam', had
tied itself to the foreign policy of the United States and had

committed itself to a rearmament programme which Britain could not afford without sacrifices in living standards, reduced investment in industry and cuts in the social services.

The Enthusiasm of 1945

The General Election of 1945 was like no other in which I have participated, either before or since. At the time I was working in a large engineering factory in the London surburban industrial belt of West Middlesex and I was an active trade unionist. In this factory and in other large engineering factories in West London and West Middlesex there was real enthusiasm for the election of a Labour government, pledged to a policy of social change. There was widespread consciousness of the kind of changes that were needed.

The first requirement was that there should be full employment and no return to the mass unemployment, depression and hunger marches of the inter-war period. This was felt all the more acutely in West Middlesex because so many of the workers had migrated there in earlier years from areas of high unemployment.

Equally as important as the determination not to return to mass unemployment was the conviction that it was within the power of government to maintain full employment. This was no idle dream. William Beveridge had produced his report *Full Employment in a Free Society* and it had achieved wide publicity. The war-time Coalition government had produced a White Paper on full employment and it had been introduced to Parliament by the then Minister of Labour, Ernest Bevin, whose reputation was based on his trade union experience.

The political parties pledged themselves to maintain full employment and Beveridge's report said that it was attainable. What was needed above all was for the government of the day to maintain, by investment, taxation policies and, if necessary, by borrowing, an adequate level of demand in the economy. Unemployment, it was explained, was caused by a deficiency of demand which had proved to be periodically inevitable if the private enterprise system were left to itself without public intervention. Among many working people, whose knowledge of economics was derived from experience rather than from textbooks, there was a belief that if unemployment were to be avoided there had to be public intervention, planning and an extension of social ownership. In practical terms this meant that there had to be a Labour government.

But it was not only full employment that was on the public agenda. The second main demand was for social security and freedom from poverty caused by industrial injuries, ill-health, temporary unemployment and other hazards of life. There was a widespread conviction that as extreme poverty had been avoided in war, by rationing and community support, then, even more, could it also be avoided in peacetime.

The third demand was for new housing. The idea that houses should be provided only if someone could make a profit out of construction would have been so ludicrous to the demobilised millions from the armed forces that even the most fanatical 'free marketeers' kept their silence. Planning was the order of the day.

On international affairs the view of the public was that the war-time coalition of Britain, the Soviet Union and the USA should be maintained. Labour, it was argued, was better placed by reason of its socialist commitment to cooperate with the Soviet Union than a Conservative Party led by Churchill. Among trade unionists Churchill was remembered for his anti-union role in the General Strike and, among Socialists, for his opposition to the Soviet Union in the years following the Russian revolution. His hysterical attacks on the Labour Party during the 1945 election campaign confirmed that he was still as anti-socialist as ever. His views were at odds not only with millions of Labour voters but also with many who voted Conservative or Liberal, who respected Churchill for his war-time contribution but were sympathetic to the need for social change.

Similarly, in relation to the empire, the anti-fascist war had profoundly affected opinion. It was felt to be inconsistent to condemn German attempts to dominate other countries if colonial domination by Britain were to continue. In India, in particular, there was a strong movement for independence and it enjoyed the sympathy of the Labour Movement in Britain.

In the big engineering factories of the western suburbs of London the campaign for the election of a Labour government was conducted vigorously. In most of the factories the trade union leadership among the shop stewards was on the left. The Communist Party was influential. The public argument at factory level was very heavily in favour of Labour. No doubt a significant minority of workers voted Conservative but my impression was that they were reluctant to engage in debate, and anyhow most sympathised with the prevailing demands for full employment, social security and economic planning. The one observation which was offered by Tory supporters was that Churchill, as the war-time leader, deserved electoral support.

Most of the press, the public commentators and even some of the Labour leaders were surprised at the extent of Labour's victory. In West Middlesex seats which the Conservatives regarded as 'safe' were lost to Labour. The constituency in which I worked, Spelthorne, and the constituency in which I lived, Heston and Isleworth, were both won by Labour by comfortable majorities. Other West Middlesex constituencies which were won by Labour included Ealing West, two seats in Willesden, Acton, Brentford and Chiswick, Harrow East, Hendon North, Wembley North, Wembley South, Southall and Uxbridge. In the area of the old London County Council Labour won forty eight seats to the Conservative's twelve. One parliamentary seat was won by the Communists and one by an Independent Labour candidate, D.N. Pritt, who stood on a strongly left-wing platform. In the rest of the south of England Labour achieved the unthinkable; it won more seats than the Tories. Labour's performance in London, Middlesex and Essex was better than in Scotland. In Essex the Conservative Party and their allies won only three out of twenty-four seats!

Labour in Action

Within a month of Labour taking office the USA cancelled all Lend-Lease contracts under which, as part of the war effort, Britain had received supplies on credit from the United States. It was a severe blow. Britain had only begun to demobilise and the peace-time industries were at a low level. Exports were nowhere near sufficient to pay for the required imports. Moreover overseas investments had been sold during the war and new debts incurred. In an attempt to meet this appalling problem the Labour government sought and secured a loan from the United States, but on conditions about freedom of trade and a return to sterling convertibility which suited American interests. Moreover, the loan lost some of its value because of the rise in prices, made worse by the removal of controls by the US government.

The Labour government carried out Labour's election pledges to bring important services and sections of industry under public ownership. The Bank of England, coal, gas, electricity, railways, some other parts of the transport industry and civil aviation were all nationalised. The Government also brought in new legislation for a comprehensive system of social insurance and for a National Health Service. In relation to India the Government accepted the demand for independence. These were all substantial achievements. There was some delay in bringing sections of the iron and steel industry under public ownership, and there was opposition from the House of Lords. Vesting date for the Iron and Steel Corporation was finally fixed for early in 1951.

Of special importance to trade unionists was the repeal of the 1927 Trade Disputes Act. This Act had been introduced by a Conservative government following the defeat of the General Strike in 1926. The main provisions of the 1927 Act were to outlaw sympathetic strikes or strikes which the courts decided were not in pursuit of a trade dispute; to enforce the severance of the civil service unions from the wider Trade Union and Labour Movement; to limit peaceful picketing in the course of a strike; to prohibit any public body from making trade union membership a condition of employment; and to substitute 'contracting in' for 'contracting out' in the payment of the unions' political levy, a measure aimed at the finances of the Labour Party.

Growing Criticism

By the summer of 1946 there were already criticisms being voiced within the Trade Union and Labour Movement about the direction of the Labour government's foreign policy. One of the first issues on which there was controversy concerned Greece. Many of us felt that the Labour government was continuing the policy of the Churchill government in favouring the restoration of political reactionaries at the expense of left-wing forces who, as in many countries occupied by the Nazis, had led the resistance.

Concern was also expressed at the decision of the USA to maintain secrecy on atomic weapons. At that stage the USA had the monopoly of the atomic bomb and it was understandable that the Soviet Union was suspicious. In his chairman's address to the 1946 Labour Party conference, Professor Harold Laski said that there was no justification for this secrecy.

In relation to Germany it became increasingly clear that American policy was to restore capitalism in the West, to obstruct proposals for the social ownership of heavy industry and to avoid any effective elimination of many of the powerful banking and industrial interests which had stood behind Hitler. In 1947 the annual report of the Labour Party, in commenting on an agreement for the economic fusion of the British and American zones of occupation, said that, 'the decision to socialise the heavy industries of Germany would not be prejudiced by the fusion agreement.'[1]

It was, however, the impact of foreign policy on Britain's economy and on living standards which had special significance for trade unionists. The year 1947 was one of very great economic difficulty. There was a fuel crisis at the beginning of the year, exacerbated by very severe weather. The mining industry was losing manpower at the rate of about a thousand a week. Arthur Horner, the General Secretary of the NUM, said in a speech to the 1947 TUC that 150,000 men in the industry were over fifty years of age. There were also severe shortages of labour in many other industries. The Minister of Labour, George Isaacs, said that in textiles and clothing, for example, there were vacancies for over 360,000 workers. The Government asked the unions to agree in principle to a lengthening of the hours of labour. The Government also reimposed control over the engagement of labour, a measure abolished after the war. The balance of payments was in deficit.

Despite these problems and the acute labour shortage, the number of people in the military services remained high. The Government planned to reduce the strength of the defence services to 1,007,000 by the end of March, 1948. In 1947 the General Council of the TUC, surprisingly, 'came to the conclusion that there is justification for the continuation of compulsory service with the Armed Forces for a limited period beyond January, 1949.'[2] This heavy commitment of manpower for military purposes was the direct consequence of the Government's view that there was a threat to peace from the Soviet Union. The British government sought military strength which, in turn, helped to produce economic weakness.

The Left of the Labour Movement did not share the Government's view that, unless deterred by overwhelming military strength, the Soviet Union was likely to invade Western Europe. Our view was that it was the United States which was determined to 'roll back' the social changes which had taken place in Eastern Europe in the countries occupied by the Red Army at the end of the war. The US argued that in Eastern Europe the democratic wishes of the people were being flouted and that communist dictatorships were being installed. The Soviet Union was equally determined that their influence in these countries should remain dominant. Soviet leaders argued that capitalism had bred fascism and that if the roots of fascism were to be eradicated the economic and social system had to be changed. The USA retained the monopoly of nuclear weapons. The Soviet Union had before it such an immense task of reconstruction that peaceful coexistence with the USA and Western Europe was a necessity. The USSR regarded the existence of friendly governments in Eastern Europe as essential for their own security. Unfortunately, the need for friendly governments was interpreted as a need for obedient governments.

Most of the Left, particularly the Left in the Labour Party, though rejecting the notion that the Soviet Union represented a military threat to Britain, were critical of some of the policies and actions of the USSR. Indeed, these actions were sometimes so indefensible that they played into the hands of 'Cold War warriors'. Thus, for example, the Soviet government introduced a ridiculous ban on marriages between Soviet women and men from certain other countries, including Britain. There were official reports of alleged plots, incredible in detail, by Soviet citizens against the lives of Stalin and other leaders. There were attempts from the highest level of the Soviet leadership to impose uniformity in thought among scientists, writers, artists and musicians. Dissidents were subject to deprivation of rights and banishment. Perhaps the most revealing of all injustices was the campaign of hostility directed against Tito and the Yugoslav government because they refused to follow slavishly every dictate from the USSR. In most of the other Communist governed countries of Eastern Europe purges were conducted, at the instigation of the USSR, against any Communist leaders who were inclined to show any independence from Moscow. A number of Communist leaders were executed or imprisoned.

The task of the Left during this period was, therefore, not an easy one. At no stage were we in anything like a majority in the trade union movement, though in the Labour Party at constituency level there was always substantial minority, and occasionally majority, support for the Left. In the constituency Labour Party of which I was a member, Heston and Isleworth, most controversial issues were vigorously debated. The Left won occasionally on foreign policy questions but the Centre and the Right were in the majority in Labour representation on the local council.

In the trade unions the controversy centred around incomes policy. In February 1948 the Government issued a White Paper on *Personal Incomes, Costs and Prices*, asking for a temporary halt to further increases in personal incomes. There were to be only very limited exceptions. The argument of the Government was that any increase in incomes without a corresponding increase in output would lead to upward pressure on prices which, in turn, would make it more difficult to sell British goods in foreign markets.

Incomes Policy and the Unions

The reality was that inflation was caused, in conditions of full employment, by an excess of demand on available resources. Employers wanted scarce resources to expand production but they also saw the opportunities to increase their profits by passing on their costs, including profit margins, in higher prices. Employees sought to protect and to improve their living standards by claims for higher wages and salaries. The Government sought to gain command over resources for public expenditure, including a heavy burden of military spending. Inflation was thus, in part, the outcome of a struggle between conflicting claims.

The TUC accepted the Government's proposals in the 1948 White Paper 'on condition that the Government pursues vigorously and firmly a policy designed not only to stabilise but to reduce profits and prices'. It was, of course, extremely unlikely that this would happen. Nevertheless, it helped to persuade the majority of unions that the policy should be supported. Moreover, the General Council of the TUC put their own interpretation on the White Paper. They said that its principles were acceptable to the extent that they: recognised the necessity for unimpaired collective bargaining; admitted the justification for wage claims based on increased output; admitted the need to adjust wages that were below a reasonable standard of subsistence; affirmed that wages should be adequate to attract labour to essential under-manned industries; and recognised the need to safeguard wage differentials required to sustain craftsmanship, training and experience.

Those on the Left who were critical of TUC policy suggested that the White Paper should be judged by what it said and not by the interpretation constructed by the General Council. Almost every union would be able to justify its claims under one or more of the TUC criteria. In negotiations, however, it would be the White Paper and not the interpretation of the TUC which would influence employers.

From that time until the downfall of the Labour government in 1951, problems of incomes policy were always at the centre of attention. The leadership of the TUC tried consistently to reconcile its support for Government policy with its wish to accommodate the demands of trade union members. It had considerable success, certainly in the early stages, but eventually in face of growing economic difficulties, and particularly when a new rearmament programme was launched, the task proved impossible.

In the second half of 1949 sterling was devalued. This gave an upward thrust to prices. Economy measures were taken, including a cut in investment, but military expenditure was increased. A national ballot of miners rejected support for Government and TUC policy on wages. This was an indication of a significant change in the attitude of working people. With the outbreak of the Korean war in 1950 prices again rose sharply. This added a further strain on the incomes policy.

The Last Stage

In August 1950 the Government published a memorandum on defence which revealed that the US government had requested information regarding the increased military effort which Britain was willing to undertake. This initiative by the USA was welcomed by the British government and a programme for substantial rearmament was put forward. Cuts in industrial investment for peaceful purposes, cuts in the social services and a reduction in living standards were inevitable. Most of us on the Left felt that the Government had signed its own death warrant.

By this time I was a full-time national official and member of the Executive Committee of the union to which I belonged, the Association of Engineering and Shipbuilding Draughtsmen. Because of the changes in the situation it had become easier for the Left to win the debates on incomes policy and the economy, but we now had to face a new difficulty. It was not the merits of the argument that mattered but our position in relation to the 'Cold War'. At best we were said to be soft on Communism; at worse we were 'fellow travellers' of the Communist Party. The pressures on individuals on the Left were very considerable.

At the 1950 TUC a resolution rejecting wage restraint was carried by a narrow majority despite opposition from the General Council. A special statement on wages policy prepared by the General Council was also rejected. To put it bluntly, there was now a substantial section of the working population which was not prepared to make the sacrifices demanded of it by the Labour government.

The 1951 Budget, introduced by Hugh Gaitskell, increased income tax, profits tax and purchase tax on some goods. Petrol was increased in price, entertainment tax was put up and health charges were introduced. This led to the resignation of Aneurin Bevan, Harold Wilson and John Freeman from the Government. At the 1951 Labour Party conference Aneurin Bevin easily topped the poll in the constituency section election for the National Executive Committee.

The National Arbitration Order (Order 1305) which, except in very special circumstances, made strikes illegal, was maintained almost throughout the period of office of the post-war Labour government. It was first introduced as a war-time measure in 1940. The TUC did not call for it to be revoked until early in 1951. At the 1950 TUC, for example, a motion that it should be revoked was defeated by 5,166,000 votes to 2,423,000. Later that year, however, a number of gas maintenance workers who had taken part in a strike fell foul of the Order and legal action was taken against them. In August 1951 the Government announced the withdrawal of Order 1305 and its replacement by a new Industrial Disputes Order which retained a provision for arbitration but did not make strikes illegal.

At the 1950 General Election Labour scraped home with a narrow overall majority of seats but at the 1951 General Election the Conservative Party won a majority of seats but with a slightly smaller total vote than for Labour. The public mood was very different from that of 1945. The enthusiasm had very largely gone. Labour's strong electoral showing, despite its defeat, was attributable to containing distrust of the Conservative Party and appreciation of the many social reforms introduced earlier by the Labour Government. Nevertheless, in my view, and in the view of many on the Left, the opportunity to go forward towards radical social change – an opportunity which had existed in 1945 – had been sacrificed in later years to a rearmament programme which was both economically damaging and politically unnecessary.

Notes

[1] Labour Party, *Annual Report*, 1947, p61.
[2] TUC, *Annual Report*, 1947, p255. This statement was made at a time when publicity campaigns were calling for more workers in coal mining, cotton textiles, iron foundries, a mobile labour building force, agriculture, nursing and domestic work in institutions, and when women were being asked to enter or rejoin industry.

Afterword

Labour's Bright Morning ... and Afternoon

Jim Fyrth

Full many a glorious morning have I seen
Flatter the mountain-tops with sovreign eye,
Kissing with golden face the meadows green,
Gilding pale streams with heavenly alchemy;
Anon permit the basest clouds to ride
With ugly rack on his celestial face,
And from the forlorn world his visage hide:
Stealing unseen to west with this disgrace ...

William Shakespeare, Sonnet lxxii.

One December morning in 1942 queues formed outside bookshops and branches of His Majesty's Stationery Office. Queues were commonplace in wartime, but these were different. People lined up, not to buy their rations, but to purchase a White Paper, Cmd. 6404, *Social Insurance and Allied Services*, popularly known as the Beveridge Report. Within a few weeks 100,000 copies were sold. In his Report Sir William Beveridge proposed an extension of social welfare that would protect all Britons, in Churchill's words, 'from the cradle to the grave'. Three years later these proposals were given life by the Labour government which had been swept into office by the electoral landslide of 1945.

Yet half a century later, in April 1993, when a Conservative government was exploring ways of dismantling the edifice built on Beveridge's principles, leading members of the Methodist churches

257

addressed a 'petition for distress from the cities' to the Queen, claiming that:

> a significant minority in this country find themselves excluded from citizenship, living in a society which is unable or unwilling to enable them to participate fully in its life, while at the same time maintaining a pretence of equal opportunities ... increasingly angry and frustrated communities are confined to ghetto areas, where all or most of the things portrayed as essentials in advertisements are denied to them.[1]

In previous months there had been much talk of a 'moral crisis', which the Prime Minister, John Major, had rather quaintly blamed on 'socialism'. Attention was frequently drawn to widespread disenchantment with the leading institutions of State and society – the monarchy, Parliament, the police, the City of London, the systems of justice and education – and to the growth of crime and people's fear of becoming victims of crime; though the crime referred to was that in city streets rather than in City boardrooms.

The Methodist petitioners pointed to the 'market-orientated, competitive, individualistic philosophy guiding government policy' as responsible. This philosophy had been the creed of the previous Prime Minister, who had told her Carlton Club audience that there was no such thing as society, only individuals and families. But the distress described by the Methodists resulted not from individualism alone. It was the consequence also of an economy which, after the 'stop-go' of the 1950s and 1960s and the 'stagflation' of the 1970s, had been severely damaged by two recessions and an equally disastrous boom which government policy had managed to effect in the space of only fourteen years. Amid the desolation and the landscapes of industrial ruin which these policies had left in their wake, one form of poverty stood out, poverty of hope for a better future and a better society.

It was very different in 1945.

Labour's Bright Dawn

On July 26th of that year, with some two dozen British Other Ranks, I sat in a hut inside the great Maratha fort at Ahmednagar, listening to the election results as they were broadcast from London. As successive Labour victories came through the cheers grew louder, reaching a crescendo when it was announced that Sir James Grigg and Leo Amery, Secretaries of State for War and India respectively – and thereby the *bêtes noires* of servicemen in India – had lost their seats. Only three members of our unit sat apart, grumbling that, 'Now we shall be controlled and directed and ordered about for another five years'. Three weeks earlier, when people in Britain were at the polls, a mock election held at Brigade HQ, with all ranks voting, had 'elected' the Labour candidate with eighty-four votes. The Communist came second with twenty-one votes, followed by the Liberal with eleven. A Conservative also ran but won only seven votes. It was a result not unrepresentative of forces opinion in 1945, and indicated a desire for, and a hope of, radical change in the direction of a better society than the one we knew.

There is no doubt that that is what people expected from the election result. A Gallup Poll shortly afterwards showed 56 per cent believing that voters had opted for radical change.[2] When, five years later, Sam Watson, the Durham Miners' leader, told the Labour Party Conference:

> Poverty has been abolished. Hunger is unknown. The sick are tended. The old folks are cherished, our children are growing up in a land of opportunity[3]

many of his hearers must have felt that those radical changes had materialised.

A more sober assessment by G.D.H. Cole in 1956 noted:

> immense improvements in the welfare of the people – above all in that of the poorer sections, and these material advances have carried with them great gains in independence and self respect.

Cole thought any reversal of the process unlikely because,

> the underdogs who have improved their status and condition will
> not easily submit to being thrust back into the ignominies of the
> old order.[4]

There had never been a government with such an extensive agenda
of Parliamentary business as that of the 1945 administration.
Seventy-five measures were put through Parliament in the first year.
Within two years 20 per cent of the economy was being taken into
public ownership. By the end of 1948 a series of measures had
replaced the old Poor Law with the Welfare State, the jewel in the
crown of which was the National Health Service. The school-
leaving age was raised to fifteen, a housing programme was launched
and legal aid in the courts extended. Among other reforms, twelve
National Parks were created in 1949 to provide 'a charter for all
lovers of the open air'.

A catalogue of legislation tells nothing about the atmosphere of
Labour's first years – that there was something new in British life
besides the rigours of austerity. Returning to my home town in
Dorset, I noticed the new clinic in what had been a large private
house at the end of the street, and the new council houses built to a
standard more comfortable than that of some of the middle-class
houses in the town. An old people's home was replacing the
workhouse. The town boasted, for the first time since 1931, a
vigorous Labour Party and, something unknown since 1926, an
active trades council. Each month there was a visit from the West of
England players, who were taking drama, much of it relevant to the
time, round small towns which had been devoid of theatre. For the
feeling of the time was not only one of better material standards, it
was also one of enhanced cultural opportunities. It seemed as
though, for the first time, society was not conducted solely in the
interests of the rich and powerful. It was a reasonable belief as long
as there was full employment, the Welfare State remained as it had
been planned, and trade union rights were protected by law.

Compared withour own times, post-war Britain was a safe place
in which to live and to walk through the streets at night. Between
1945 and 1950 crime diminished – indictable offences fell by 3.6 per

cent, crimes against property by 6.1 per cent, crimes per head of the population by 4.8 per cent.[5] It is worthwhile to compare with more recent events the embarrassment caused to the Government at that time, and the furore in the Conservative press, when a junior minister and a Bank of England director were found to have taken very minor favours from a spiv; the latter's evidence before the tribunal of inquiry provided light relief amind the austerities of 1948.[6]

But what of the economy?

Labour's Economic Inheritance and Achievement

The economic legacy inherited by the Labour government was not an enviable one. The state of the balance of payments was alarming. Imports were only 60 per cent of their pre-war level, but would be bound to rise as food and raw materials needed for recovery were imported. Exports, on the other hand, had fallen to 30 per cent of their pre-war level. They had naturally been restricted in wartime by shipping problems and the priority given to production for the home front. To add to the difficulty the American government had insisted that Lend-Lease imports could not be used for making exports that might compete with American goods.[7]

American terms for aid were dictatorial. By 1940, after the retreat from France, Britain had no longer had enough gold and dollars to pay for the imports needed to carry on the war. Churchill's Coalition government had been faced with the alternatives of making a humiliating peace with Germany or begging aid from the USA. Making peace had been discussed but rejected, although some Conservatives would have preferred it.[8] Among the harsh conditions accepted for American help had been the sale of British overseas assets, which were snapped up by US firms. So by 1945 Britain had lost 28 per cent of pre-war overseas assets and was burdened by the largest overseas debt in history. Gold and dollar reserves, it was forecast, would cover only two-thirds of the balance of payments over the next three years.[9] The nation's capital stock was run down. Shipping losses, even after wartime building and purchase, amounted to 28 per cent of pre-war tonnage. Half-a-million houses had been destroyed or made uninhabitable, and another four million damaged, by bombs.[10]

Even in 1939 the economy was not in a condition where it could carry the weight of a major war. Before 1914 home investment had been neglected in favour of overseas investment. Two major depressions between the wars had left Britain, in spite of the new industries of the Midlands and South, having to import the machine-tools needed for war production. The battle of El Alamein was fought with American Sherman tanks because the British tanks were not able to stand up to the German panzers. The reports of the seventeen Working Parties which Stafford Cripps set up between 1945 and 1947 revealed how much of Britain's industrial equipment was outdated; in textiles much of it was over forty, and some over eighty, years old.

On the other hand, Britain had no rivals in world markets apart from the USA, and the Government's export drive had considerable success. It was creditable that, in spite of the difficulties, exports reached 150 per cent of their pre-war value by 1948, and that, thanks to the exploitation of colonial resources, by the outbreak of the Korean War in the summer of 1950 the 'dollar gap' in the balance of payments had almost disappeared. Production was increasing at a rate unprecedented in this century, price controls had kept inflation within reasonable bounds and there was full employment.[11]

Ken Alexander, in this book, points to the benefits which Scotland's economy reaped from the Government's regional policy. The same was true of South Wales where the Government sponsored the building, or expansion, of 112 of 179 new factories constructed between 1945 and 1949.[12]

Alec Cairncross, who as a Civil Servant was involved in policy making in those years, gives as his verdict that the Government:

> pointed the economy in the right direction, rode out the various crises that the years of transition almost inevitably gave rise to, and by 1951 had brought the economy near to eventual balance.[13]

The historian Kenneth Morgan goes further and credits Cripps with having 'created the basis for a new affluence'.[14]

Labour's Afternoon

In spite of these successes, all did not bode well for the economy. Cairncross also pointed to the crucial lack of growth in productivity, the lack of success in changing long-standing attitudes in industry, and the 'serious error over the scale of rearmament that was feasible'.[15] G.D.H. Cole in his 1956 assessment warned that things might get worse rather than better because:

> the combined demands of consumption, investment and rearmament add up to more than can be met out of current resources ... I believe that the right course is to make drastic cuts in armament expenditure.[16]

No post-war British government would do this. Guns were preferred not only to butter but to industrial equipment as well.

Nor was Sam Watson's 'poverty has been abolished' true. In 1951 two-and-a-half million people (one in twenty of the population) were being supported by the National Assistance Board after submitting to a means test.[17] Indeed, 1950 was not a propitious time for such euphoria as Watson's. Defence expenditure had been trebled, the unions were rejecting the Government's incomes policy and both the Government and the Labour Party were divided. Most ominous of all, in the General Election in February the Government's majority had slumped to five.

Support for Labour had continued to grow for six months after the 1945 election, giving a 19 per cent lead by January 1946.[18] By May the lead had fallen to 3 per cent, as support ebbed from Labour but did not flow to the Conservatives.[19] During those January to May months, rations had been reduced, and in May bread rationing was announced, even though the scheme was not necessary and would not have worked if it had been.[20] By March 1947, during the fuel crisis, the Labour lead had been lost, and by November the Conservatives were eleven points ahead. Marginal opinion was very volatile, swinging against Labour after the devaluation crisis of 1949, but back to Labour for the 1950 election. The 1951 election, which brought the Conservatives back, was a paradox. Labour polled more votes than the Conservatives, indeed more votes, and a higher proportion of the votes, than any party has had since, yet lost. The higher Labour vote was partly the result of a higher turnout than in 1945, and one cause of this may have been that service men and women who had not registered in 1945 were now voting. The Conservatives gained from the collapse of the Liberal vote to its lowest ebb ever, and from changes in constituency boundaries. But within the figures there were interesting indications. Labour votes increased in traditional Labour areas, possibly because memories of the 1930s were stronger there and Labour's social programme more appreciated, but declined in the South and in suburban areas, probably because middle-class voters saw austerity as a reduction in their living standards. The Conservative vote was up by 9 per cent on 1945 among both men and women. But there had also been a strong swing against Labour among working-class men, though working-class women had mostly remained loyal to Labour. Raymond Plant, Labour Party Research Officer, commented that, 'Labour dropped more votes from working-class men than from the whole of the middle-class.'[21] It seems likely that the Government's 'wage-freeze' and its frequent use of troops to break strikes[22] had alienated many working-class men. Working-class women had benefitted more than men from family allowances and from the National Health Service, as most men were previously covered by the 'panel'.

Since the defeat of 1951 Labour has held office for only ten years, the Conservatives for thirty-two. It was to be thirteen years before there was another Labour government. This cannot be explained solely by the effects of austerity or the 'wage-freeze'. In 1945 Labour's programme, and the political atmosphere in which it was proposed, had offered a vision. In 1950 and 1951 there was none. The programme was one of 'consolidation', put forward by what Kenneth Morgan calls, 'an ageing team intent on grim, bunker-like survival and little else'.[23] Even in 1945 Attlee's team was made up of Labour veterans whose political outlook was more conservative than that of the young MPs who constituted a good part of the 1945 intake. The team had included some of the left-wing rebels of the 1930s, but except for Aneurin Bevan they had tended to move to the right. Now, in 1951, most of the leaders were in their late sixties and some had held office through ten stressful years. Cripps was terminally ill, Ernest Bevin and Ellen Wilkinson were dead. The one new man heading a senior ministry was Hugh Gaitskell as Chancellor. He was an able intellectual, but his economic policies were orthodox and conservative, so that his name was soon to be linked with that of the Conservative Chancellor 'Rab' Butler in the term 'Butskellism', which indicated the similarity of the economic policies of two parties in the 1950s. The Labour Party could justly congratulate itself on having carried out most of its 1945 manifesto, but it was now backward-looking, smugly recalling its 'magnificent journey'. Its slogan, 'Ask your Dad', called on the young to learn from their elders how much better things were than before the war, as indeed they were. But the Conservative slogan, 'Set the People free', even if it was meretricious, looked to the future and offered a vision of some sort.

The French, recovering from the devastation of occupation, were developing new techniques of economic planning. Germany and Japan were beginning to rebuild their economies on the foundation of new technology and new industrial structures. Britain did neither. Yet from 1945-51 Britain was ahead of the world in many branches of technology, especially in aeronatics and automobiles. In 1951 Ferranti's made the first commercial mainframe computer, Leo. Wartime experience had shown the scope of electronics, optics, anti-biotics, artificial fibres, detergents and many new industrial techniques. The future was to lie with science-based industries, and in 1945 the Barlow Committee on *Scientific Manpower* had urged a doubling of the number of science graduates coming from universities. But not until Harold Wilson's adminsitration of 1964 was there a British government which took the scientific revolution seriously. Interestingly, it was Wilson who, as President of the Board of Trade in 1950, produced a paper for senior ministers, 'The State and Private Industry', which offered a coherent programme for the next stage of Labour's economic policy. After considerable discussion it was turned down.[24]

Fatal Illusions

Ultimately the fate of post-war Labour Britain, and the settlement it bequeathed to the Conservatives, was determined by three illusions which shaped what the Attlee governments did and what they did not do. These were:

- the belief that Britain was, and could remain, a Great Power politically and financially, the hub of an Empire stretched around the globe
- the belief that the Soviet Union was planning to over-run Europe in a war of aggression
- the belief that it was possible to create a democratic socialist society while leaving intact the structures of the State, the Establishment and the class hierarchy.

The first two of these illusions were the premises on which was built a level of expenditure on armaments, including the luxury of the 'independent deterrent', which has been the albatross around the neck of the British economy ever since the Second World War. More than half of Britain's research and development effort has gone to the defence industries, while Germany and Japan have directed theirs towards industrial technology. In 1950 defence spending began to eat into the National Health Service, so leading to a split in the Government and the Party, which remained an electoral liability.

It can, of course, be argued that no British government could have been persuaded to follow the 'Scandinavian road', of small nation neutrality and prosperity, when Britain had just taken part in winning a world war – even though it was obvious that without American aid and the Red Army the story would have been very different. Certainly the Labour Party, with the exception of individual socialists, had always been keen on what Herbert Morrison called 'the jolly old Empire', and in this it reflected the views of most of its working-class voters. But there were warning voices. In February 1946 Maynard Keynes, in a minute to 'Otto' Clarke, of the Treasury's Overseas Finance Department, warned that, unless it were drastically cut, military expenditure would swallow up the whole of the American loan which he had negotiated: 'it comes out in the wash that the American loan is primarily required to meet political and military expenditure overseas'. It should be remembered that a chunk of this military spending was to try to win Indonesia and Indo-China back for their Dutch and French masters, and to put the Greek king back on his throne. Keynes warned the Cabinet that the loan was, 'going down the drain at an alarming pace', and that the public would be alarmed if they knew that, 'not a single bean of sustenance for themselves or of capital equipment for British manufacturers was likely to be left over from the U.S. credit'.[25] As rations had just been cut at that time the public would certainly have been alarmed if they had known the truth.

In 1949 Sir Henry Tizard, Chief Scientific Advisor to the Ministry of Defence, warned the Government that:

> We persist in regarding ourselves as a Great Power, capable of anything and only temporarily handicapped by economic difficulties. We are not a Great Power and never will be again. We are a great nation, but if we continue to behave like a Great Power we shall cease to be a great nation. Let us take warning from the fate of the Great Powers of the past and not burst ourselves with pride. (See Aesop's fable of the frog.)[26]

The advisors were right, the ministers were wrong.

Denis Healey, who was International Secretary of the Labour Party at the time, concedes in his autobiography that the Labour government was wrong in its estimate of the Soviet Union:

> Like most western observers at the time, I believed that Stalin's behaviour showed he was bent on military conquest of western Europe. I now think we were all mistaken. We took too seriously some of the Leninist rhetoric pouring out of Moscow, as the Russians took too seriously some of the anti-Communist rhetoric favoured by American politicians.

The extent of the Soviet losses, he writes, made it 'most unlikely that Stalin could have contemplated another war against the west,'[27] and it was these losses which motivated the Soviet policy of creating a buffer zone in Eastern Europe. This buffer zone, it could be added, was the reverse of the *Cordon Sanitaire* of right-wing states with which the Allies had sought to contain Soviet Russia in 1919. It is also probable that the Soviets feared attack because their Intelligence knew of the preparations that were being made, long before 1945, for a possible war against the Soviet Union. As Soviet Intelligence had penetrated the Manhattan (atom bomb) Project, it presumably knew what General Leslie R. Groves, the leading administrator of the project, told the Oppenheimer hearings in 1954, that from its inception in 1942 the Project was based on the assumption that Russia was the enemy.[28]

Today it is fairly clear that the Soviet Union's fear of attack was the basis of its policy in Eastern Europe; but, sadly, the brutality with which the policy was carried out, and the intransigence of Soviet diplomacy, gave credence to Western allegations of aggression, and helped Cold War propaganda in converting the pro-Soviet feelings of the British people in 1945 to the hostility of the following years.[29]

Healey blames the 'mistaken' estimate of Soviet intentions on Stalin's secrecy over the extent of Russia's losses, but the devastation of western Russia and the immensity of human losses were well known to journalists and public alike. The Joint Intelligence Committee estimate of 1948 was that the Soviet Union would be unlikely to have the resources to wage large scale warfare until 1957.[30] Nor did all the Cabinet members agree with Ernest Bevin's extreme anti-Soviet policy. At various times, Attlee, Hugh Dalton, Aneurin Bevan, Manny Shinwell and even Herbert Morrison, had serious doubts, but the Foreign Office and Bevin prevailed.[31]

Here the illusion of a Soviet threat links with the Labour illusion about the State, which they made no effort to reform. The Foreign Office in 1945 was staffed by much the same people, including Sir Alexander Cadogan, Chamberlain's appointment as Permanent Under-Secretary, as in 1939. They were, almost to man (and it was 'man') Old Etonians.[32] The same was not so true of the Treasury and other economic Departments, where there were a number of Keynesians and some Labour supporters during and after the war. But, until the Fulton Commission of 1966, the Civil Service at decision-making level remained unreformed and staffed by (mainly) men and women of the same social and educational backgrounds as before the war.[33] When Labour appointed administrators and advisers to economic posts, they were drawn, almost exclusively, from among private business executives.[34]

Labour's deference to the State was apparent from the moment when Attlee, on his first day, bowed to the wishes of King George VI and appointed Bevin as Foreign Secretary in place of his own choice of Dalton.[35] It was soon evident, in matters great and small, that the Government would not stand up to the State. Attlee withdrew his objections to Bevin's Middle Eastern strategy when Field Marshall Montgomery threatened the resignation of the whole General Staff, while John Strachey, the Air Minister, withdrew his proposal that Air Force personnel should be able to send their grievances to their MPs or the Minister, when he was opposed by Sir John Slessor, Vice Chief of Air Staff.[36]

The Government did take one step towards a fuller Parliamentary democracy in 1948 when, for the first time, Britain adopted the basic principle of 'one person, one vote'. University graduates and business people lost their second vote, and those – such as seafarers – whose jobs or travels had prevented them from meeting the old residential requirements, were now able to register. The following year the power of the House of Lords to hold up legislation was reduced from two years to one. But further reform, or abolition, of the Lords was blocked by Morrison's view that, 'we should not set up something different from the past', a statement that embodied Labour's attitude to 'our old institutions'.[37]

There was no challenge to the seats of Conservative influence and power in the public schools, the universities and the press. A Royal Commission of the Press gave the newspaper barons a clean bill of health, although some of the evidence it produced pointed in a different direction.[38] No whisper of 'workers' control' or even 'workers' participation' was allowed in the nationalised industries, nor were the Joint Production Committees, on which in wartime workers' representatives had discussed production questions with managements in private industry, encouraged to continue in peacetime. Any direct action by working people, such as squatting in disused army camps by homeless families, was vigorously opposed.[39]

The Labour governments, in short, did a great deal *for* the people, but were not willing to see things done *by* the people. Consultation with workers' representatives was confined to the 'praetorian guard' of trade union leaders. It was a fatal flaw, which meant that the nationalised industries and Welfare State were bureaucratic, and that people's experience of the bureaucracy did not enthuse them to defend the institutions of post-war Britain when they began to be savaged in the 1980s.

Peter Hennessy, the principal historian of the era, thinks it 'absurd' to think that the Labour governments, with all else they had to do, could have taken on the public schools and universities.[40] He is, I think, mistaken. The failure to challenge the State and the class structure was more the result of lack of will than lack of time. Such aims were not known to the philosophy of the Mainstream British Labour Movement. Even with 'Red' Ellen Wilkinson at the Ministry of Education, state schools continued to celebrate Empire Day on Queen Victoria's birthday.

If ever there was a time when the conservatism and deference of the British was shaken it was during the Second World War. Far form being the united and loyal nation of myth at the time when Britain 'stood alone', and during the blitz, Ministry of Information reports revealed low morale, there was extensive looting and the rich were accused of dodging rationing.[41] As the war progressed, factory workers and service people had less trust in the ability of their managers and officers, and learned to have more confidence in themselves. Joint Production Committees, Shelter Committees, Civil Defence and the Home Guard were schools of practical democracy, while forces education, the popular press and films contributed to the mood of self-confidence, and to criticism of traditional 'superiors' among people whose subordinate role had always been taken for granted. Without this change the Labour victory of 1945 would not have been possible. The tragedy was that this democratic mood was squandered after that victory. Failure to challenge the class hierarchy or its values left the field open to supporters of the old class domination to reassert those values.

One group in particular had been crucial to the success of 1945. These were the 'activists' who, in the forces, in Civil Defence and the factories, had spread socialist and progressive ideas during the war, and so had contributed to the eclipse of the pre-war conservative hegemony. Some of this group were shop stewards or trade union lay officers, others had taken part in forces education, formal and informal, or had just talked politics. Some were Labour, some others Communists. Many had had their political apprenticeship in the pre-war unemployed or Aid Spain campaigns, or in the Left Book Club. After 1945 a few became Labour MPs, many trained as teachers, some went into university or adult education. In a more democratic Britain, their talents and dedication could have been used in many different ways. As it was, by 1950 many of them were no longer in a mood to campaign enthusiastically for Labour, as Jim Mortimer shows in a previous chapter. Labour's foreign policy and 'wage freeze', and the anti-Communist purge, had disenchanted many. So had controversial Government actions such as the refusal to allow Seretse Khama to take up his Chieftainship of the Bamangwato people in 1950, because his marriage to an English woman might offend Dr Malan's South African government. Also hard to swallow, in the same year, was the ban on entry into Britain of Paul Robeson, Dmitri Shostakovich, the poets Louis Aragon and Pablo Neruda and other intellectuals who were bound for a peace conference in Sheffield.[42] Standard histories of the time do not record either the importance of the enthusiasm of the activists in the run-up to 1945, or the significance of their lack of enthusiasm in 1950 and 1951; but their role was crucial to the fortunes of the Labour Movement.

Then and Now

What then was the nature of Labour's achievement? John Strachey, who was a Minister from 1945-51 wrote:

> My real heroes are the English leaders of 1688 and, above all, 1832 ... and I don't think Mr Attlee's first administration is an unworthy successor to them.[43]

271

The parallel was significant. The patrician Whig leaders at those dates had carried through 'revolutions' that were essentially conservative and stabilising and which consciously excluded the majority of people from political power and influence. The historian Kenneth Morgan also holds Strachey's view of a preserving revolution, 'the final endorsement of the enduring triumph of the Whigs.'[44]

It would be more generous to see the Attlee governments as having completed the work of the great Liberal and Conservative reformers of the nineteenth century, the Liberal governments of 1906 and 1910, and the Fabians Sidney and Beatrice Webb; as having rounded off the history of Liberal reformism, rather than as having begun the history of democratic socialism, even though the Health Service and family allowances could be said to have socialist characteristics. The achievement was an historic one, and no one who knows about the hunger marches and malnutrition of the 1930s, and what happened after the First World War can fail to salute what was accomplished in both human and economic terms. But neither should we underestimate the importance of the missed opportunity, or the long-term weaknesses of Labour's politics.

Has Labour a future? This is not the same as asking whether Labour can win a general election. Labour could win office because of reaction against a Conservative government, but still have no long-term future. The successes of 1945-51 were possible because the Government energetically attacked the problems that had engaged reformers for a century – unemployment, boom and slump, ill health and 'poverty amid plenty'. The failures arose from Labour's inability to address the new problems of a world irrevocably changed from that of 1939 – the need to construct a democratic Britain, able to play the role of a great nation that was no longer a Great Power (to recall Sir Henry Tizard's words), and one which could help to build an international order accommodating the legitimate concerns of both the Western nations and the Soviet Union.

The question now is whether Labour can develop policies for the problems of the late twentieth and the twenty-first century. Some of these have old names such as 'poverty' and 'unemployment', but are different from their counterparts of half a century ago. Some concern the necessity for restructuring the economy, but on very different lines from the post-war 'consensus'. The democratic reforms urgently needed in State and society also have new dimensions, with Britain part of Europe, ethnic changes in the population, and changing gender relations. Over everything hang questions about the environment, peace, Third World poverty and the turning over of industries which forged the swords of the Cold War to the production of ploughshares – questions which are unlikely to find answers within existing capitalist frameworks.

If Labour can co-operate with all groups interested in finding bold, even if partial, solutions, and if these solutions can be translated into a political programme, there is a future for Labour. It is a challenge which calls for imagination, and also for a knowledge of Labour's successes and failure between 1945 and 1951.

Notes

[1] *Guardian*, 22.4.93.
[2] *Quoted in* Andrew Davies, *Where did the 'Forties Go*, Pluto, London 1984, p70.
[3] Labour Party Conference Report, 1950.
[4] G.D.H. Cole, *The Post-War Condition of Britain*, Routledge and Kegan Paul, London 1956, p238.
[5] Peter Hennessy, *Never Again, Britain 1945-1951*, Cape, London 1992, p445.
[6] For this episode, see John Gross, 'The Lynskey Tribunal', in Michael Sissons and Philip French (eds)., *The Age of Austerity*, Penguin Books, Harmondsworth 1964.
[7] Alec Cairncross, *Years of Recovery*, Methuen, London 1985, pp8 and 6.
[8] Clive Ponting, *1940: Myth and Reality*, Hamish Hamilton, London 1990, Chap. 6 and Chap. 9 *passim* and p75.
[9] Cairncross, *op cit*, pp7-9.
[10] *Ibid*, pp7 and 13.
[11] Kenneth Morgan, *The People's Peace*, OUP, 1990, pp72-3; Cairncross, *op cit*, pp500 and 503.
[12] Arthur Marwick, *British Society Since 1945*, Penguin, Harmondsworth 1982, p33.
[13] Cairncross, *op cit*, p509.
[14] Morgan, *op cit*, p74.
[15] Cairncross, *op cit*, p509.
[16] Cole, *op cit*, p447.
[17] James Harvey ahnd Katherine Hood, *The British State*, Lawrence and Wishart, London 1958, p237.
[18] James Hinton, 'Women and the Labour Vote, 1945-1950', in *Labour History Review*, Vol. 27, Part 3, 1992. Except where otherwise stated, information on

Labour's electoral support is from this article.

[19] Tom Harrison, in *Public Opinion Quarterly*, Vol II, No. 3, Fall 1947, quoted in Davies, *op cit*, p78.

[20] Hugh Thomas, *John Strachey*, Harper and Row, New York and London 1973, pp236-7.

[21] Hinton, *op cit*.

[22] See Peter Hennessy and Keith Jeffery, 'How Attlee stood up to strikers', *Times*, 21.11.79.; 'By 1948 strike breaking had become almost second nature to the cabinet.'

[23] Morgan, *op cit*, p84.

[24] Ben Pimlott, *Harold Wilson*, HarperCollins, London 1992, pp129-30.

[25] Cairncross, *op cit*, p111 and 111n.

[26] Quoted in Hennessy, *op cit*, p431.

[27] Denis Healey, *The Time of My Life*, Penguin Edn., Harmondsworth 1986, p101.

[28] P.M.S. Blackett, *Atomic Weapons and East-West Relations*, Cambridge 1956, p70.

[29] A Gallup Poll following Churchill's 'Iron Curtain' speech at Fulton in March 1946 showed that even then only 36 per cent approved of standing up to Russia, 39 per cent disapproved and 16 per cent had no opinion.

[30] Hennessy, *op cit*, p247.

[31] *Ibid*, pp256 and 261-2; Morgan, *op cit*, p43.

[32] Gladwyn Jebb, memoirs, Weidenfeld & Nicholson, London 1972, p106.

[33] A.A. Rogow and Peter Shore, *The Labour Government and British Industry, 1945-51*, Blackwell, Oxford 1955, p14; Morgan, *op cit*, pp107-8.

[34] Rogow and Shore, *op cit*, Appendices I and II.

[35] For a full account of this episode, see Ben Pimlott, *Hugh Dalton*, Macmillan, London 1985, Chapter 24.

[36] For Montgomery, see F. Carr in this volume, p.140; for Strachey, see Hugh Thomas, *op cit*, p227.

[37] Quoted Morgan, *op cit*, p108.

[38] See, for example, Cmd. 7318, Royal Commission on Press, Evidence, Third Day, 15.10.47.

[39] James Hinton, 'Self-help and Socialism; the Squatters' Movement, 1946', in *History Workshop Journal*, Spring 1988, No 25; Noreen Branson, *London Squatters, 1946, Our History*, No 80, Communist Party History Group, August 1989.

[40] Hennessy, *op cit*, p434.

[41] Ponting, *op cit*, pp160-164; Angus Calder and Dorothy Sheridan (eds), *Speak for Yourself, A Mass Observation Anthology*, Cape, London 1984, p99.

[42] Bill Moore, *Cold War in Sheffield*, Sheffield Trades Council, 1990. The PRO documents relating to this incident are still withheld from the public.

[43] Thomas, *op cit*, p243.

[44] Morgan, *op cit*, p111.

Subject Index

275

SUBJECT INDEX

SUBJECT INDEX

Ministry of Town and Country Planning, 41
Ministry of Works, 10

National Advisory Council on Education for Industry and Commerce, 101
National Agricultural Advisory Service, 78, 82, 90, 91, 92
National Arbitration Order 1305, (1940), 17, 180, 253
National Coal Board, 37, 39, 45, 46, 47, 51, 54, 56-7, 63
National Farmers' Union, 78, 81, 84, 85, 91, 92
National Government, 84, 86
National Health Service, xxvii, xxxiii-iv, 27, 145, 186, 247, 260, 264, 266, 272
National Insurance, 24, 27
Nationalisation (general), xxvii, xxix, 37-60, 186, 247, 260; Bank of England, 37, 48; Cable and Wireless, 37; Civil aviation, 37, 39; coal, xxix, 37, 38, 39, 51, 55, 61-77, 88; inland waterways, 37, 48; iron and steel, 37, 39, 48; electricity, xxix, 37, 39, 48, 57; gas, xxix, 37, 39, 48, 55, 57; land, 86-90; railways, xxix, 37, 39, 48; transport, 37, 38, 39, 55, 56, 57
National Union of General and Municipal Workers, 166-7, 181
National Union of Mineworkers, 61-77 passim, 167, 181, 183, 248
National Union of Railwaymen, 43, 45, 167
National Union of Vehicle Builders, 172
New Deal, 22, 40
New Fabian Essays, xxxi
New Propellor, xix
News Chronicle, 78
New Statesman, 43, 243
North Atlantic Treaty Organisation (NATO), 139, 144, 153, 157
North of Scotland Hydro-Electric Board, 39, 45, 47, 56, 200, 202, 203
Nuclear power, 57
Nuclear weapons, 125, 142, 248, 249, 266, 268

Oil industry, sources, 125, 129
Organisation for European Economic Co-operation (OEEC), 12-13, 157, 158
Overseas Development Corporation, 47
Overseas Food Corporation, 130
Overseas Resources Act (1948), 130
Oxford Institute of Statistics, xxxiii

Parliamentary Scientific Committee, 101
Percy Committee Report (1945), 97, 100-1, 102
Personal Incomes, Costs and Prices, 174, 223, 250
Potsdam Conference, xx, 152
Polish workers, 229, 237-8
Post-war Plan for Scotland (1942), 200
Principles of Economic Planning, 5
Progressive Farming, 78
Public schools, xx, 269, 270

Race, racism, racial discrimination, 227-242
Rationing, 79-80, 263, 267, 270
Reid Report (coal industry), 64
Ridley Committee (1952), 51
Road Transport Executive, 47
Robbins Report (higher education) (1963), 108
Royal Commission on Equal Pay (1946), 222
Royal Commission on the Press (1947), 269
Royal College of Art, 102
Ruhr Authority, 151

Saltire Society, 199
Schuman Plan, 148-61
Science, and industry, research, 201, 265, 266
Scottish Council of State, 199
Scottish Convention, 206, 211
Scottish National Party, National Party of Scotland, 196, 201, 202, 212
Scottish Office, 199, 202
Scottish (Self-Government) Party, 196
Scottish TUC, 201, 205
Sex Discrimination Removal Act (1919), 215

Name and Place Index

NAME AND PLACE INDEX

Name and Place Index